BLUE HAND MOJO

HARD TIMES ROAD

story and art by

JOHN JENNINGS

Published by Rosarium Publishing
P.O. Box 544
Greenbelt, MD 20768-0544
www.rosariumpublishing.com
Printed in Canada

INTRODUCTION

It goes without saying—or at least it should go without saying—that I loved *Blue Hand Mojo*. The fact that I'm writing the introduction for this graphic novel should say all that needs to be said. No one writes an intro for a book they didn't like. You know what this part is about—it's a combination of singing the praises of the work and the creative talent responsible, with the hope that my words will lend some greater level of legitimacy to both. Honestly, I wouldn't be offended if you stopped reading the intro right now and skipped right to *Blue Hand Mojo*. Seriously … you can come back and read this after you've the read the book. I say this because I've already read *Blue Hand Mojo*, and I can't help but feel this introduction is standing between you and greatness. Still, I was asked to write something, and to be a part of this work, in even such a minor capacity, is a great honor.

I went into *Blue Hand Mojo* not fully knowing what to expect. I've known John Jennings for several years and am familiar with his work as an artist, a writer, a college professor, and a champion of diversity and representation in pop culture. John and I have been on numerous panels together. In my office, his art hangs on the walls, and books that he has contributed to sit on the shelves. But all of this familiarity with the man and his work did not prepare me for *Blue Hand Mojo*, because, if I'm going to be truly honest, *Blue Hand Mojo* is John Jennings taking it to some next level shit.

Sometimes, when I'm reading a comic book or graphic novel, I feel a sting. It may be the sting of single yellow jacket or the concentrated attack of an entire swarm, but it is real. And I feel it. The sting is awe. The sting is envy. The sting is jealousy. The sting is that feeling I get when I've read something really good, and I'm upset that I didn't come up with the idea myself. It is my bruised ego and my fragile self-esteem getting together for a little conference and coming to the conclusion that I just don't work hard enough. But then I stop—gathering up all that jealously and envy and awe, pushing it aside for the inevitable moment when I must own up to what is really gnawing at me. I'm talking about that moment when I really examine what I've just read, and I say to myself, ***"You could not have done it this good."***

Blue Hand Mojo was a roller coaster ride that started with awe. John Jennings is an incredible artist and a gifted writer—there's no way you can't be in awe of his work. Awe soon gave way to envy, but I was able to reconcile that feeling—after all, John does the art, and the artist who can also write is the envy of every writer who can't draw. But then it started to dawn on me that for all of John's art that I've seen, and for all his writing that I have read, *Blue Hand Mojo* was a completely different beast.

Deeply rooted in history and Southern folklore, with a pulp novel sensibility and a healthy dose of hoodoo, *Blue Hand Mojo* defies easy classification. It merges familiar genres in a new and refreshing way, drawing from a deep well of culture and sensibility that is missing from most comics. As much as this is a book about crime and the supernatural, it is also a book steeped in the Black experience in America. And that is something we just don't get enough of in comics.

People talk about the importance of diversity and representation in comics, but it is mostly talk; and too often that which passes for diversity and representation is merely superficial window dressing. That's not the case with *Blue Hand Mojo*. John Jennings has crafted a graphic novel that puts on the page what is missing from so many other comics—heart and soul. There is life in these pages, and death—and you can feel it resonating in a way that conjures feelings of awe, and envy and even a twinge of jealousy because not every writer or artist can do what John has done.

After I finished reading *Blue Hand Mojo*, the feelings of jealousy started to fade, and I slowly came to peace with the knowledge that I could not have done it this good. And then a new feeling came over me—one that I don't feel nearly as often as I'd like to when reading comics. To put it quite simply, I felt inspired to be a better writer.

David F. Walker
Portland, OR
2016

CHAPTER 1

A SHARK IN THE DARK

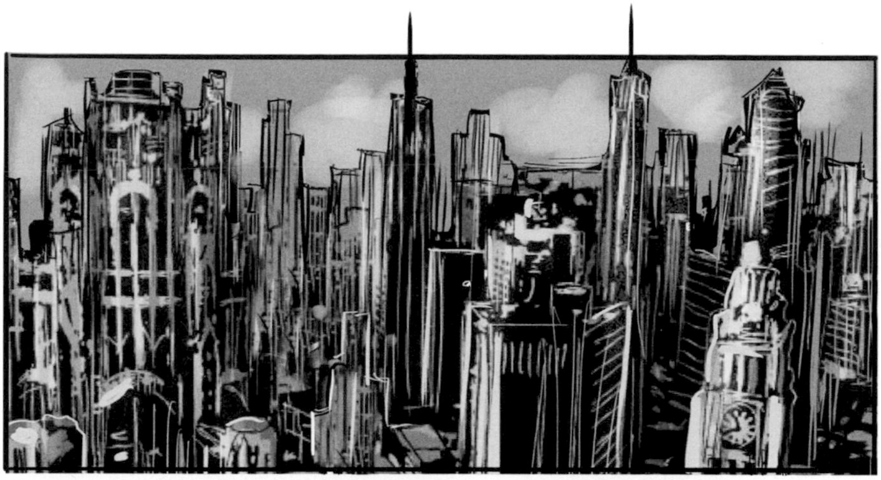

My body and **what's left** of my soul live in **Chicago, Illinois.** The year is **1931.** It's fall and **the Hawk** is already starting to claim victims with its cold breath.

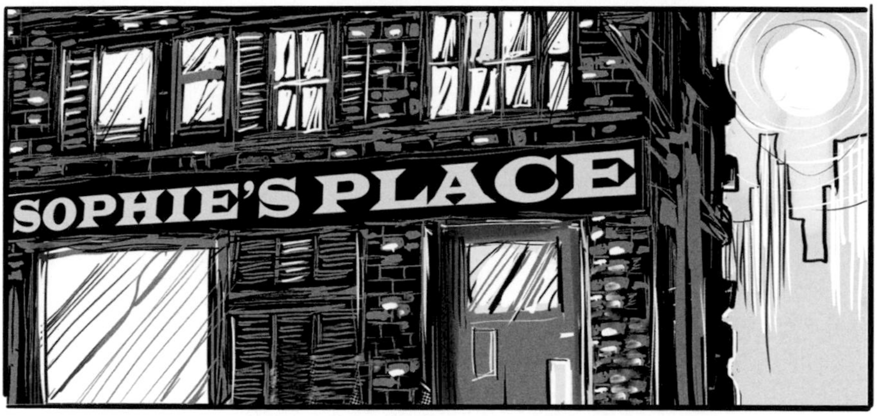
SOPHIE'S PLACE

I'm laid up in my **main squeeze's** joint.

It's **Saturday morning,** and I can still feel **Flapjack Martin and the Mason's** homespun blues deep in my bones from last night's cuttin' up.

My spirit is **restless** as I enter into a dream.

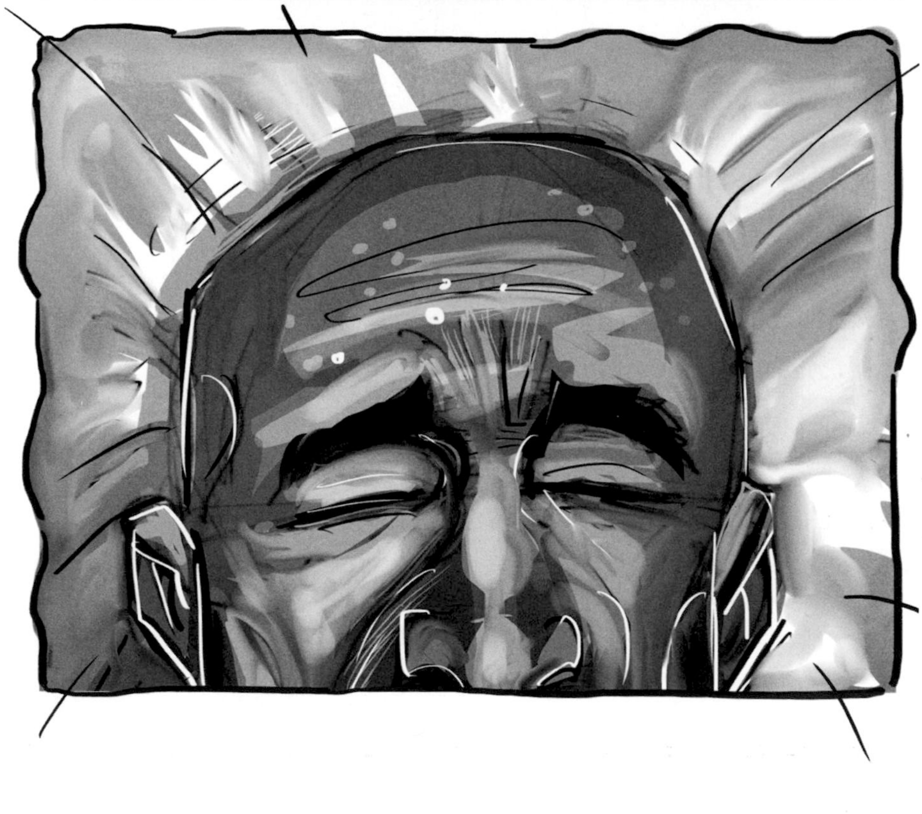

It's restless because of what comes **next.**

You see, I have a real **love/ hate relationship** with the dream world, but I think it goes one way. It only seems to **hate** me.

I dream each and every night. The **nightmares** come at me hard, vivid, and full of anger and dread. However, when you make a living playing **the wheel,** dreams get you **paid** and mine always pay off.

So, there's the **love.**
There's the **hate.**

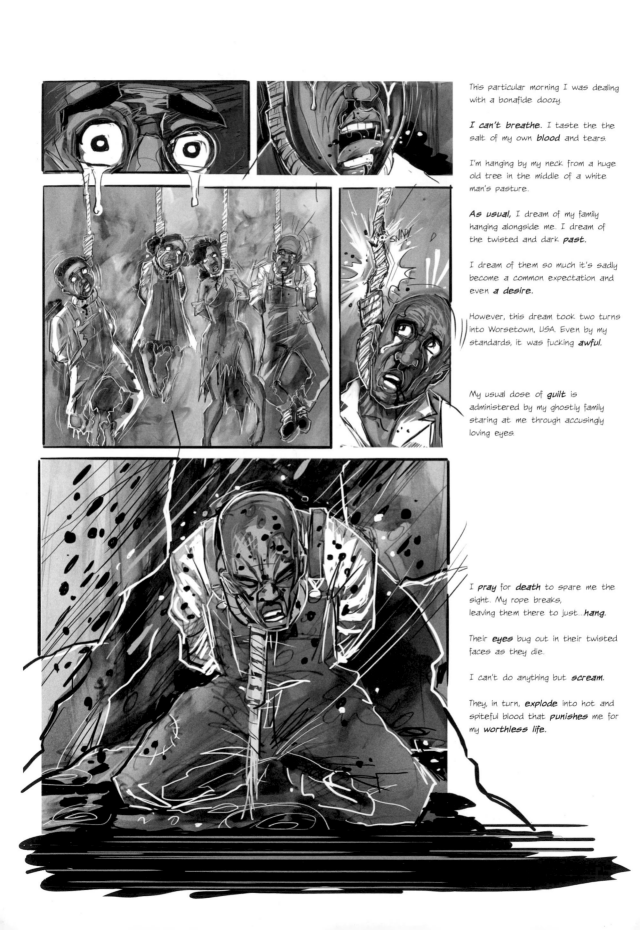

This particular morning I was dealing with a bonafide doozy.

I can't breathe. I taste the the salt of my own *blood* and tears.

I'm hanging by my neck from a huge old tree in the middle of a white man's pasture.

As usual, I dream of my family hanging alongside me. I dream of the twisted and dark *past*.

I dream of them so much it's sadly become a common expectation and even *a desire*.

However, this dream took two turns into Worsetown, USA. Even by my standards, it was fucking *awful*.

My usual dose of *guilt* is administered by my ghostly family staring at me through accusingly loving eyes.

I *pray* for *death* to spare me the sight. My rope breaks,
leaving them there to just...*hang*.

Their *eyes* bug out in their twisted faces as they die.

I can't do anything but *scream*.

They, in turn, *explode* into hot and spiteful blood that *punishes* me for my *worthless life*.

Then the **blood** comes down **harder.** It pours down like punches from the sky. The storm of blood makes the ground beneath the **tree** into a swamp of mud and **hateful redness.**

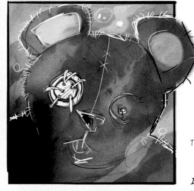

Then I **sink** into the abyss.

I **choke** like I should have in that fucking tree some **ten years** ago.

I am **thankful. That is**...until I understand that I will survive this. This is just a dream. My rage **shatters me.**

A **wolf** howls in the distance. Licking the blood from its **greedy lips.**

A one-eyed **teddy bear** floats over to me and **knocks** on my head like it's filled with some great secret.

That's when I wake up...all maladjusted and **empty.**

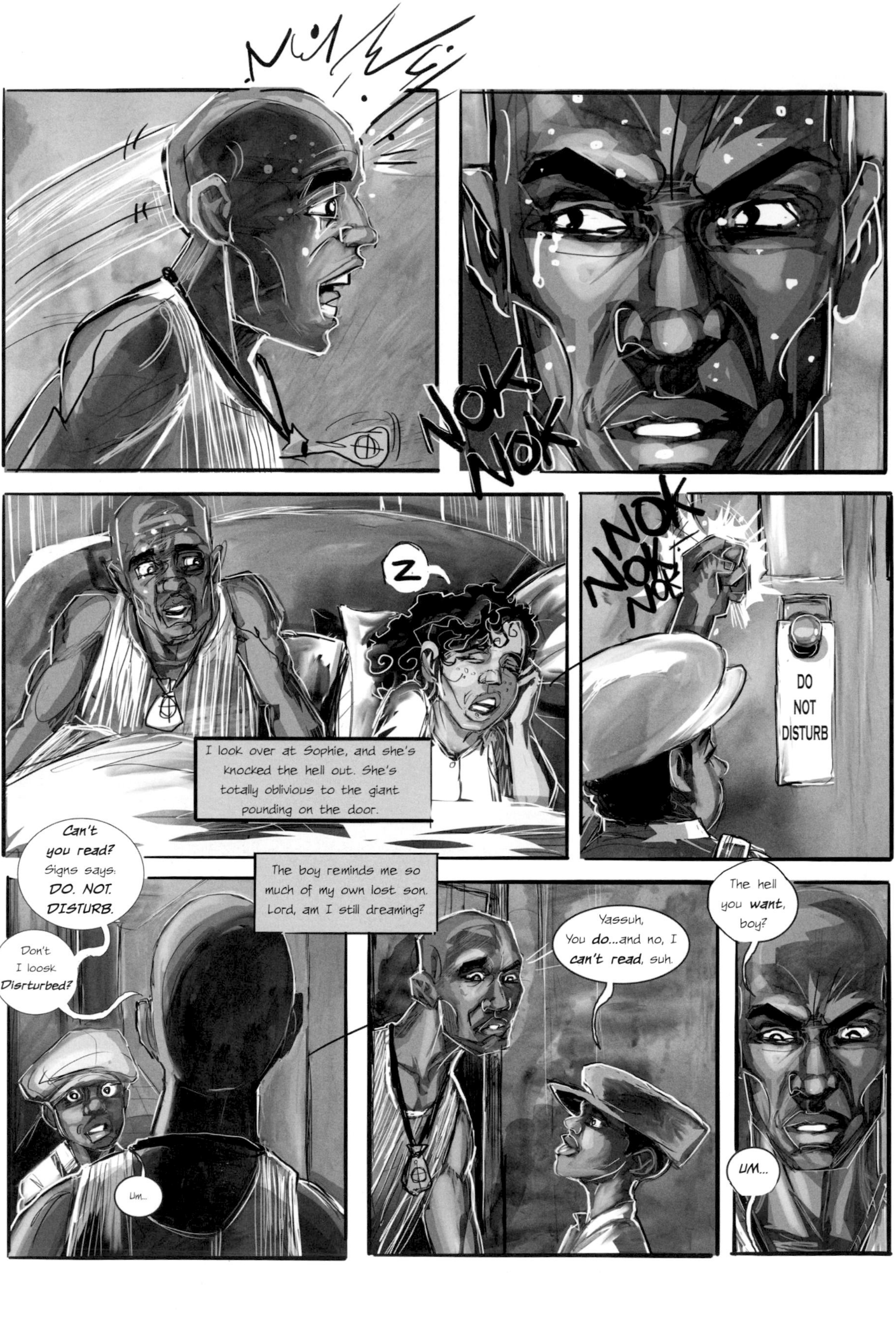
NOK NOK
NOK NOK NOK
Z
DO NOT DISTURB
I look over at Sophie, and she's knocked the hell out. She's totally oblivious to the giant pounding on the door.
Can't you read? Signs says: DO. NOT. DISTURB.
Don't I loosk Disrturbed?
Um...
The boy reminds me so much of my own lost son. Lord, am I still dreaming?
Yassuh, You do...and no, I can't read, suh.
The hell you want, boy?
UM...

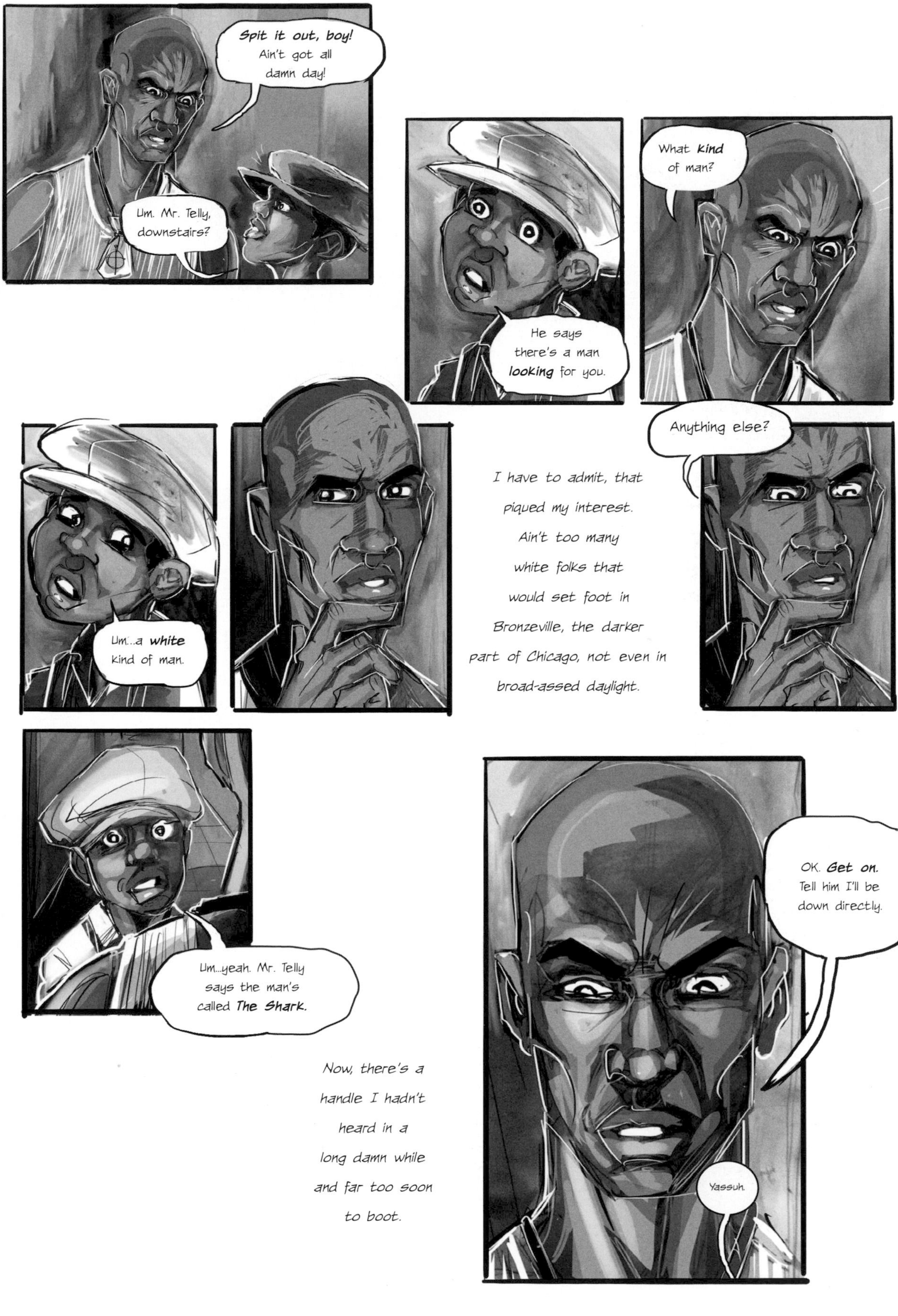
Spit it out, boy! Ain't got all damn day!
Um. Mr. Telly, downstairs?
He says there's a man looking for you.
What kind of man?
Um...a white kind of man.
I have to admit, that piqued my interest. Ain't too many white folks that would set foot in Bronzeville, the darker part of Chicago, not even in broad-assed daylight.
Anything else?
Um...yeah. Mr. Telly says the man's called The Shark.
Now, there's a handle I hadn't heard in a long damn while and far too soon to boot.
OK. Get on. Tell him I'll be down directly.
Yassuh.

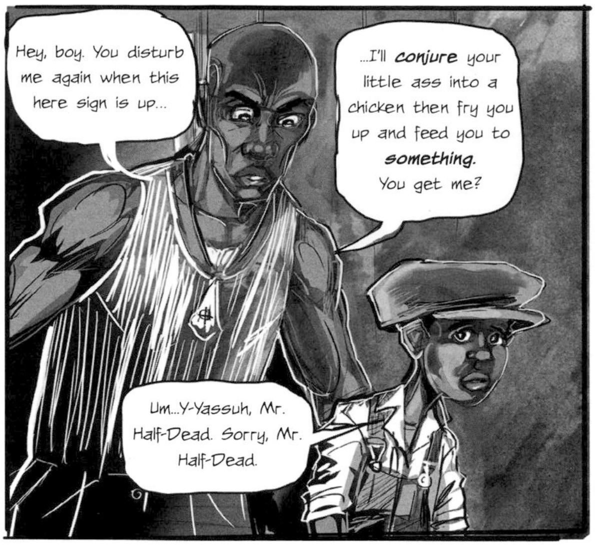
Hey, boy. You disturb me again when this here sign is up...
...I'll **conjure** your little ass into a chicken then fry you up and feed you to **something.** You get me?
Um...Y-Yassuh, Mr. Half-Dead. Sorry, Mr. Half-Dead.

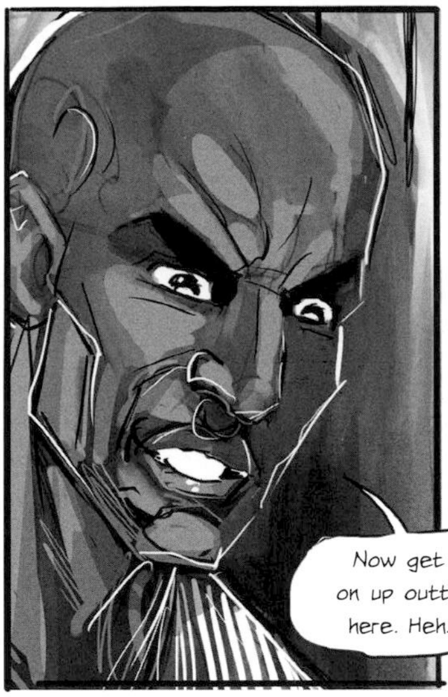
Now get on up outta here. Heh.

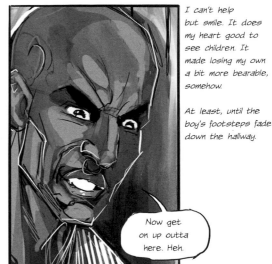

I can't help but smile. It does my heart good to see children. It made losing my own a bit more bearable, somehow.

At least, until the boy's footsteps fade down the hallway.

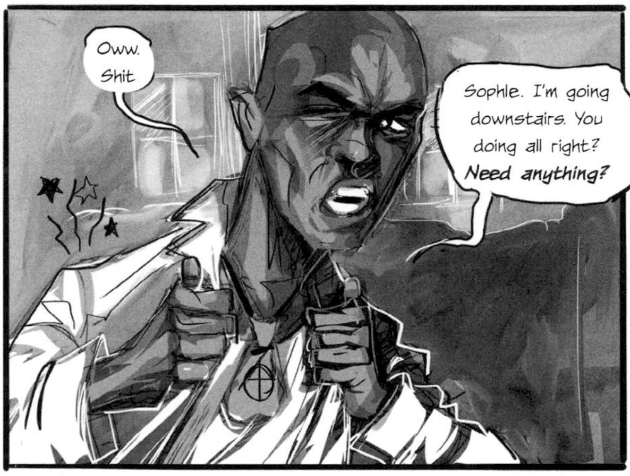
Oww. Shit
Sophie. I'm going downstairs. You doing all right? **Need anything?**

I get moving and start putting on some clothes.

My arm hurts from where Sophie took some blood last night.

It's part of our arrangement, you see. She makes me my tonic that I need to stay real. I give her some of my blood for her passing potion.

A conjure man's blood, especially one that regularly speaks to the Devil himself, is some powerful ***mojo shit.***

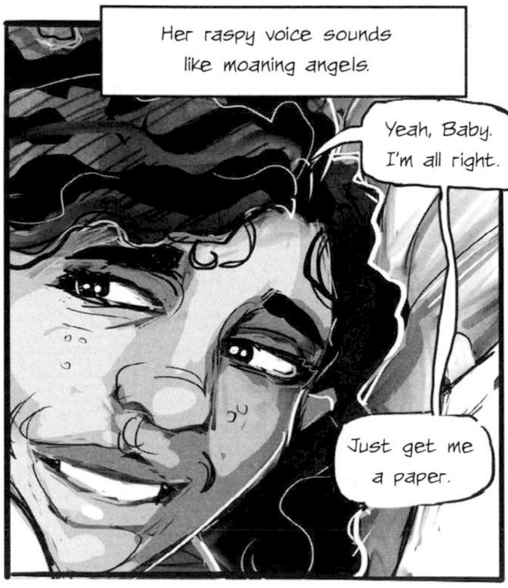
Her raspy voice sounds like moaning angels.
Yeah, Baby. I'm all right.
Just get me a paper.

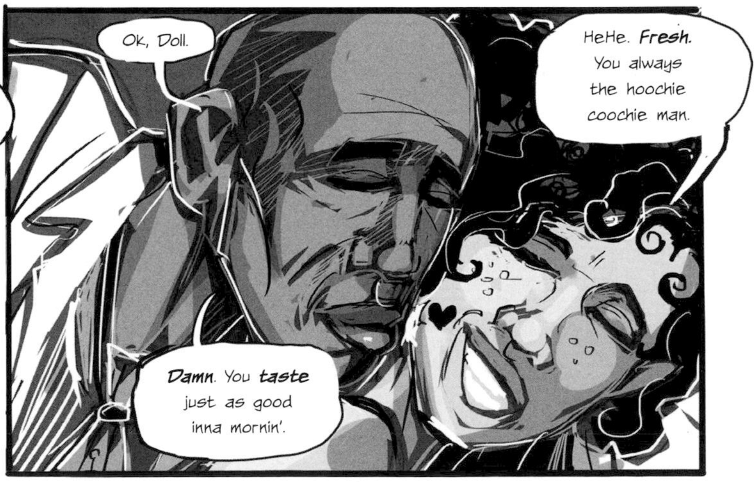
Ok, Doll.
HeHe. ***Fresh.*** You always the hoochie coochie man.
Damn. You ***taste*** just as good inna mornin'.

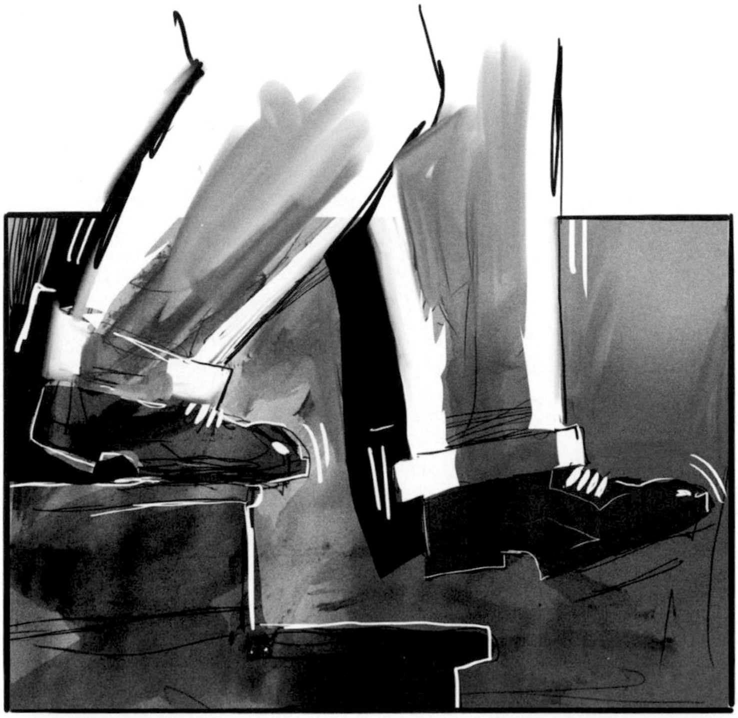

I make my way down the stairs.

The hooch, sex, and blood loss make the way a rocky one at best.

My body works way different than most these days but I still gotta lay off the booze.

When the Devil's got you on the hunt for wayward souls and escaped demons you gotta stay sharp... or else.

Still though, I likes my liquor.

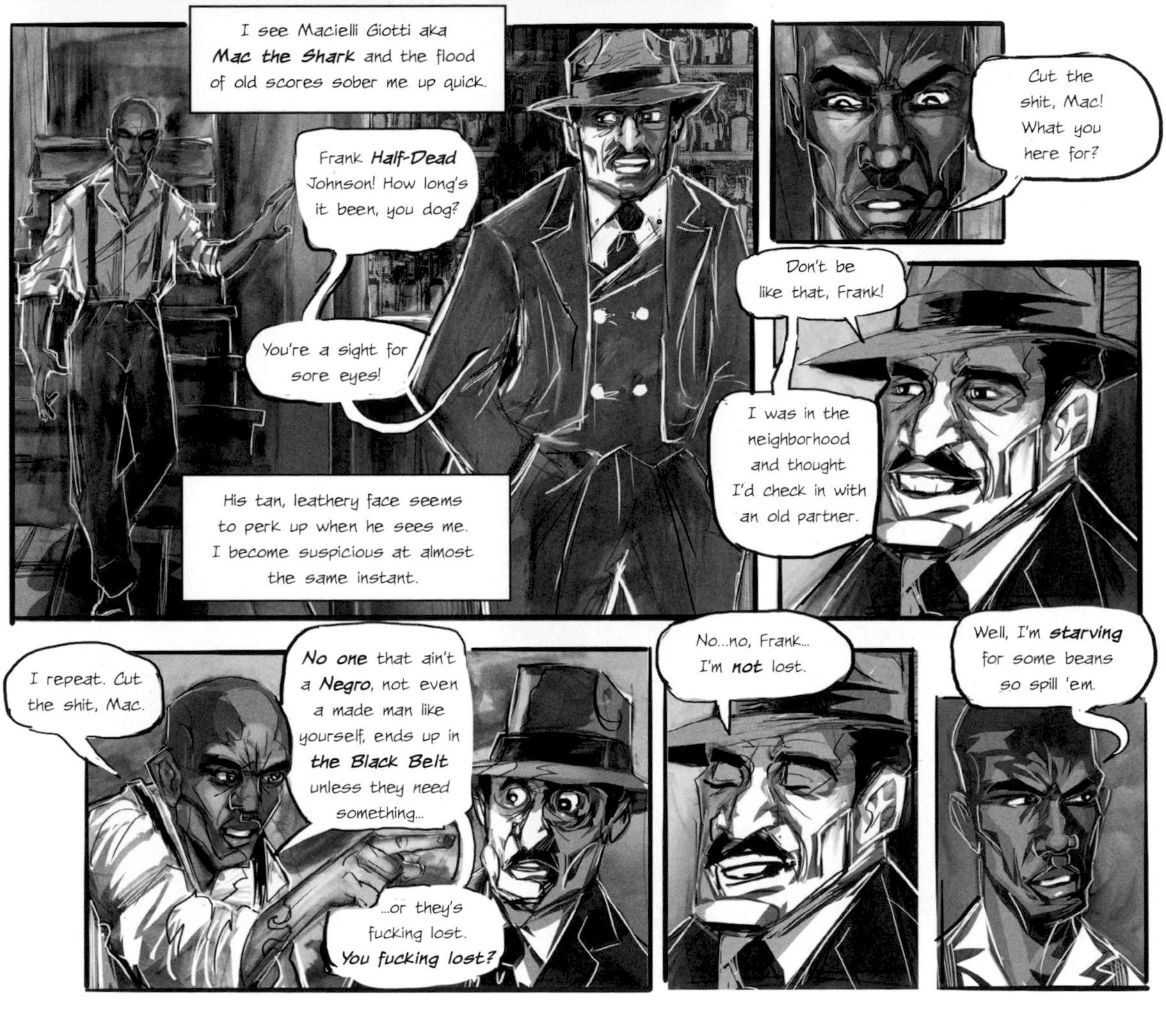

I see Macielli Giotti aka **Mac the Shark** and the flood of old scores sober me up quick.
Frank **Half-Dead** Johnson! How long's it been, you dog?
You're a sight for sore eyes!
His tan, leathery face seems to perk up when he sees me. I become suspicious at almost the same instant.
Cut the shit, Mac! What you here for?
Don't be like that, Frank!
I was in the neighborhood and thought I'd check in with an old partner.
I repeat. Cut the shit, Mac.
No one that ain't a **Negro**, not even a made man like yourself, ends up in **the Black Belt** unless they need something...
...or they's fucking lost. **You fucking lost?**
No...no, Frank... I'm **not** lost.
Well, I'm **starving** for some beans so spill 'em.

CHAPTER 2

OLD SCORES

I hate to be rude to an old friend. My momma taught me better.

However, when one of Capone's own is standing in one of the top policy wheels on the South Side, let's just say I get a bit anxious. By "anxious," I mean, "looking-over-my- shoulder-sleeping-with-one-eye-open" suspicious.

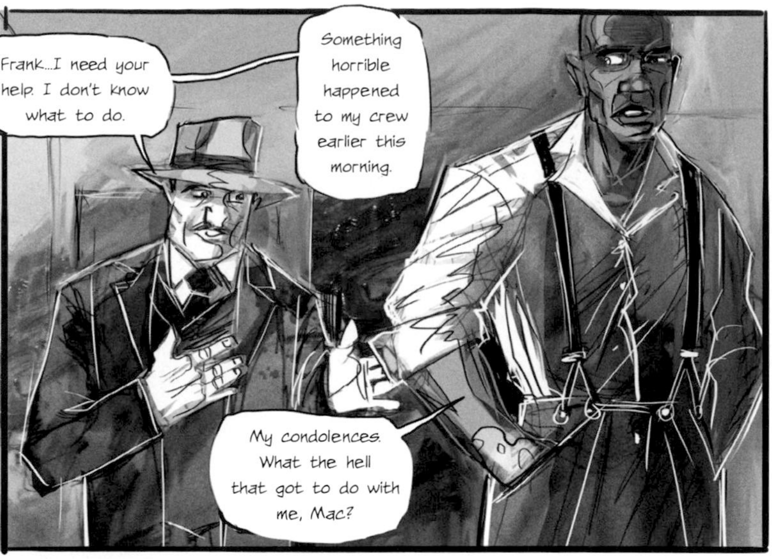

Frank...I need your help. I don't know what to do.
Something horrible happened to my crew earlier this morning.
My condolences. What the hell that got to do with me, Mac?

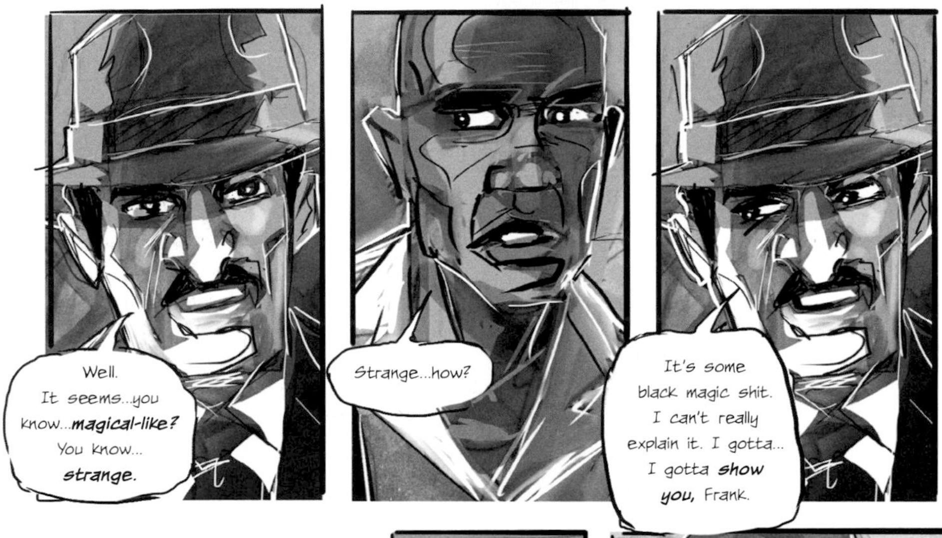

Well. It seems...you know...**magical-like?** You know... **strange.**
Strange...how?
It's some black magic shit. I can't really explain it. I gotta... I gotta **show you,** Frank.

The Shark ain't the kinda man that ***scares*** easily.

Honestly, when we used to run hooch together for Capone, he had nerves of steel. Earned the name ***the Shark*** because he was always after the next score.

I was tempted just by the fact that he was about to piss himself in fear right here in Sophie's bar.

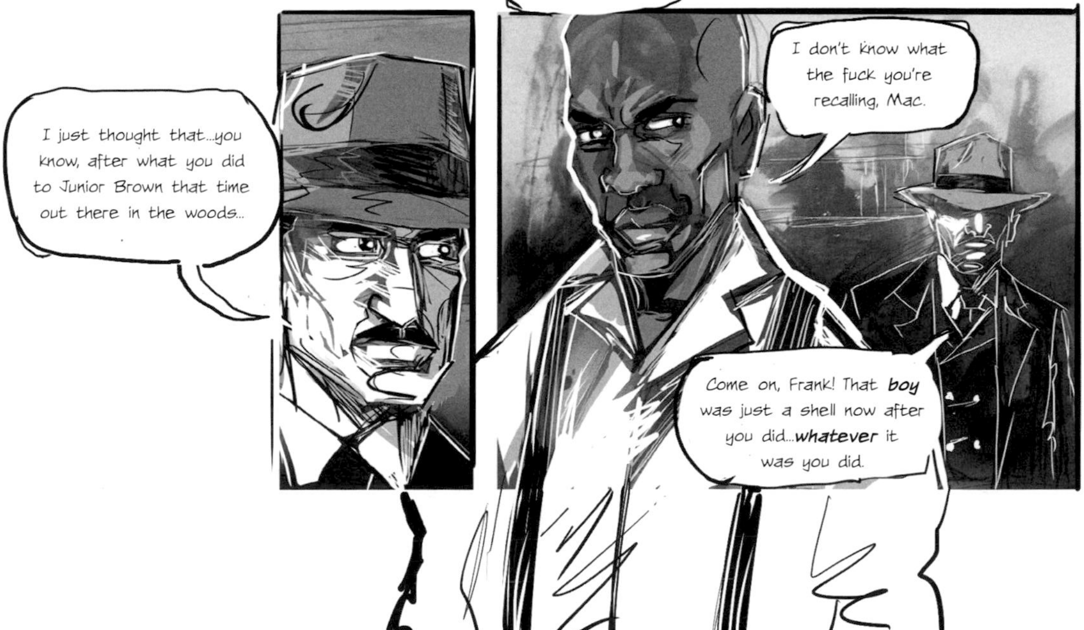

I just thought that...you know, after what you did to Junior Brown that time out there in the woods...
I don't know what the fuck you're recalling, Mac.
Come on, Frank! That **boy** was just a shell now after you did...**whatever** it was you did.

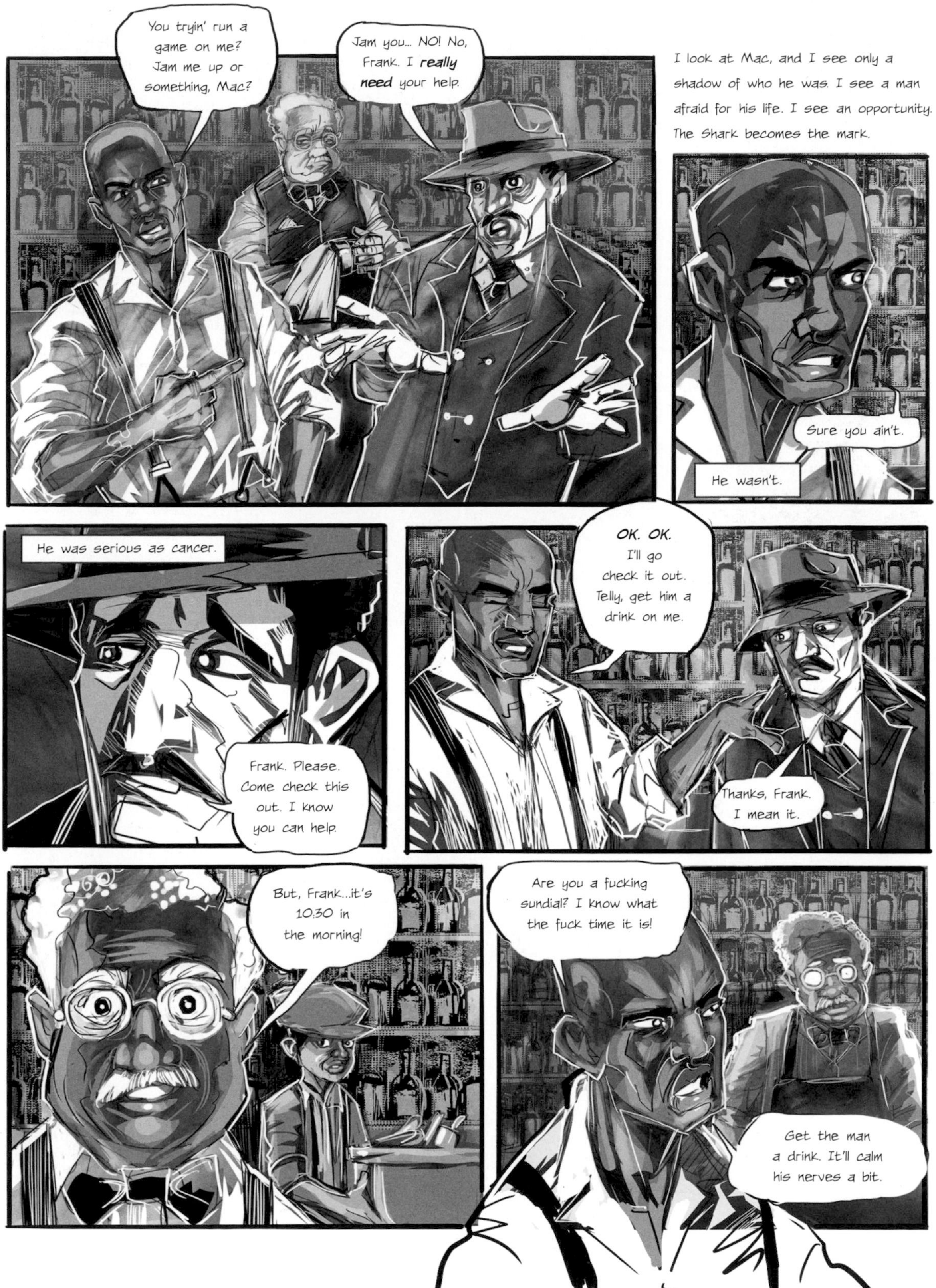

You tryin' run a game on me? Jam me up or something, Mac?
Jam you... NO! No, Frank. I **really need** your help.
I look at Mac, and I see only a shadow of who he was. I see a man afraid for his life. I see an opportunity. The Shark becomes the mark.
Sure you ain't.
He wasn't.
He was serious as cancer.
Frank. Please. Come check this out. I know you can help.
OK. OK. I'll go check it out. Telly, get him a drink on me.
Thanks, Frank. I mean it.
But, Frank...it's 10:30 in the morning!
Are you a fucking sundial? I know what the fuck time it is!
Get the man a drink. It'll calm his nerves a bit.

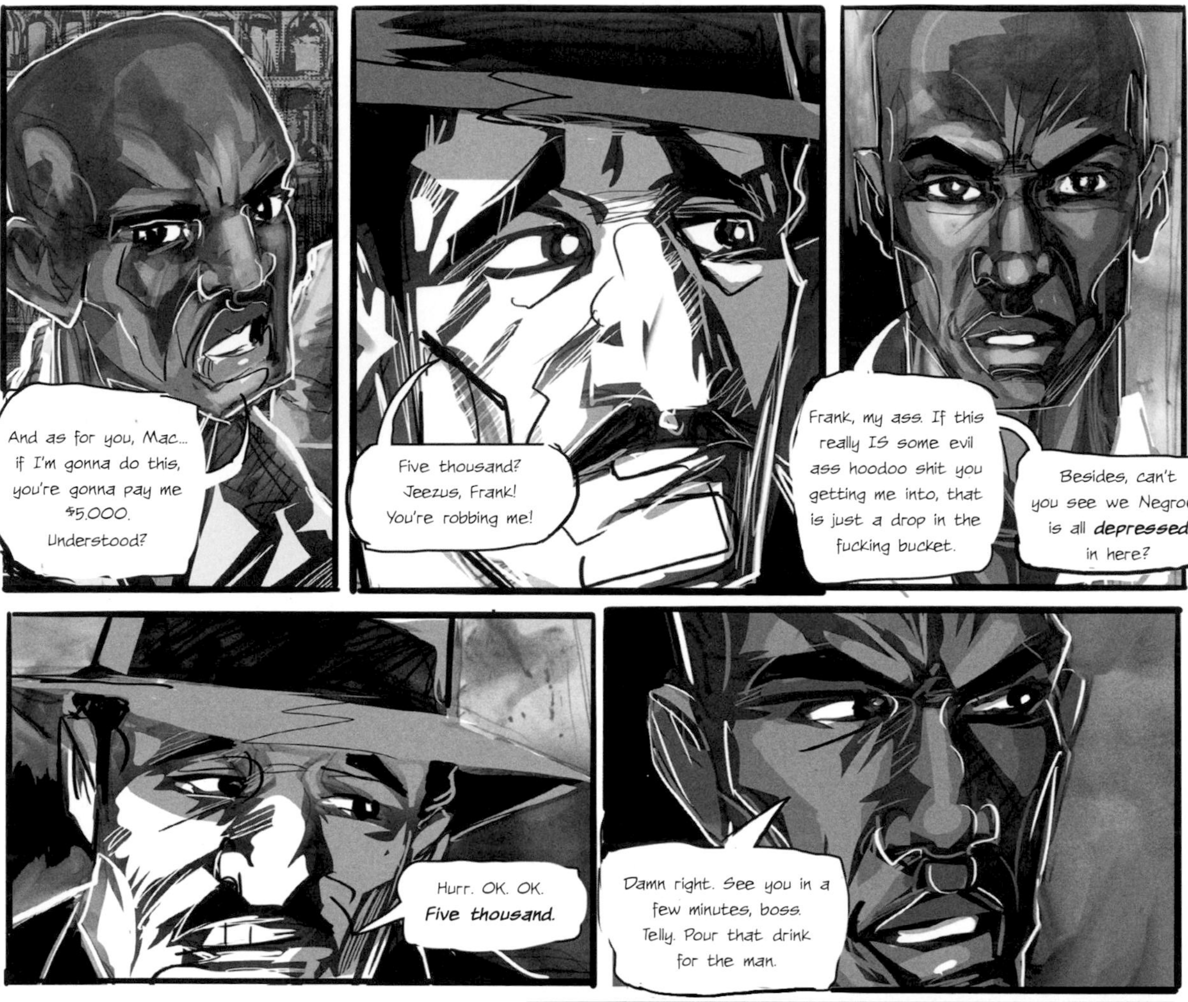
And as for you, Mac... if I'm gonna do this, you're gonna pay me $5,000. Understood?
Five thousand? Jeezus, Frank! You're robbing me!
Frank, my ass. If this really IS some evil ass hoodoo shit you getting me into, that is just a drop in the fucking bucket.
Besides, can't you see we Negroes is all **depressed** in here?
Hurr. OK. OK. **Five thousand.**
Damn right. See you in a few minutes, boss. Telly. Pour that drink for the man.

I make my way back upstairs kind of pleased with myself and my haggling skills, at first. Then a cold shiver goes from my ass to the base of my thick skull. He barely bat an eye at a five-grand price tag. Shit. I shoulda demanded more money.

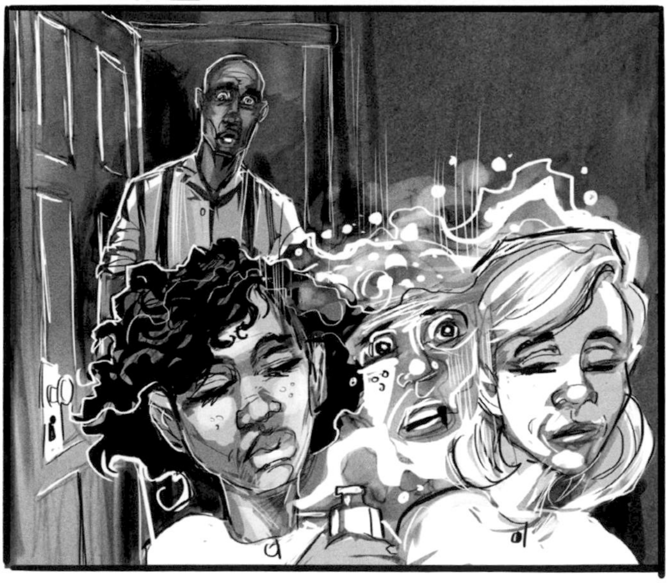

I come into the room just as Sophie is making her change. She's in mid-swallow of her passing potion. I watch the woman I know slip from the high yella brunette beauty to a blonde, blue-eyed white girl.

She does it because of this nice job she does downtown. Pays good money, even in these hard times...but only if you got the right complexion.

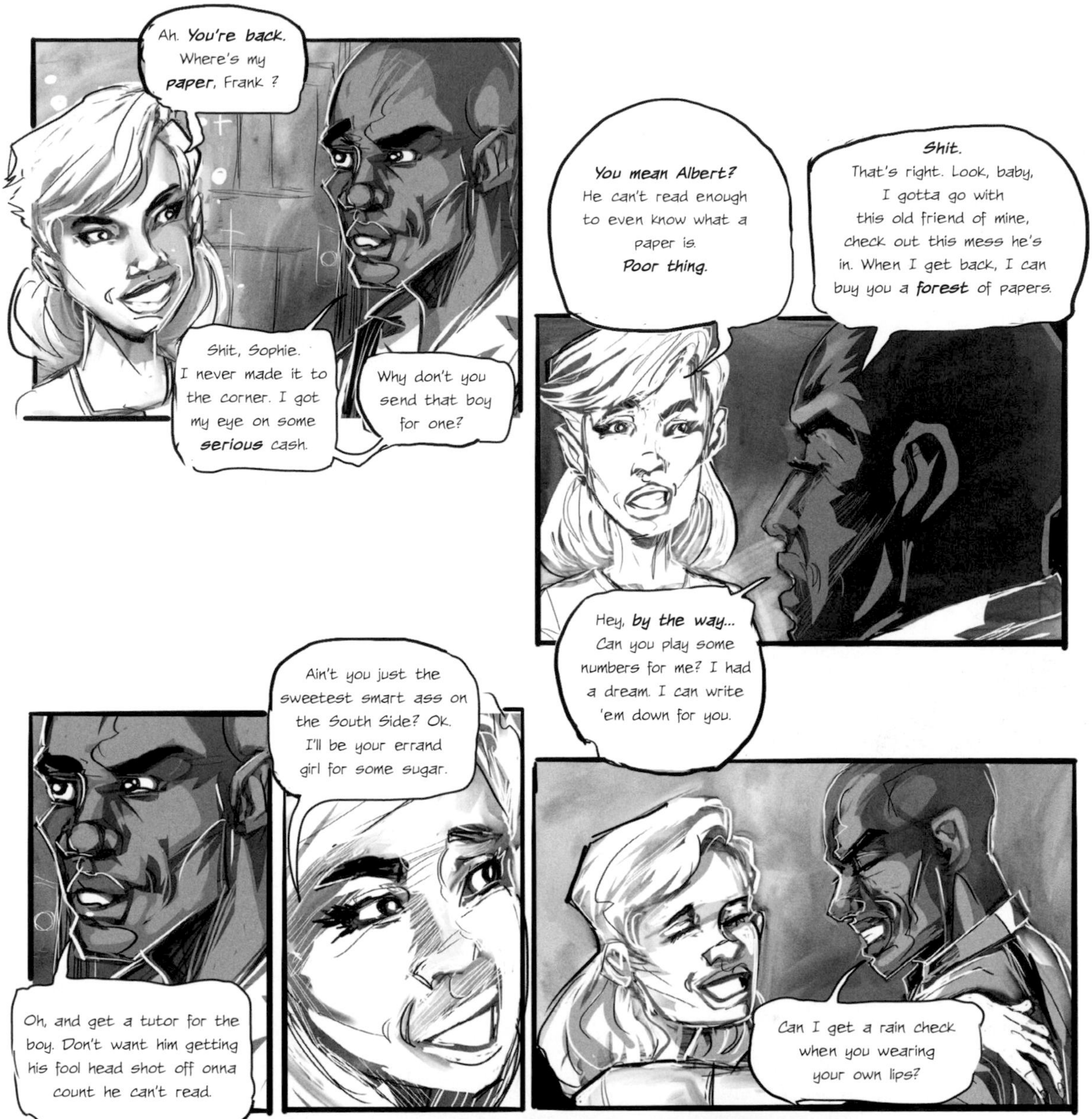
Ah. **You're back.** Where's my **paper**, Frank ?
Shit, Sophie. I never made it to the corner. I got my eye on some **serious** cash.
Why don't you send that boy for one?
You mean Albert? He can't read enough to even know what a paper is. **Poor thing.**
Shit. That's right. Look, baby, I gotta go with this old friend of mine, check out this mess he's in. When I get back, I can buy you a **forest** of papers.
Hey, **by the way...** Can you play some numbers for me? I had a dream. I can write 'em down for you.
Ain't you just the sweetest smart ass on the South Side? Ok. I'll be your errand girl for some sugar.
Oh, and get a tutor for the boy. Don't want him getting his fool head shot off onna count he can't read.
Can I get a rain check when you wearing your own lips?

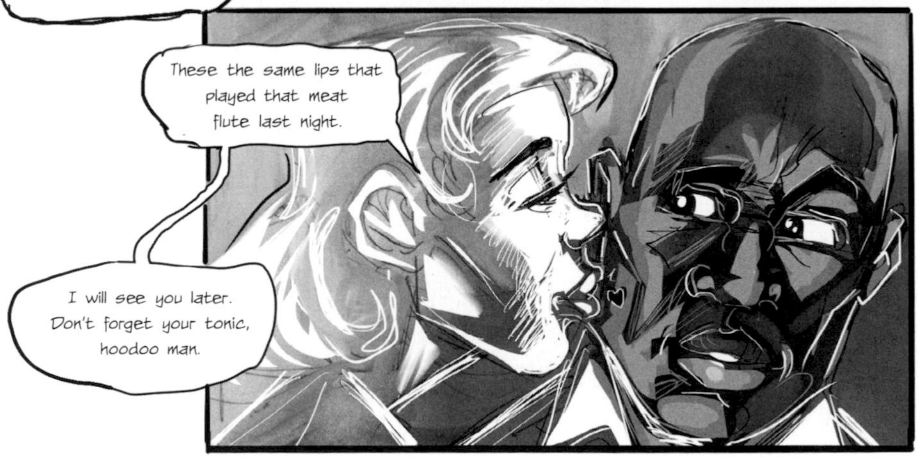
These the same lips that played that meat flute last night.
I will see you later. Don't forget your tonic, hoodoo man.

Sophie is as sweet as honey and loves me more than I think she even knows. She's a right strong rootworker, too. The tonic must be made by the hands of a lover. Sophie's good at both roles.

She's been a hell of a comfort to me, for sure. I think I may love her some, too. Who's to say? But her kiss makes my mojo hand twitch. That's **HER** hand. The Noir's hand and she gets mighty jealous. That's never good.

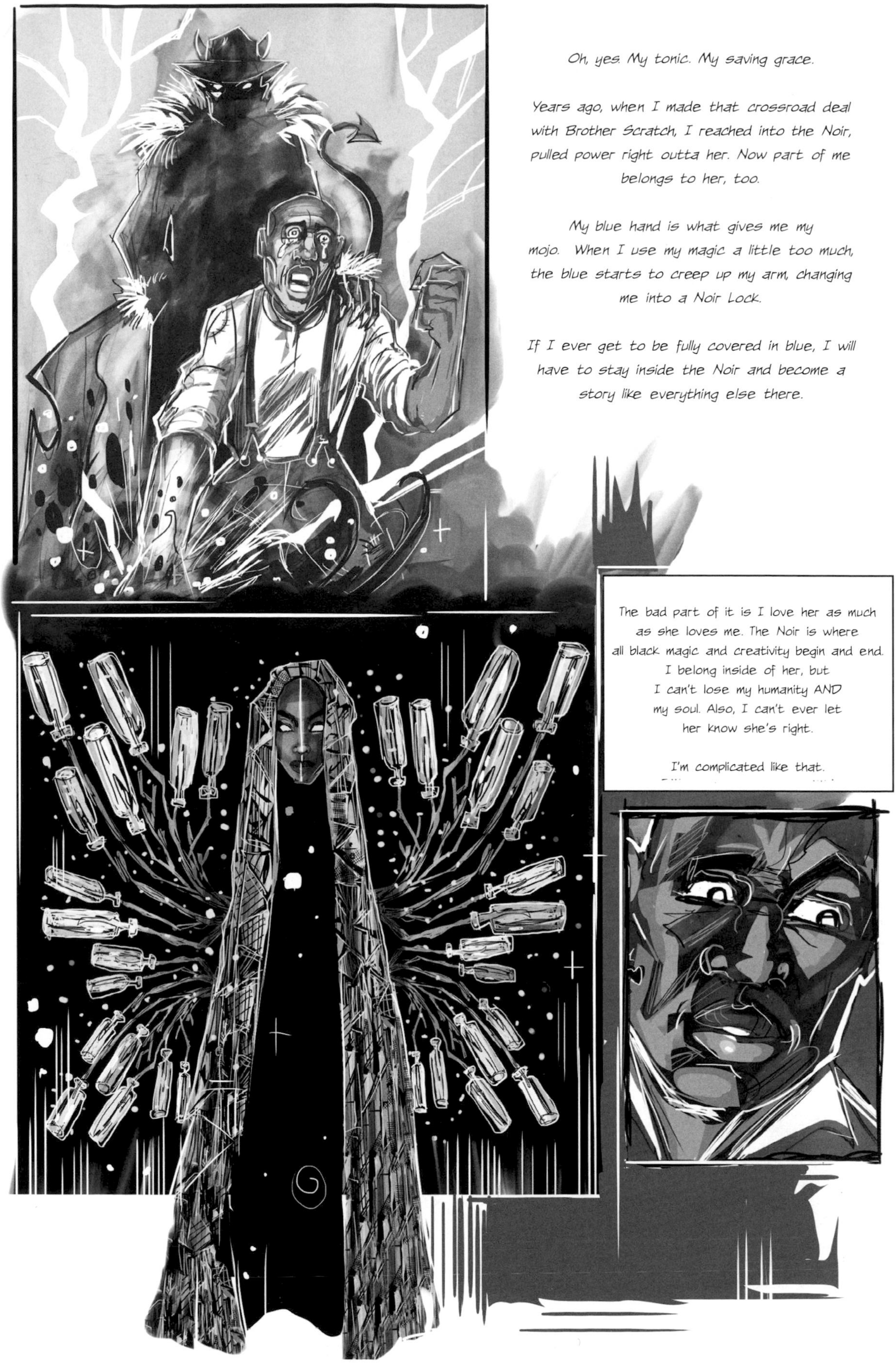
Oh, yes. My tonic. My saving grace.
Years ago, when I made that crossroad deal with Brother Scratch, I reached into the Noir, pulled power right outta her. Now part of me belongs to her, too.
My blue hand is what gives me my mojo. When I use my magic a little too much, the blue starts to creep up my arm, changing me into a Noir Lock.
If I ever get to be fully covered in blue, I will have to stay inside the Noir and become a story like everything else there.
The bad part of it is I love her as much as she loves me. The Noir is where all black magic and creativity begin and end. I belong inside of her, but I can't lose my humanity AND my soul. Also, I can't ever let her know she's right.
I'm complicated like that.

CHAPTER 3
A Muddy Massacre

I jot down the gig numbers for
Sophie, grab my flask of tonic, and get
dressed for business..

Mac and me take his ride back to the
place where whatever scared the shit
out of him happened.

We don't talk much outside of some
idle chatter about current events.
At first he seems in good spirits. I
know it's just a front.

I have to admit. It is good to see
him. It reminds me of our times running
white lightning and mash for Capone.
Those were the days.

His mood gets darker as we get closer
to our destination.

He gets distant and cold, and I can't
help but feel it. The car becomes a
tomb on wheels. Mac just stares out
at the road as we leave the city limits.

We park at an old warehouse that the
mob has "redistributed" for their uses.
God only knows what darkness this
place has seen.

I guess I will know it soon myself.

We go into the double doors, and the
damp smell hits me full in
the face. Death lives here, and It's
taking visitors.

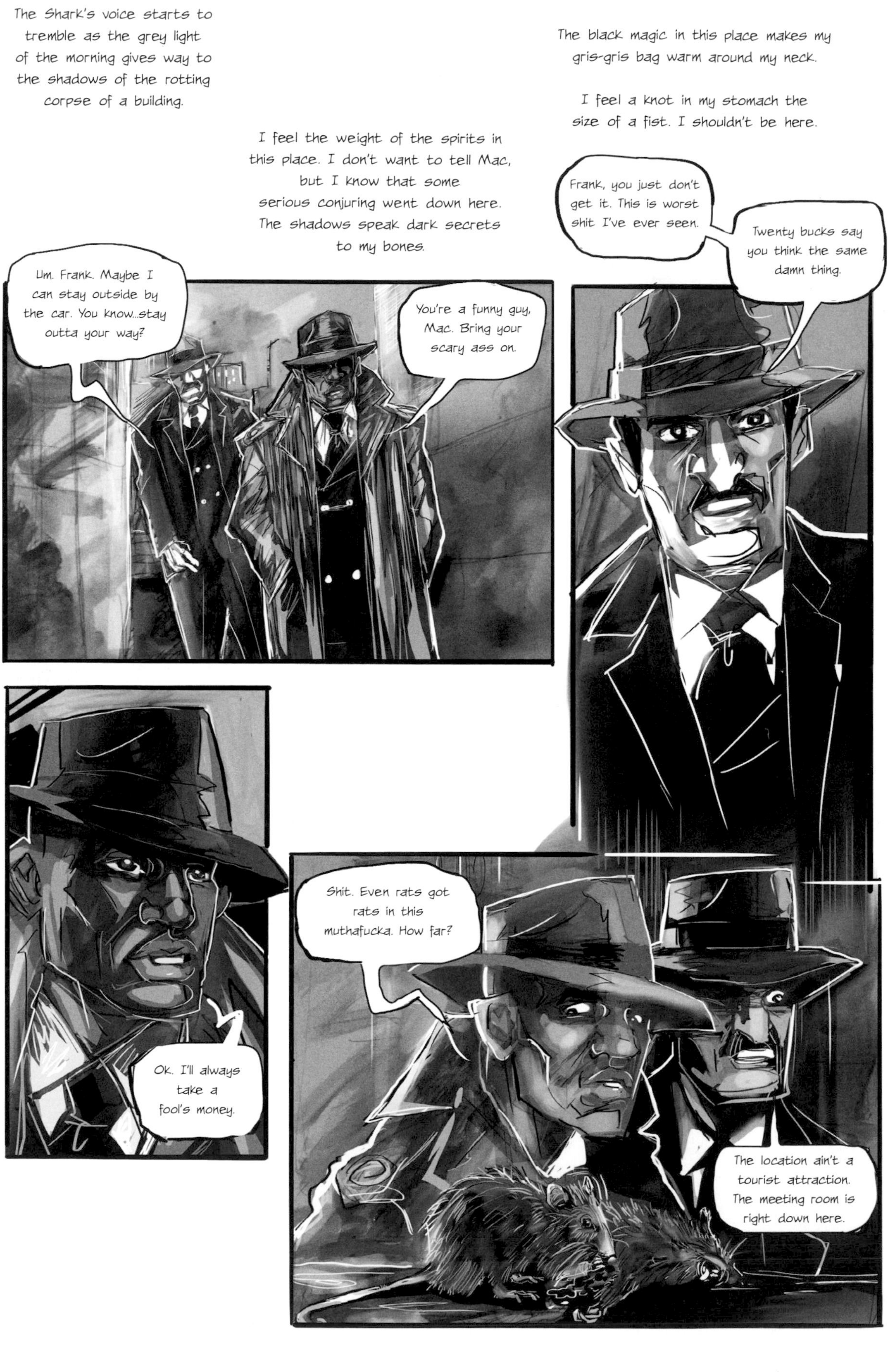
The Shark's voice starts to tremble as the grey light of the morning gives way to the shadows of the rotting corpse of a building.
I feel the weight of the spirits in this place. I don't want to tell Mac, but I know that some serious conjuring went down here. The shadows speak dark secrets to my bones.
The black magic in this place makes my gris-gris bag warm around my neck.
I feel a knot in my stomach the size of a fist. I shouldn't be here.
Um. Frank. Maybe I can stay outside by the car. You know...stay outta your way?
You're a funny guy, Mac. Bring your scary ass on.
Frank, you just don't get it. This is worst shit I've ever seen.
Twenty bucks say you think the same damn thing.
Ok. I'll always take a fool's money.
Shit. Even rats got rats in this muthafucka. How far?
The location ain't a tourist attraction. The meeting room is right down here.

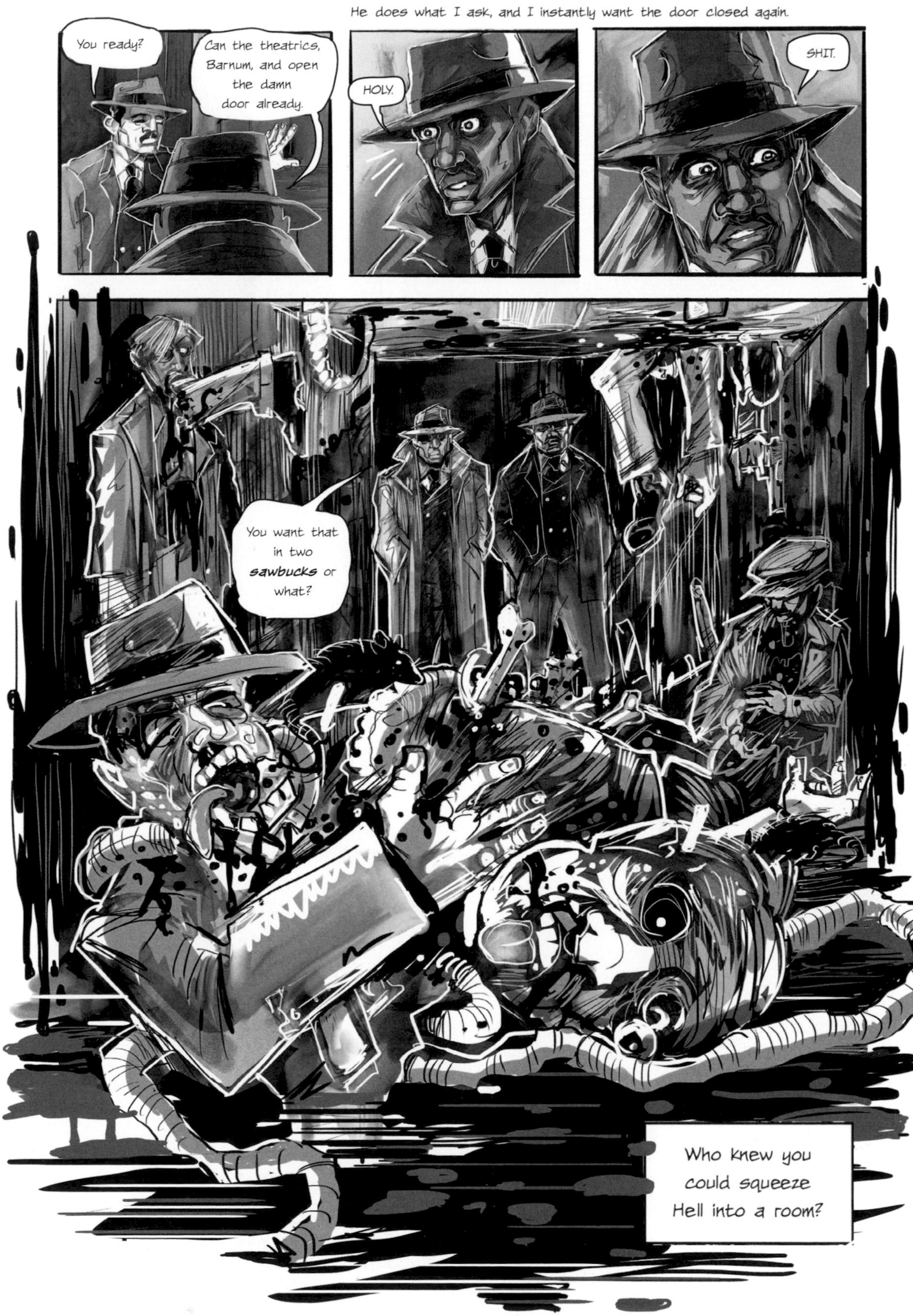
He does what I ask, and I instantly want the door closed again.
You ready?
Can the theatrics, Barnum, and open the damn door already.
HOLY.
SHIT.
You want that in two **sawbucks** or what?
Who knew you could squeeze Hell into a room?

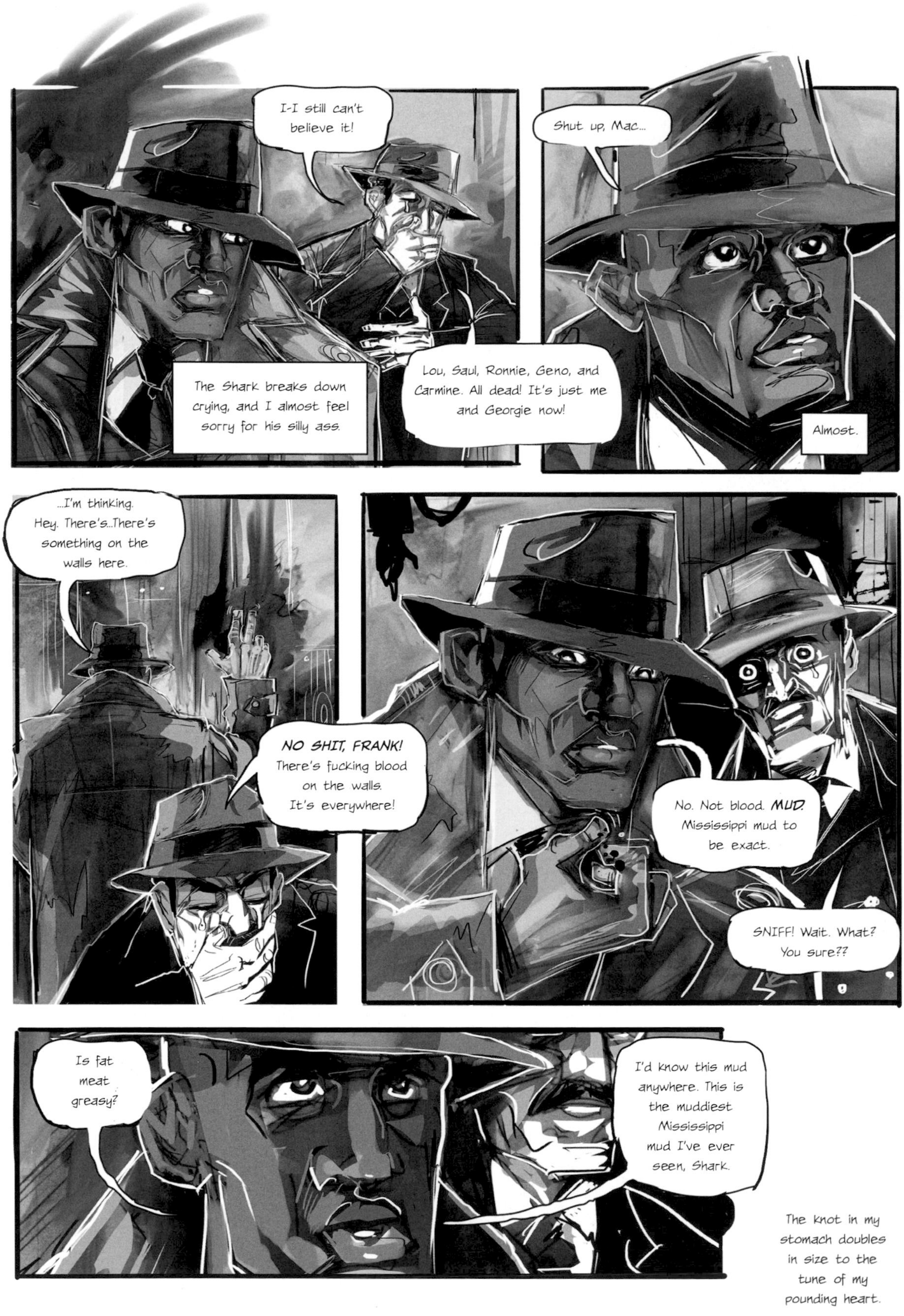
I-I still can't believe it!
The Shark breaks down crying, and I almost feel sorry for his silly ass.
Lou, Saul, Ronnie, Geno, and Carmine. All dead! It's just me and Georgie now!
Shut up, Mac...
Almost.
...I'm thinking. Hey. There's...There's something on the walls here.
NO SHIT, FRANK! There's fucking blood on the walls. It's everywhere!
No. Not blood. MUD. Mississippi mud to be exact.
SNIFF! Wait. What? You sure??
Is fat meat greasy?
I'd know this mud anywhere. This is the muddiest Mississippi mud I've ever seen, Shark.
The knot in my stomach doubles in size to the tune of my pounding heart.

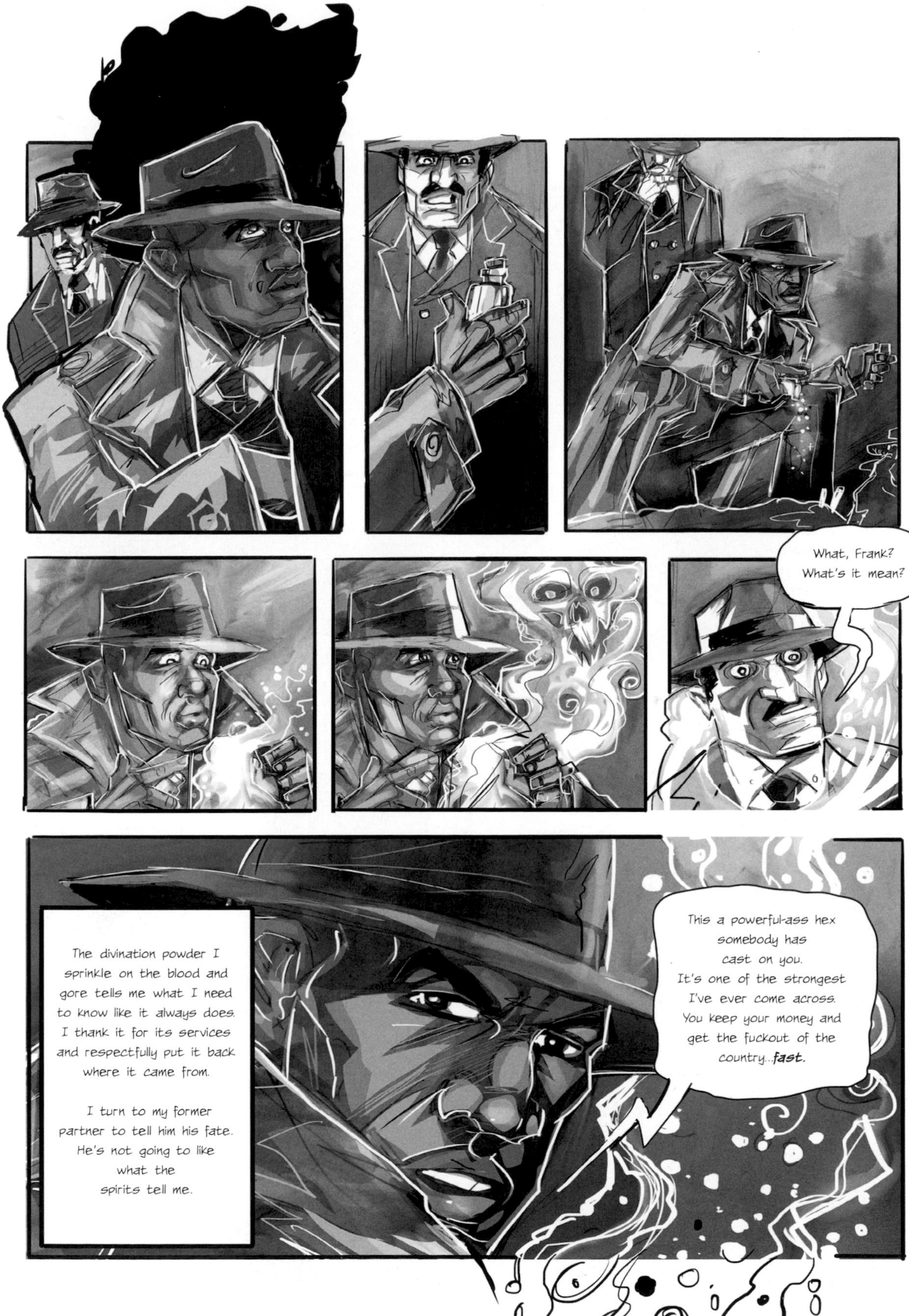
What, Frank? What's it mean?
The divination powder I sprinkle on the blood and gore tells me what I need to know like it always does. I thank it for its services and respectfully put it back where it came from.
I turn to my former partner to tell him his fate. He's not going to like what the spirits tell me.
This a powerful-ass hex somebody has cast on you. It's one of the strongest I've ever come across. You keep your money and get the fuckout of the country...*fast.*

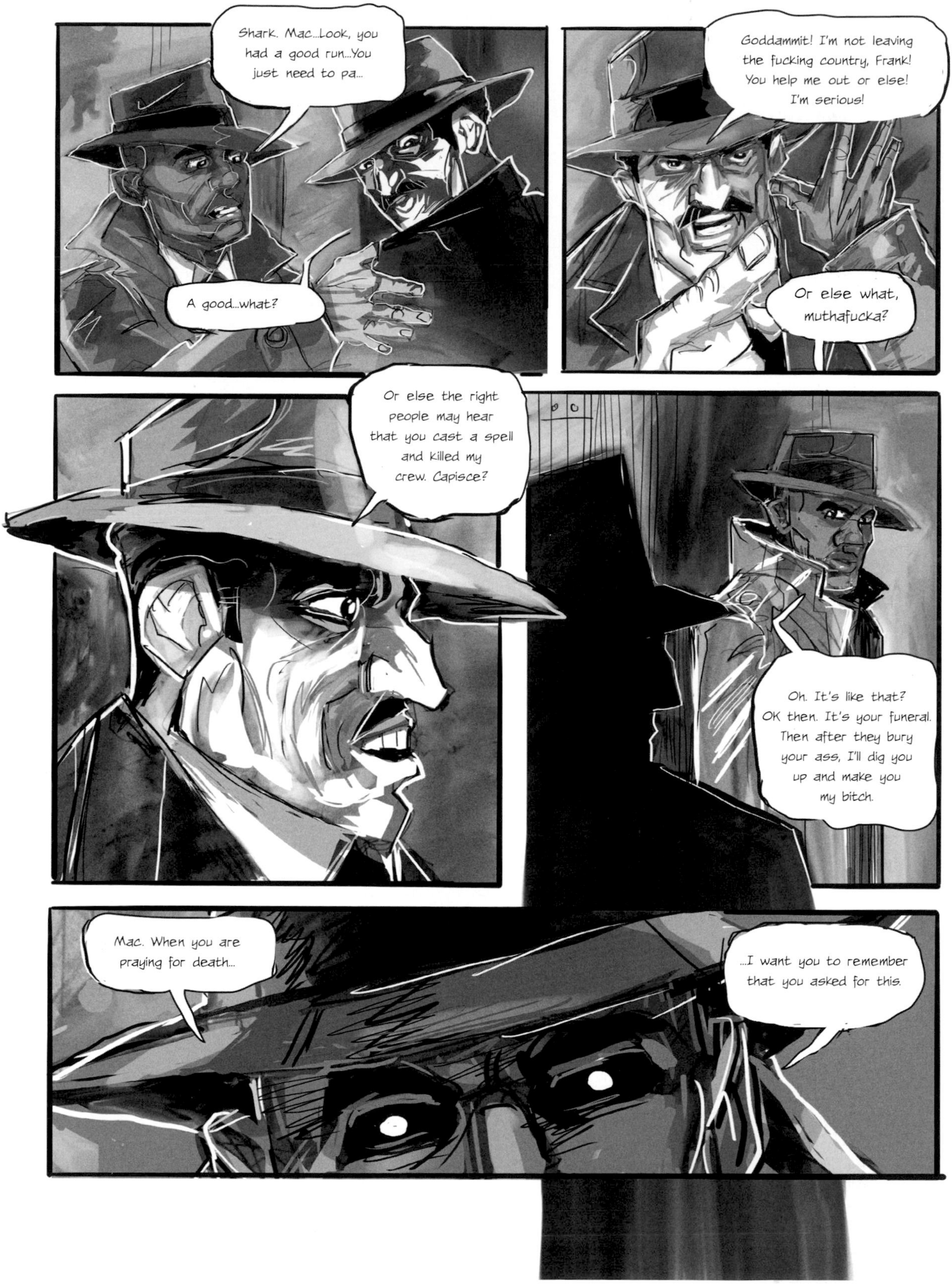

Shark. Mac...Look, you had a good run...You just need to pa...
A good...what?
Goddammit! I'm not leaving the fucking country, Frank! You help me out or else! I'm serious!
Or else what, muthafucka?
Or else the right people may hear that you cast a spell and killed my crew. Capisce?
Oh. It's like that? OK then. It's your funeral. Then after they bury your ass, I'll dig you up and make you my bitch.
Mac. When you are praying for death...
...I want you to remember that you asked for this.

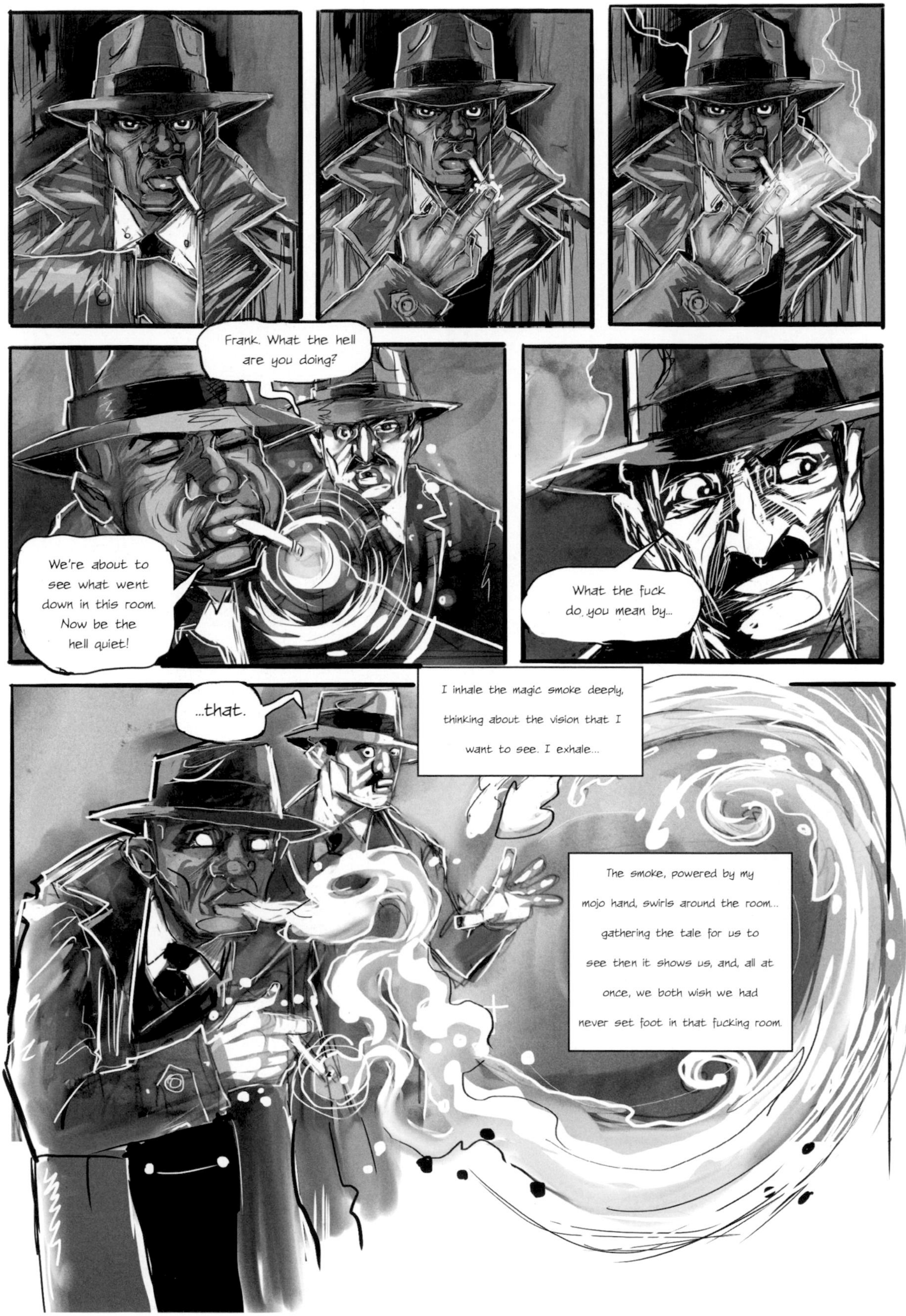
Frank. What the hell are you doing?
We're about to see what went down in this room. Now be the hell quiet!
What the fuck do you mean by...
...that.
I inhale the magic smoke deeply, thinking about the vision that I want to see. I exhale...
The smoke, powered by my mojo hand, swirls around the room... gathering the tale for us to see then it shows us, and, all at once, we both wish we had never set foot in that fucking room.

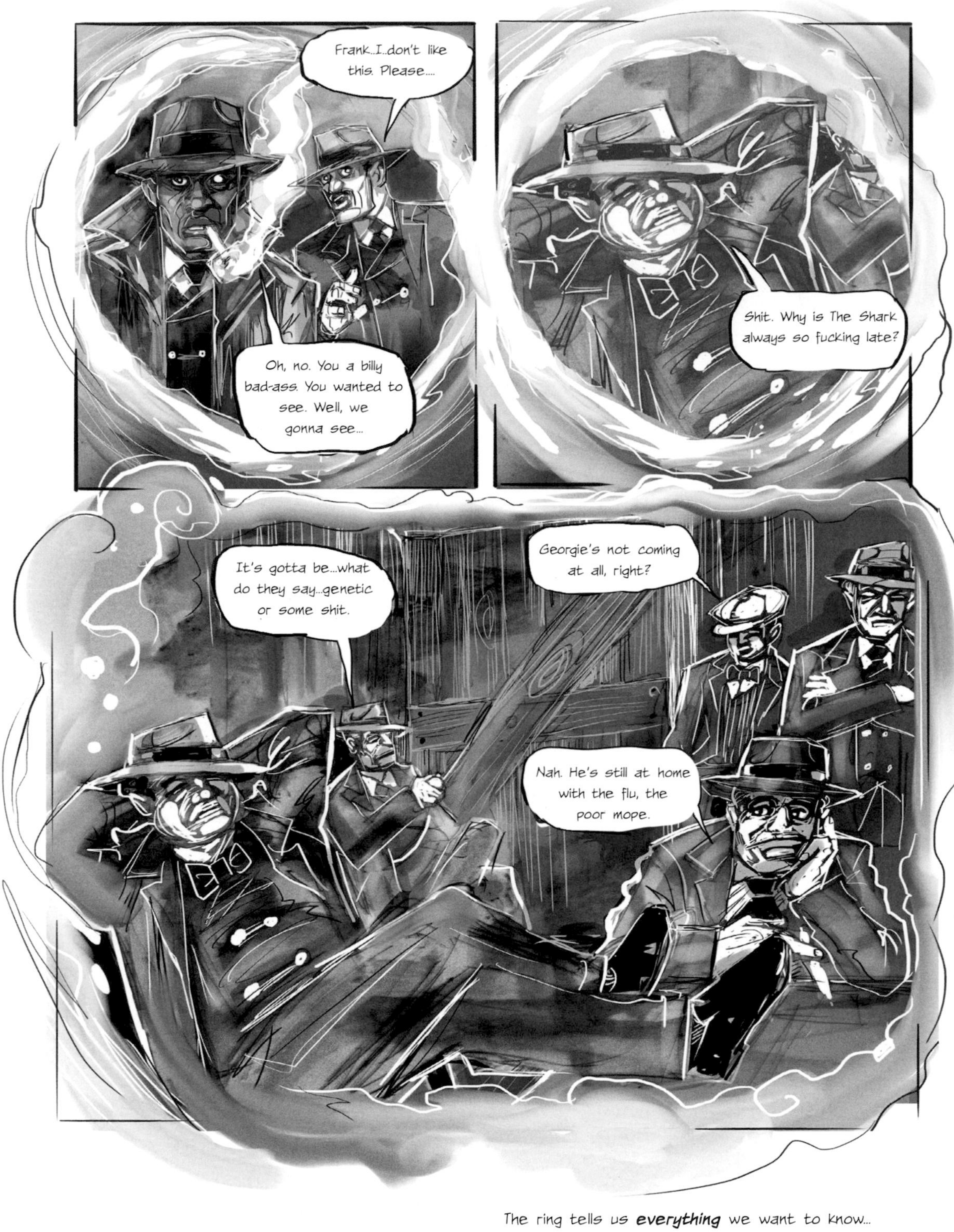
Frank...I...don't like this. Please....
Oh, no. You a billy bad-ass. You wanted to see. Well, we gonna see...
Shit. Why is The Shark always so fucking late?
It's gotta be...what do they say...genetic or some shit.
Georgie's not coming at all, right?
Nah. He's still at home with the flu, the poor mope.

The ring tells us ***everything*** we want to know...
or everything ***we thought*** we wanted to know.
To this day I wish I hadn't seen ***any of it.***

But that's nothing compared to actually being there...
I guarantee you that.

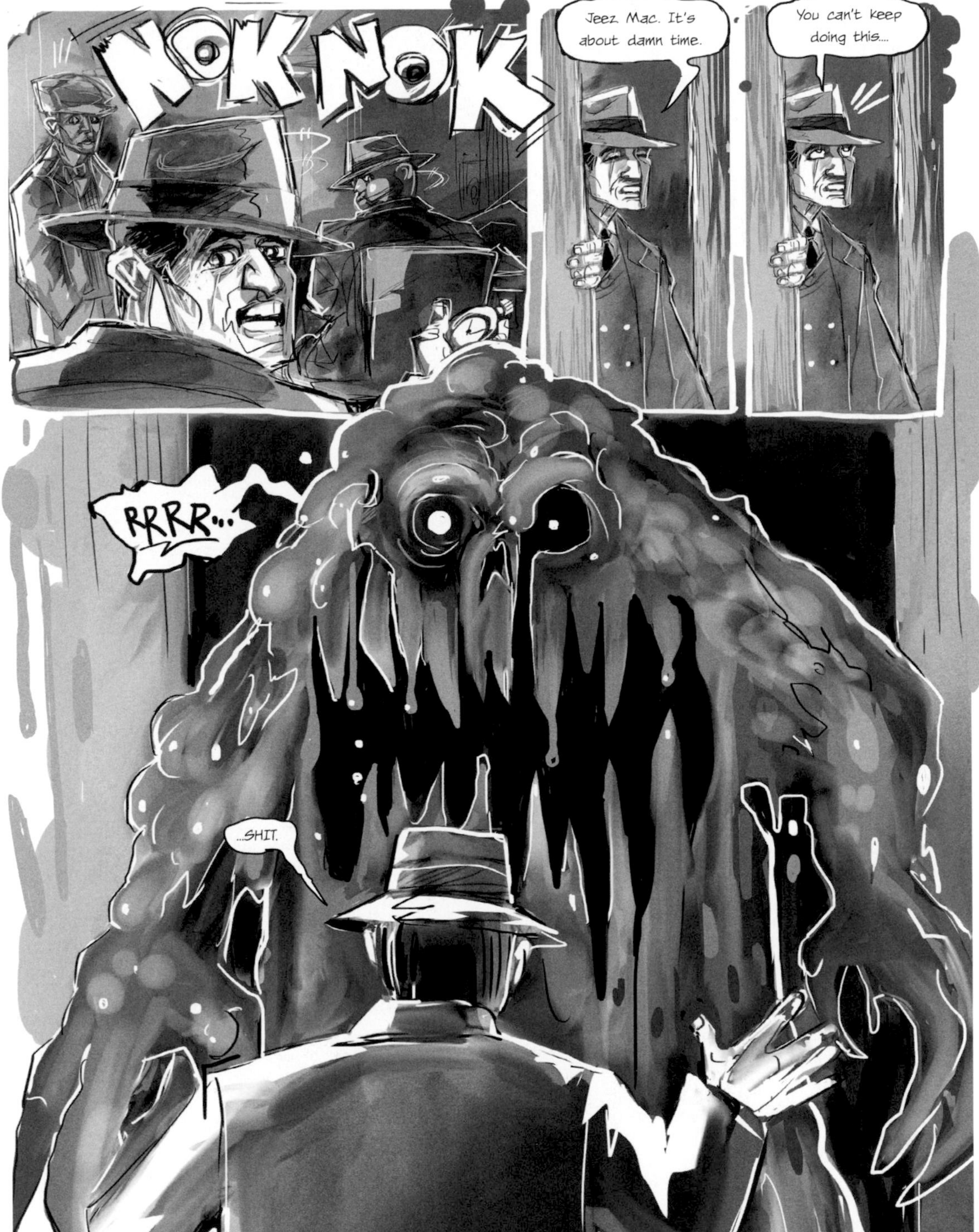
NOK NOK
Jeez Mac. It's about damn time.
You can't keep doing this...
RRRR...
...SHIT.

Time stops. Just enough of a moment
to see a glimpse of your life flash...

...then the devil laughs somewhere and
Hell makes itself known...

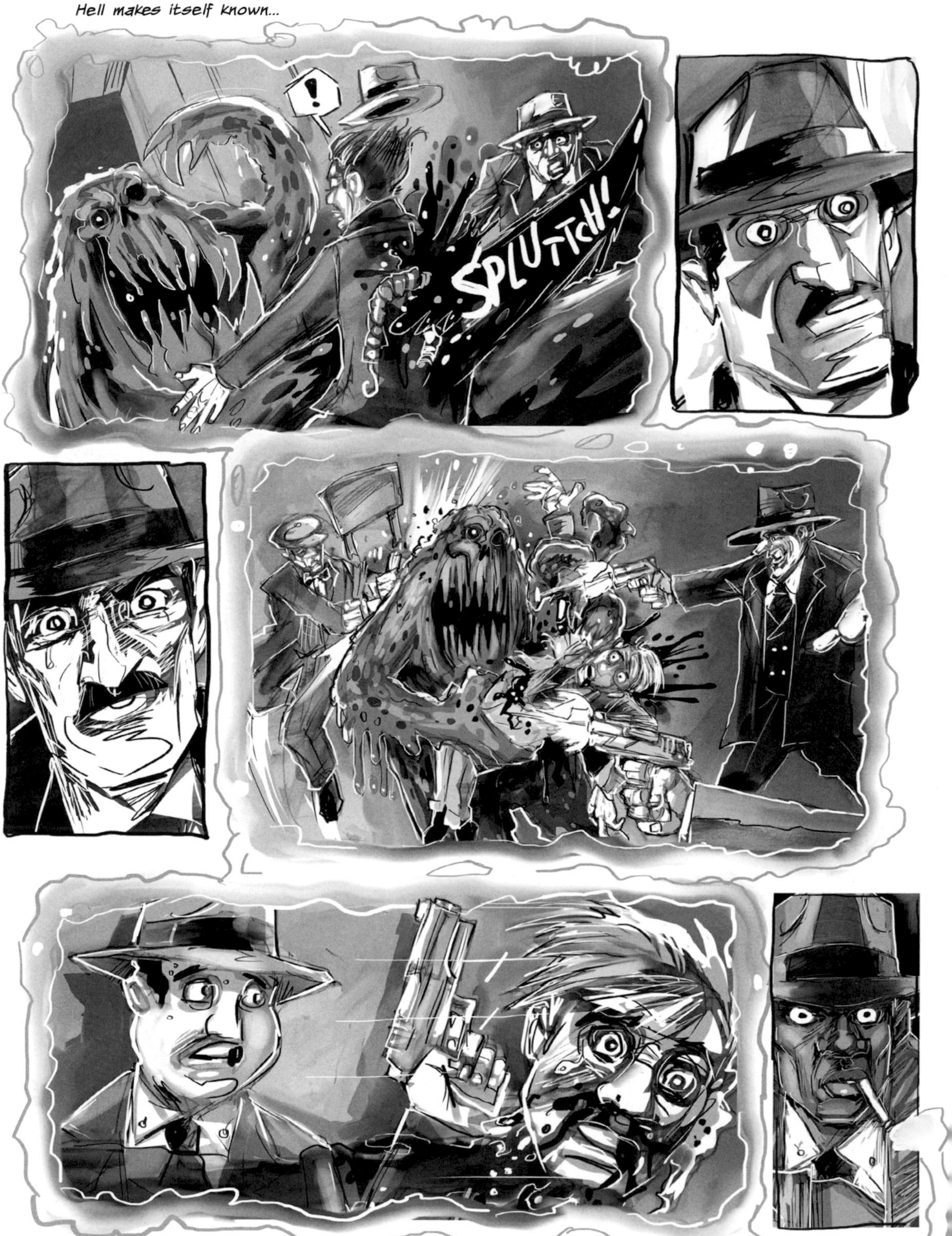
!
SPLUTTCH!

One by one, **each man** was reduced to just the stink of **fear and shit...**

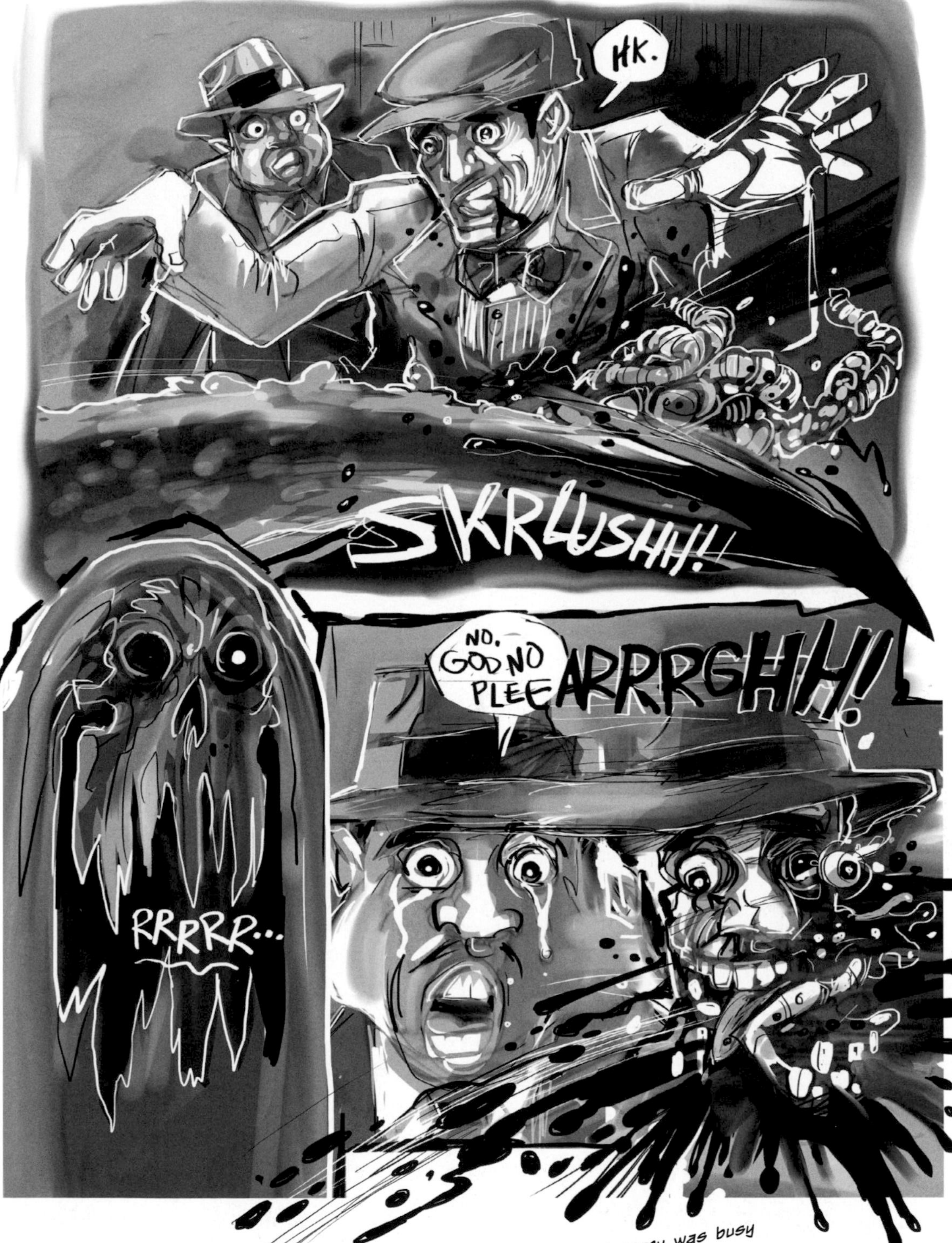
HK.
SKRUSHH!
NO, GOD NO PLEE
ARRRGHH!
RRRRR...

...and mercy was busy that day.

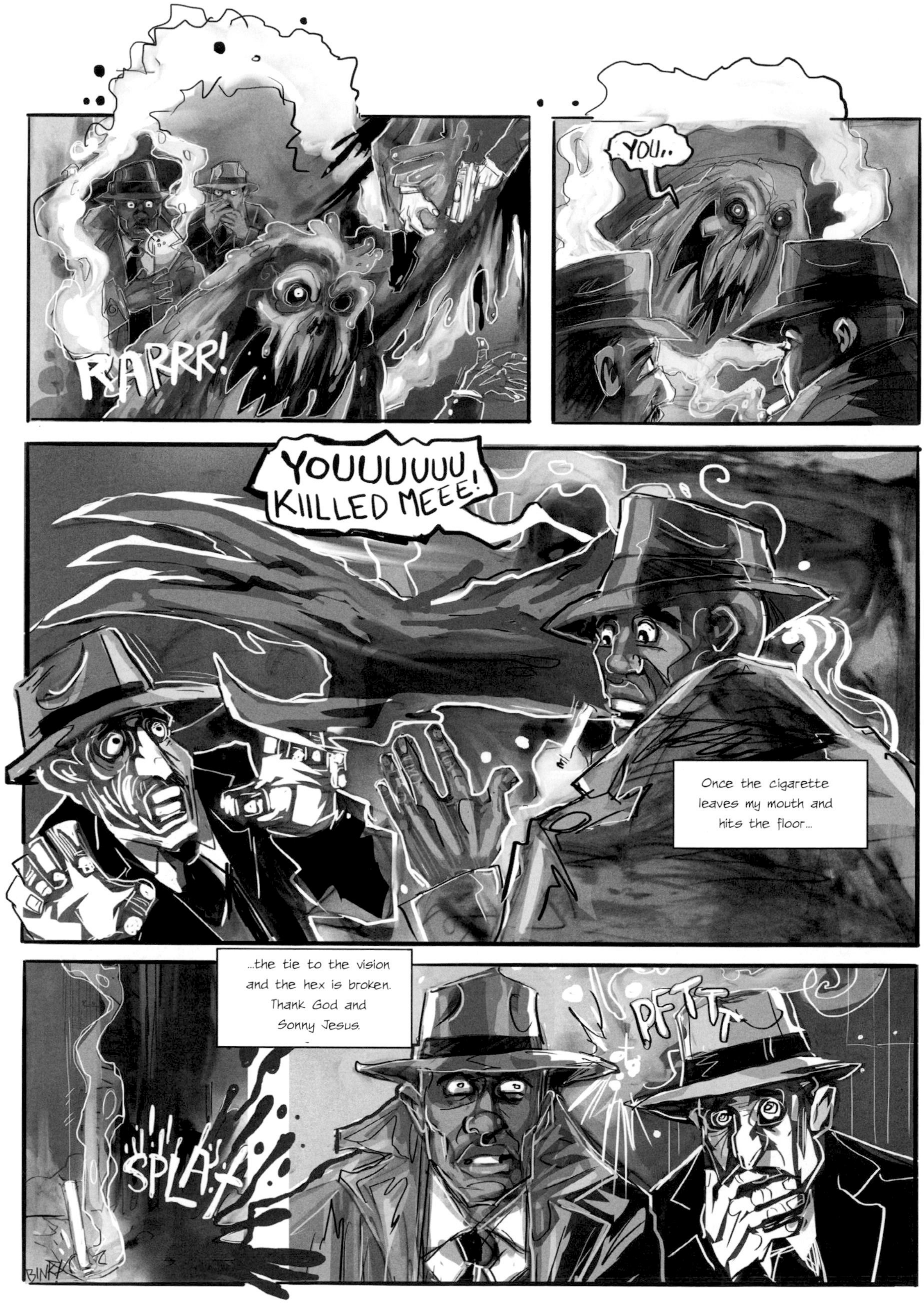
RARRR!
YOU..
YOUUUUUU, KIILLED MEEE!
Once the cigarette leaves my mouth and hits the floor...
...the tie to the vision and the hex is broken. Thank God and Sonny Jesus.
PFTTT
SPLAT

We both strain to keep down the last thing we ate...

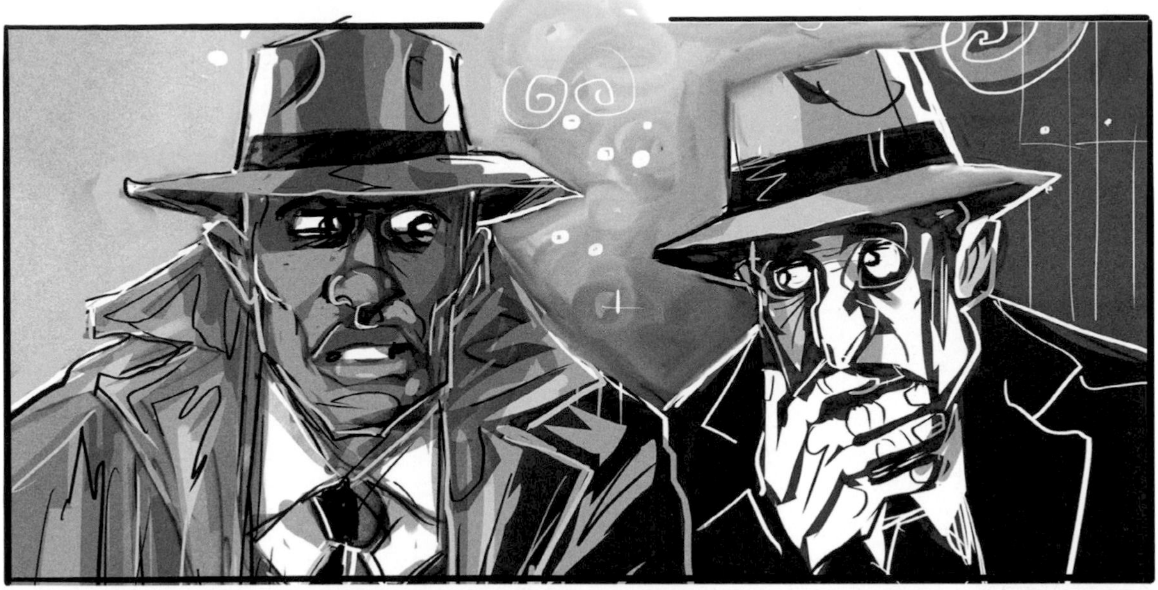

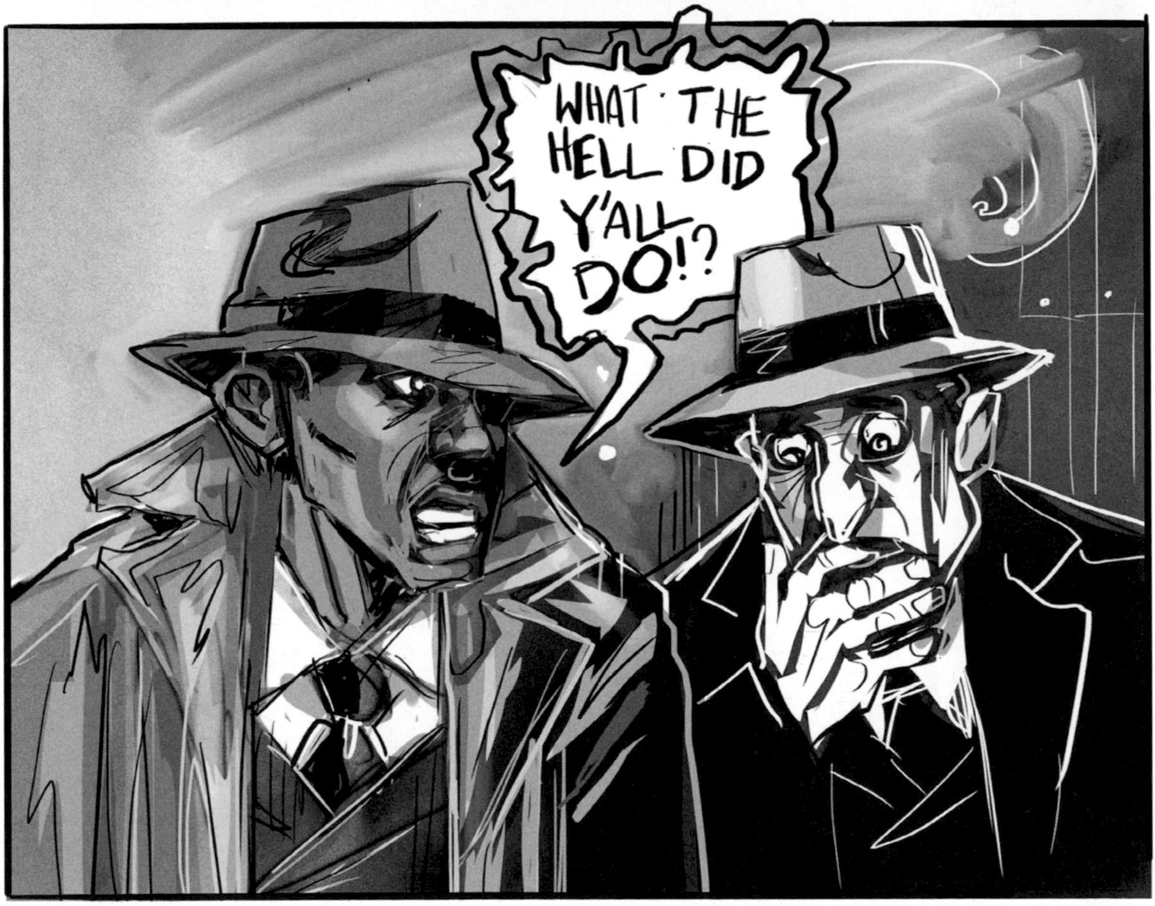
WHAT THE HELL DID Y'ALL DO!?

CHAPTER 4

WHAT THE HELL THEY DID

We both can't wait to get out of that room for some clean air. The light doesn't help much.

I light up another square while Mac loses his lunch all over the ground. I can't blame him. What we saw wasn't meant for human eyes.

I've never seen so much pain and rage in a thing in my life. It's hell-bent on revenge.

The darkest thing there is.

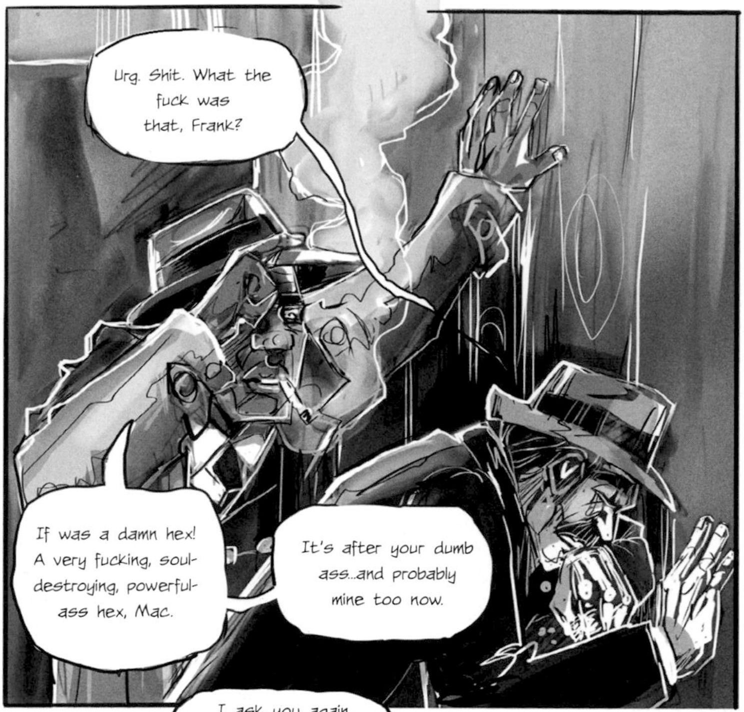

Urg. Shit. What the fuck was that, Frank?
If was a damn hex! A very fucking, soul-destroying, powerful-ass hex, Mac.
It's after your dumb ass...and probably mine too now.

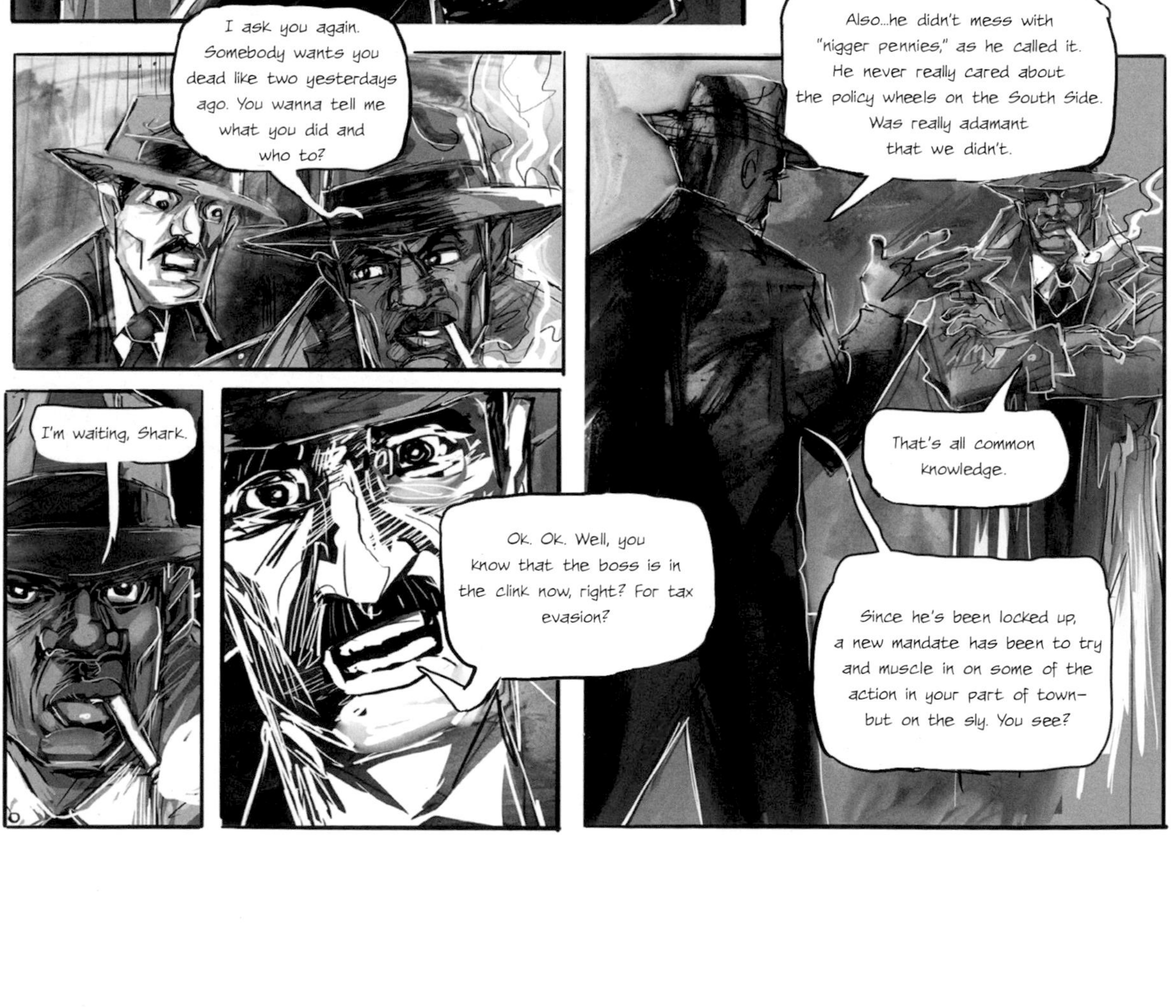

I ask you again. Somebody wants you dead like two yesterdays ago. You wanna tell me what you did and who to?
I'm waiting, Shark.
Ok. Ok. Well, you know that the boss is in the clink now, right? For tax evasion?
Also...he didn't mess with "nigger pennies," as he called it. He never really cared about the policy wheels on the South Side. Was really adamant that we didn't.
That's all common knowledge.
Since he's been locked up, a new mandate has been to try and muscle in on some of the action in your part of town–but on the sly. You see?

SOYE
LIN

xxxxxxx3736

4/16/2021

Item: ï¿½0010090280511 ((book)

The Shark rambles on, and I get more and more worried about the end of this mess..

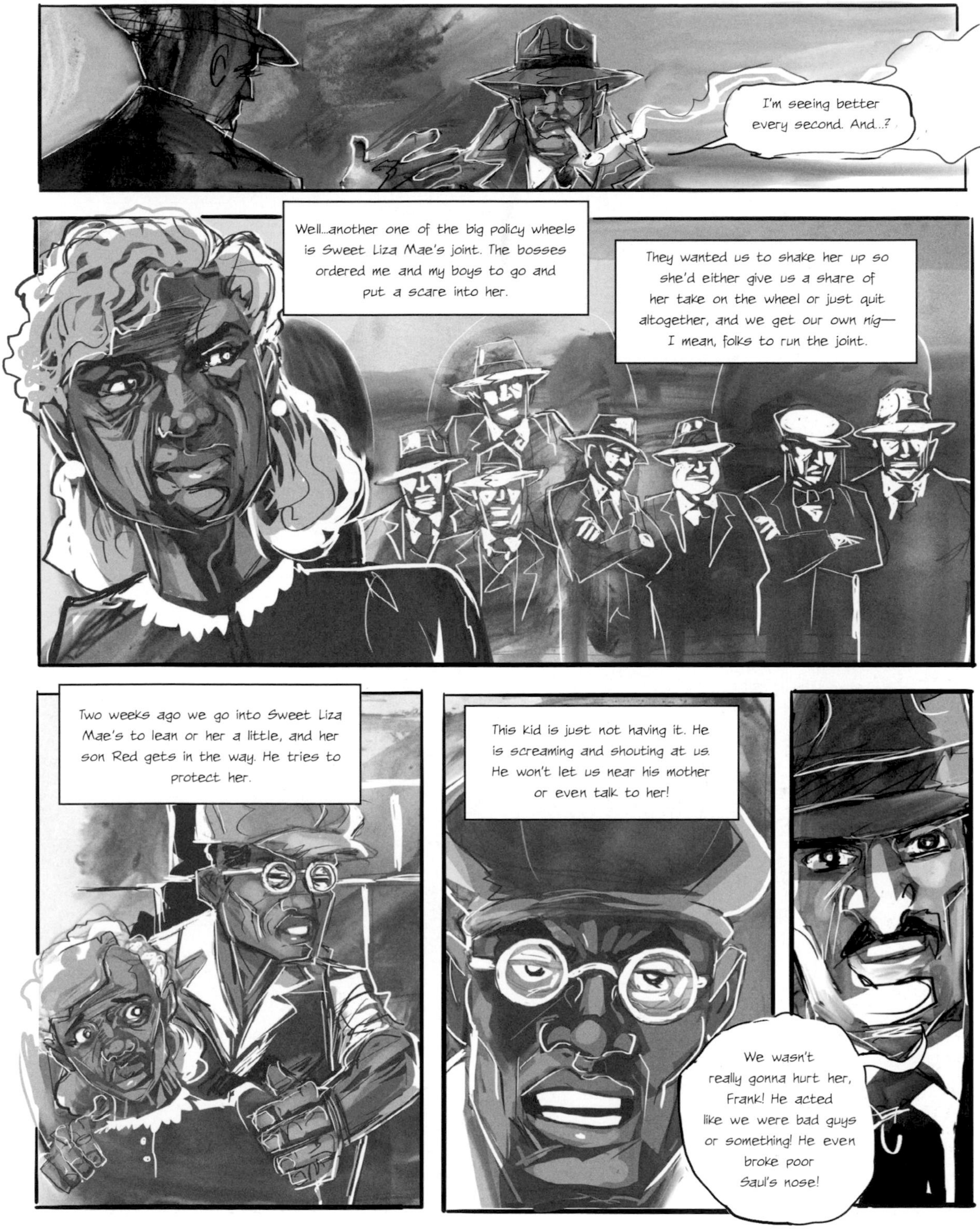
I'm seeing better every second. And...?
Well...another one of the big policy wheels is Sweet Liza Mae's joint. The bosses ordered me and my boys to go and put a scare into her.
They wanted us to shake her up so she'd either give us a share of her take on the wheel or just quit altogether, and we get our own *nig*— I mean, folks to run the joint.
Two weeks ago we go into Sweet Liza Mae's to lean or her a little, and her son Red gets in the way. He tries to protect her.
This kid is just not having it. He is screaming and shouting at us. He won't let us near his mother or even talk to her!
We wasn't really gonna hurt her, Frank! He acted like we were bad guys or something! He even broke poor Saul's nose!

He got really physical, and he ended up rushing us. Before you know it, Carmine pulled his piece and plugged the kid. It wasn't supposed to go down like that! He shouldn't have rushed us like that! I think he was slow or something, you know?

We had no choice, Frank.

The kid..Red..he died right there in his mother's arms. I never heard wailing like that. Never.

Then. Then, all of a sudden, she stopped and stared at us with this...look. She didn't say a word. She just...looked right through us like we werent there.

We got outta there quick. We ddin't even look back. I think we were all in shock. It all went to hell so fast, Frank.! Right to Hell.

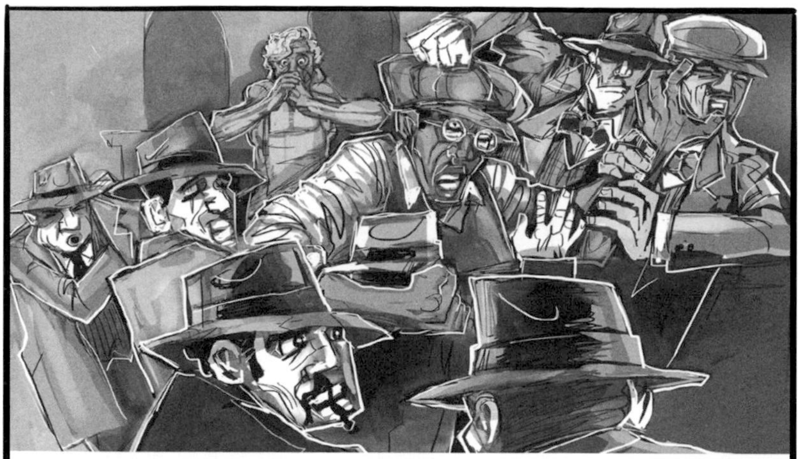

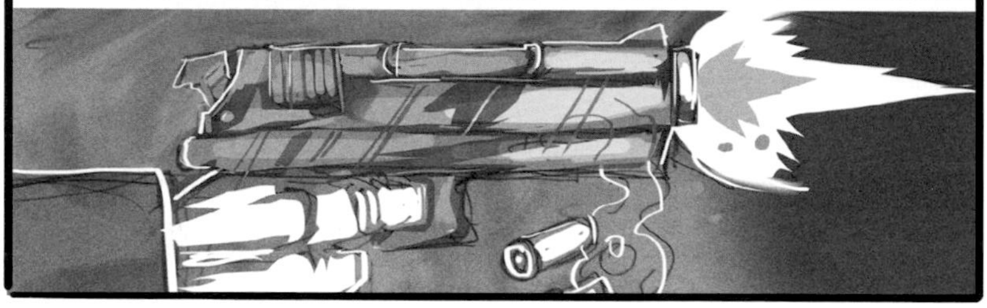

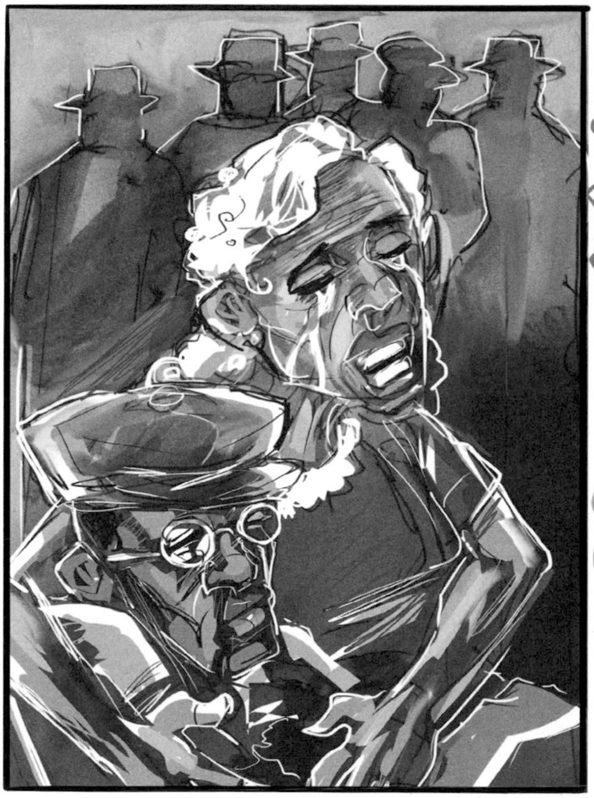

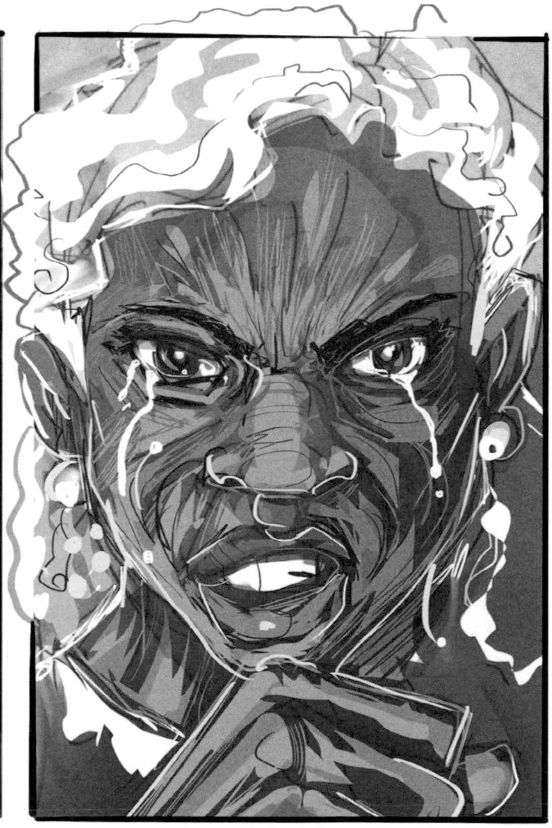

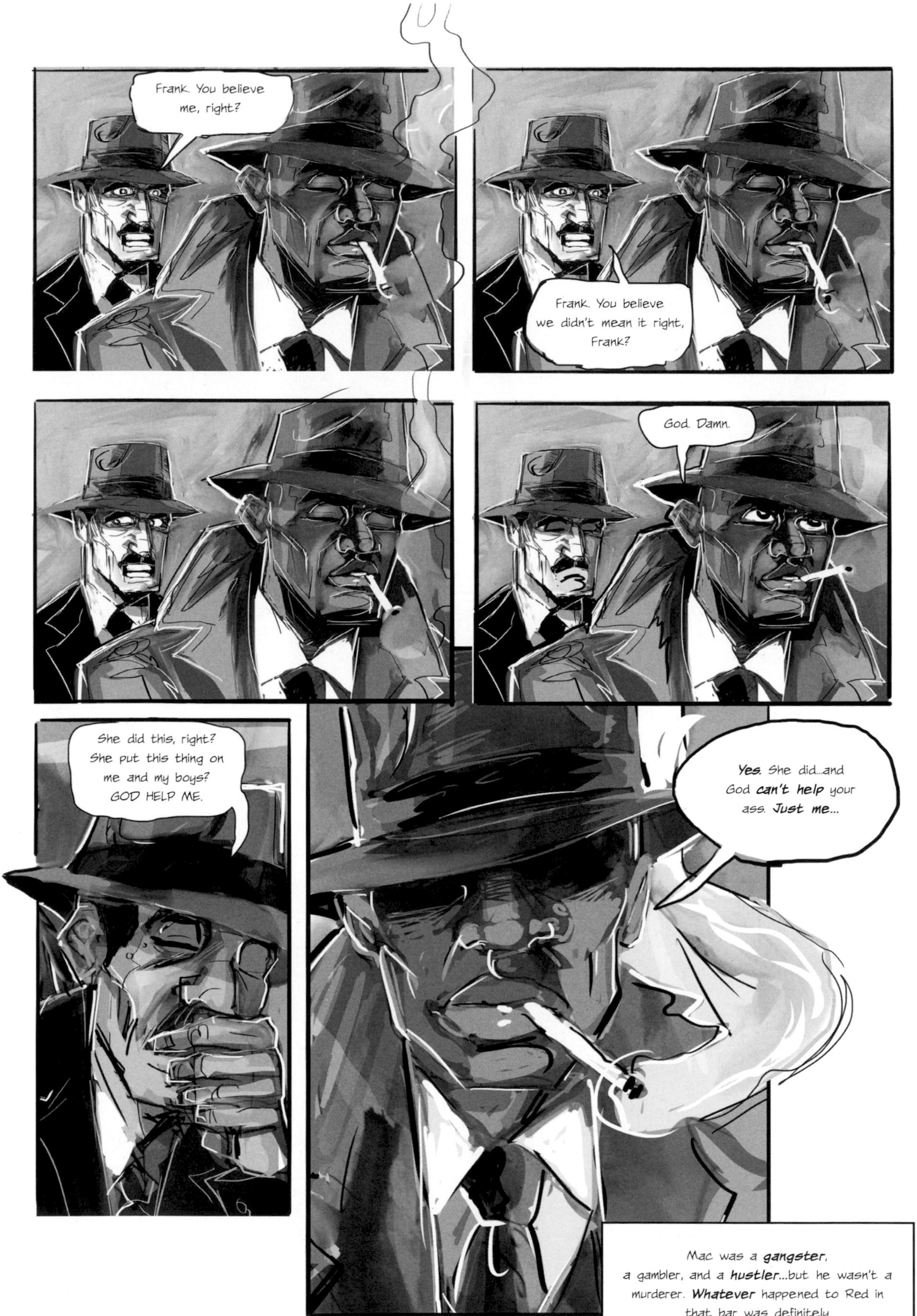
Frank. You believe me, right?
Frank. You believe we didn't mean it right, Frank?
God. Damn.
She did this, right? She put this thing on me and my boys? GOD HELP ME.
Yes. She did...and God **can't help** your ass. **Just me...**
Mac was a **gangster**, a gambler, and a **hustler**...but he wasn't a murderer. **Whatever** happened to Red in that bar was definitely an accident.

HOWEVER...

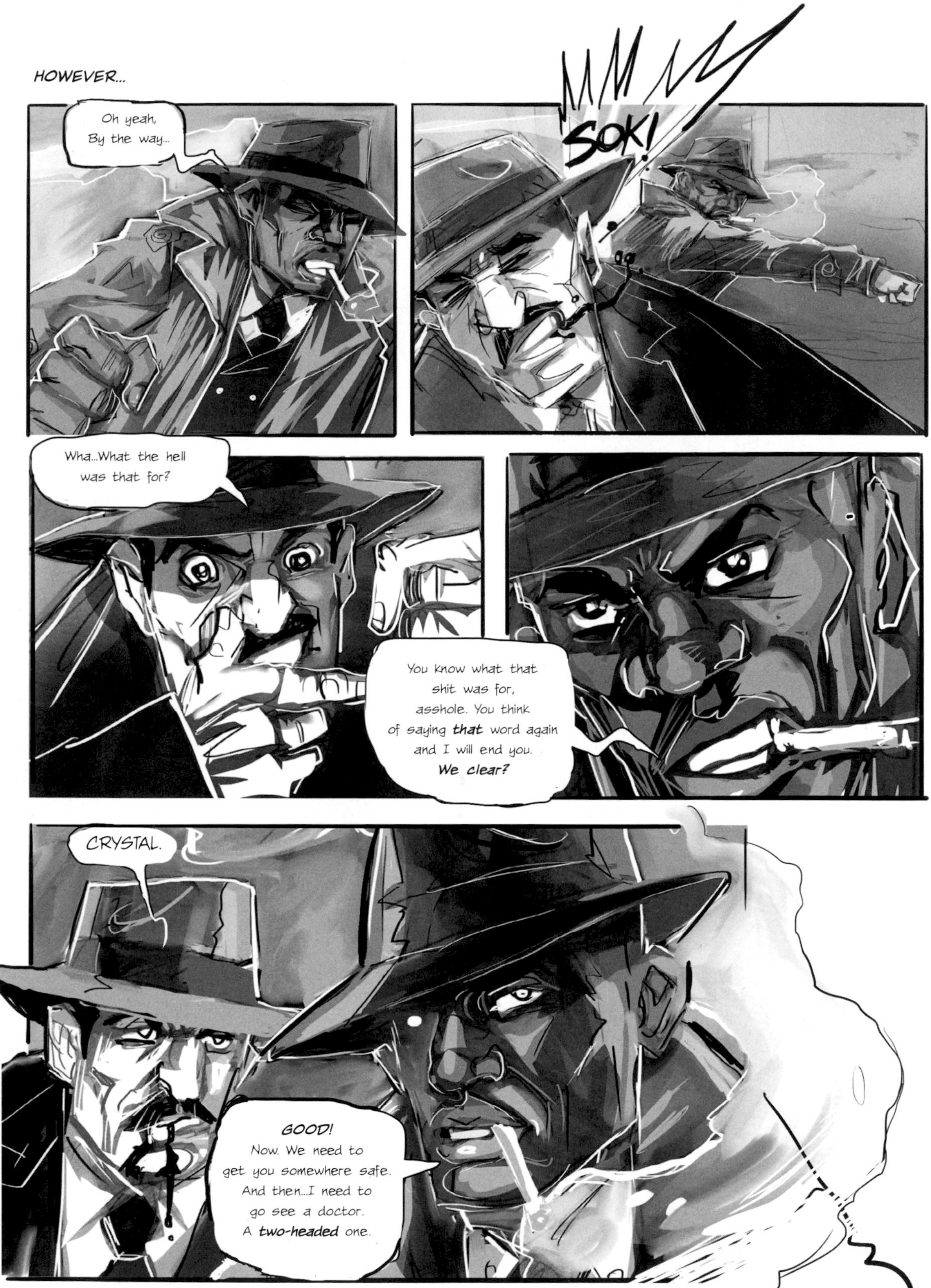

Oh yeah, By the way...
SOK!
Wha...What the hell was that for?
You know what that shit was for, asshole. You think of saying **that** word again and I will end you. **We clear?**
CRYSTAL.
GOOD! Now. We need to get you somewhere safe. And then...I need to go see a doctor. A **two-headed** one.

We head **back** to the city...and the hell we just saw **goes back** wiith us.

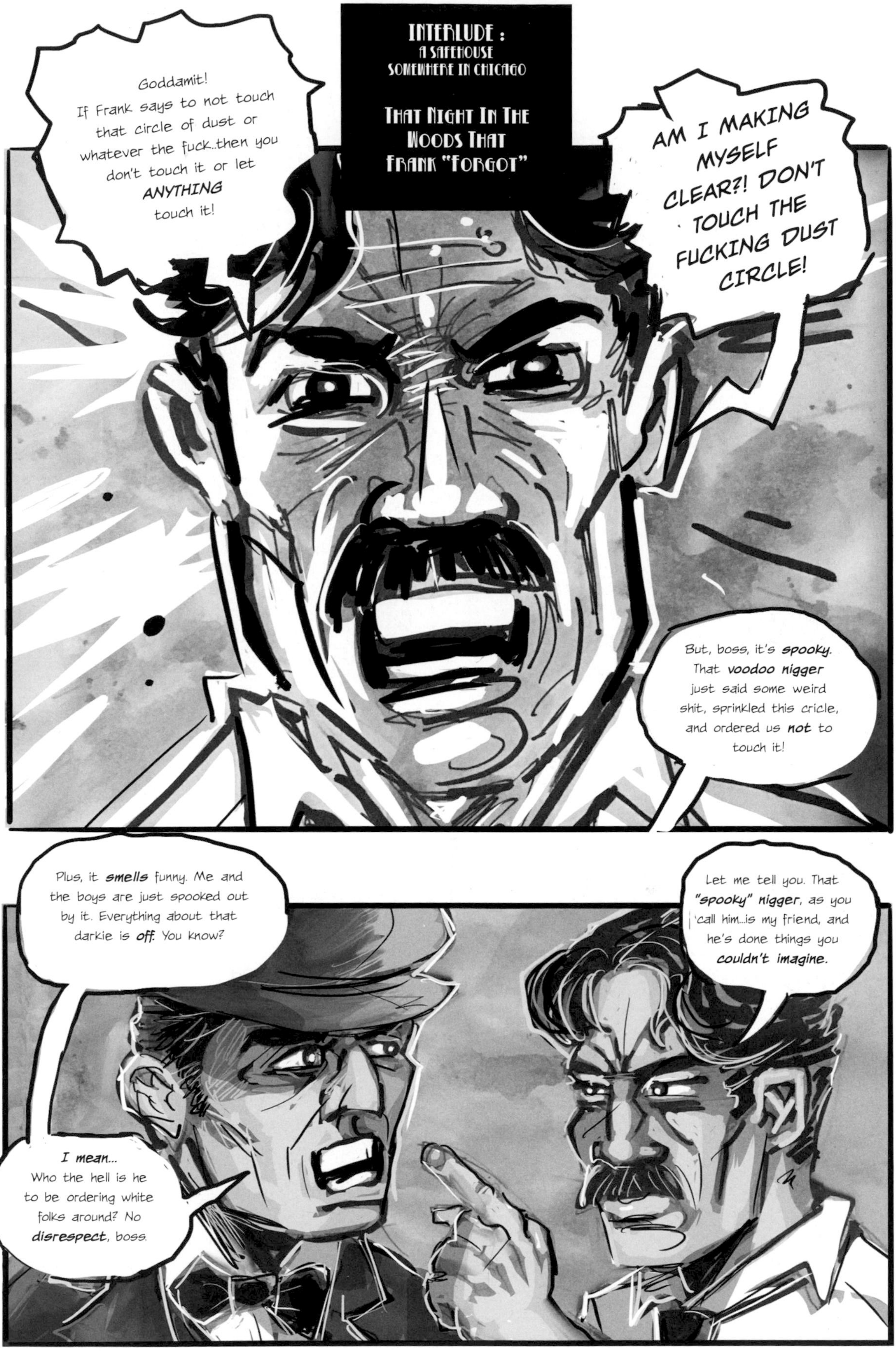
INTERLUDE :
A SAFEHOUSE
SOMEWHERE IN CHICAGO
THAT NIGHT IN THE WOODS THAT FRANK "FORGOT"
Goddamit! If Frank says to not touch that circle of dust or whatever the fuck..then you don't touch it or let ANYTHING touch it!
AM I MAKING MYSELF CLEAR?! DON'T TOUCH THE FUCKING DUST CIRCLE!
But, boss, it's spooky. That voodoo nigger just said some weird shit, sprinkled this cricle, and ordered us not to touch it!
Plus, it smells funny. Me and the boys are just spooked out by it. Everything about that darkie is off. You know?
I mean... Who the hell is he to be ordering white folks around? No disrespect, boss.
Let me tell you. That "spooky" nigger, as you call him...is my friend, and he's done things you couldn't imagine.

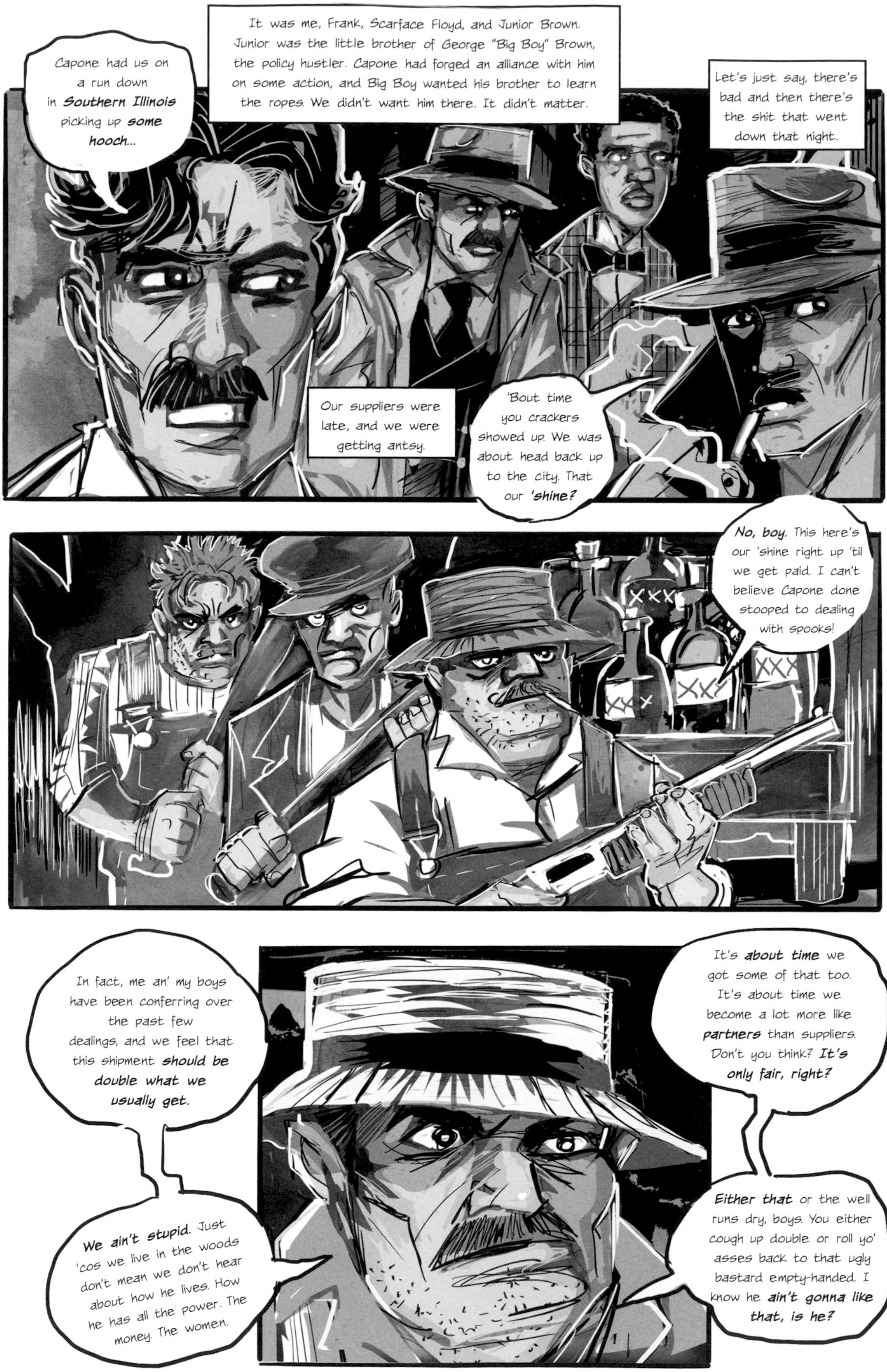
Capone had us on a run down in **Southern Illinois** picking up **some hooch...**
It was me, Frank, Scarface Floyd, and Junior Brown. Junior was the little brother of George "Big Boy" Brown, the policy hustler. Capone had forged an alliance with him on some action, and Big Boy wanted his brother to learn the ropes. We didn't want him there. It didn't matter.
Let's just say, there's bad and then there's the shit that went down that night.
Our suppliers were late, and we were getting antsy.
'Bout time you crackers showed up. We was about head back up to the city. That our **'shine?**
No, boy. This here's our 'shine right up 'til we get paid. I can't believe Capone done stooped to dealing with spooks!
In fact, me an' my boys have been conferring over the past few dealings, and we feel that this shipment **should be double what we usually get.**
It's **about time** we got some of that too. It's about time we become a lot more like **partners** than suppliers. Don't you think? **It's only fair, right?**
We ain't stupid. Just 'cos we live in the woods don't mean we don't hear about how he lives. How he has all the power. The money. The women.
Either that or the well runs dry, boys. You either cough up double or roll yo' asses back to that ugly bastard empty-handed. I know he **ain't gonna like that, is he?**

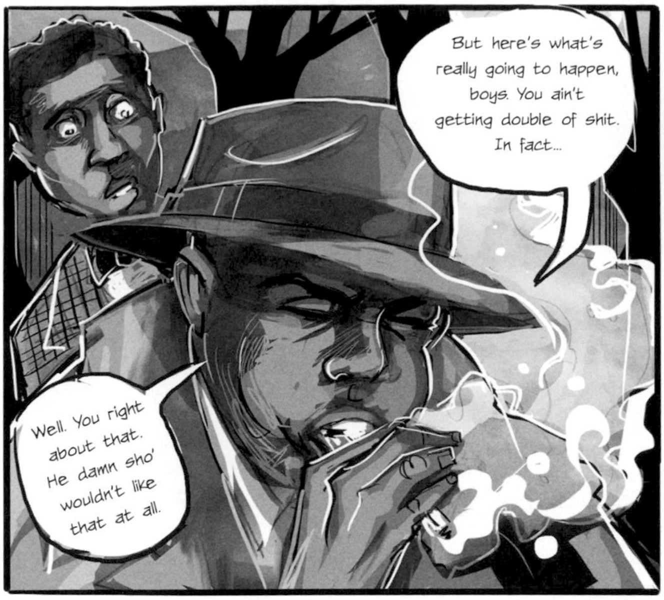
Well. You right about that. He damn sho' wouldn't like that at all.
But here's what's really going to happen, boys. You ain't getting double of shit. In fact...

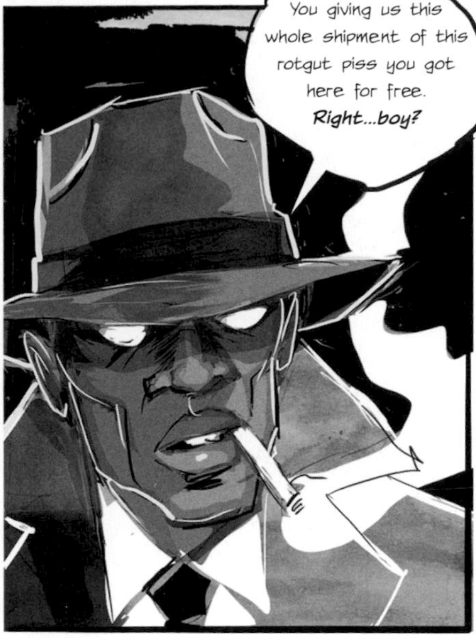
You giving us this whole shipment of this rotgut piss you got here for free. ***Right...boy?***

I don't know what Frank did. It was...well, it was magic for lack of a better more saner word. He put a whammy on those rednecks. He took a puff of his cigarette and closed his eyes like he was concentrating...

He turned them into his lap dogs...right there in front of themselves. I never seen anything like it. I've heard of mesmerism and whatever the fuck. But this, this was something frightening...something dark.

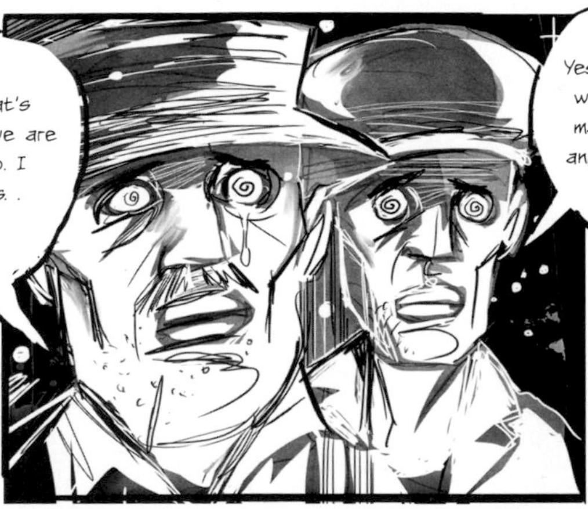
Y-Yessuh. That's exactly what we are about to do. I t's all yours. .
Yessuh. How can we serve you, master? I'll do anything for you.

Frank just laughed and said "I know you do, boy. I know you do." His eyes were all stange and white, and I could see sparks around him like fireflies. He just smiled because he knew what was coming next.

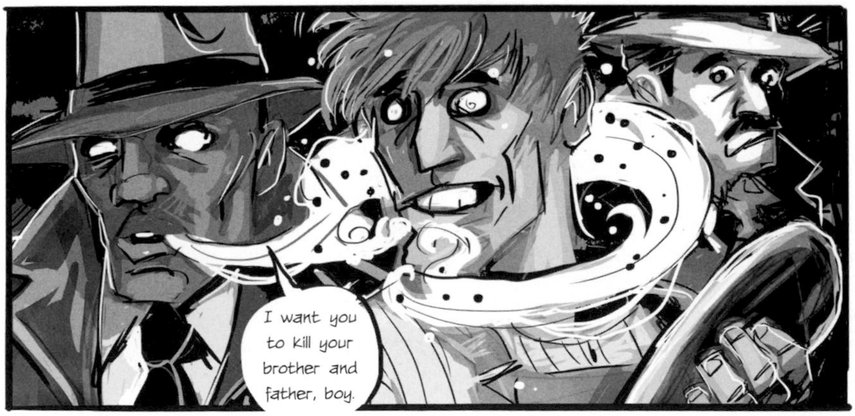
I want you to kill your brother and father, boy.

You see, these good ole boys had been disrespecting Capone for a while now. He didn't like that. So, we were supposed to come back with the shipment and their heads. Junior Brown didn't know that. Turns out, Junior Brown didn't know shit from nothing and more's the pity.

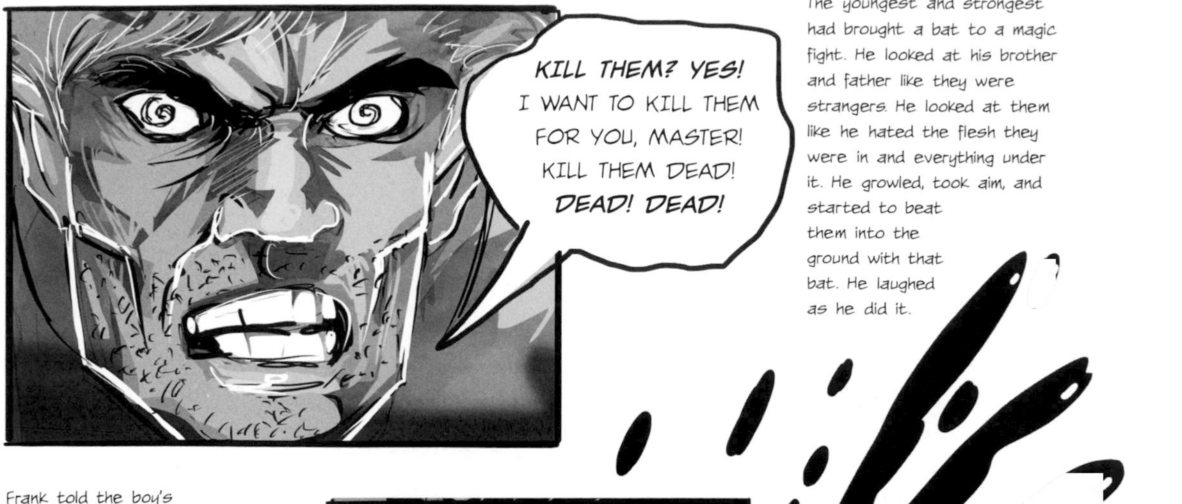
KILL THEM? YES! I WANT TO KILL THEM FOR YOU, MASTER! KILL THEM DEAD! DEAD! DEAD!

The youngest and strongest had brought a bat to a magic fight. He looked at his brother and father like they were strangers. He looked at them like he hated the flesh they were in and everything under it. He growled, took aim, and started to beat them into the ground with that bat. He laughed as he did it.

Frank told the boy's father and brother to be still and to be quiet.

They did just that. Even when pieces of skull and muck exploded from them. Even when bones became bloody powder.

They said not one word.

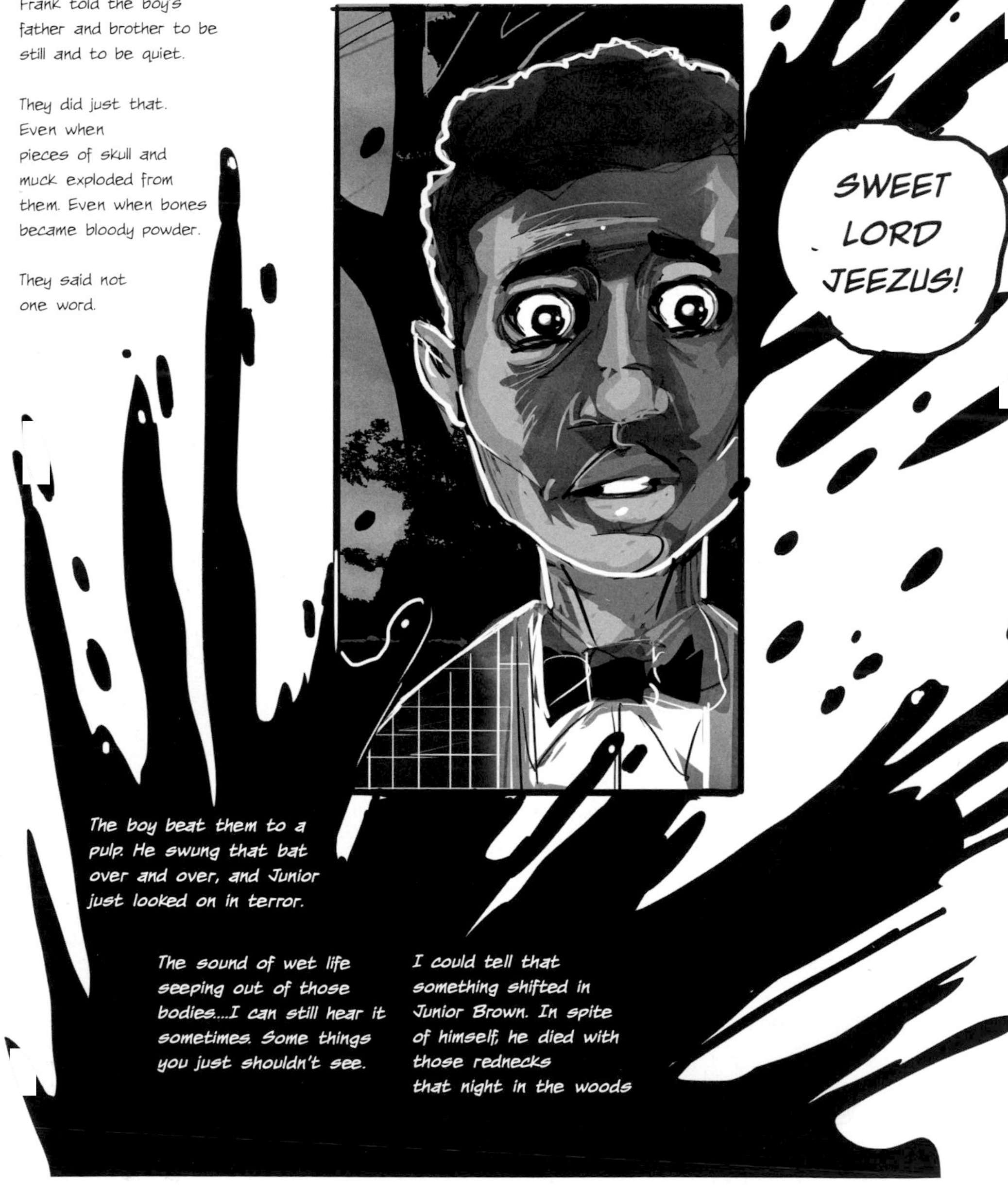
SWEET LORD JEEZUS!

The boy beat them to a pulp. He swung that bat over and over, and Junior just looked on in terror.

The sound of wet life seeping out of those bodies...I can still hear it sometimes. Some things you just shouldn't see.

I could tell that something shifted in Junior Brown. In spite of himself, he died with those rednecks that night in the woods

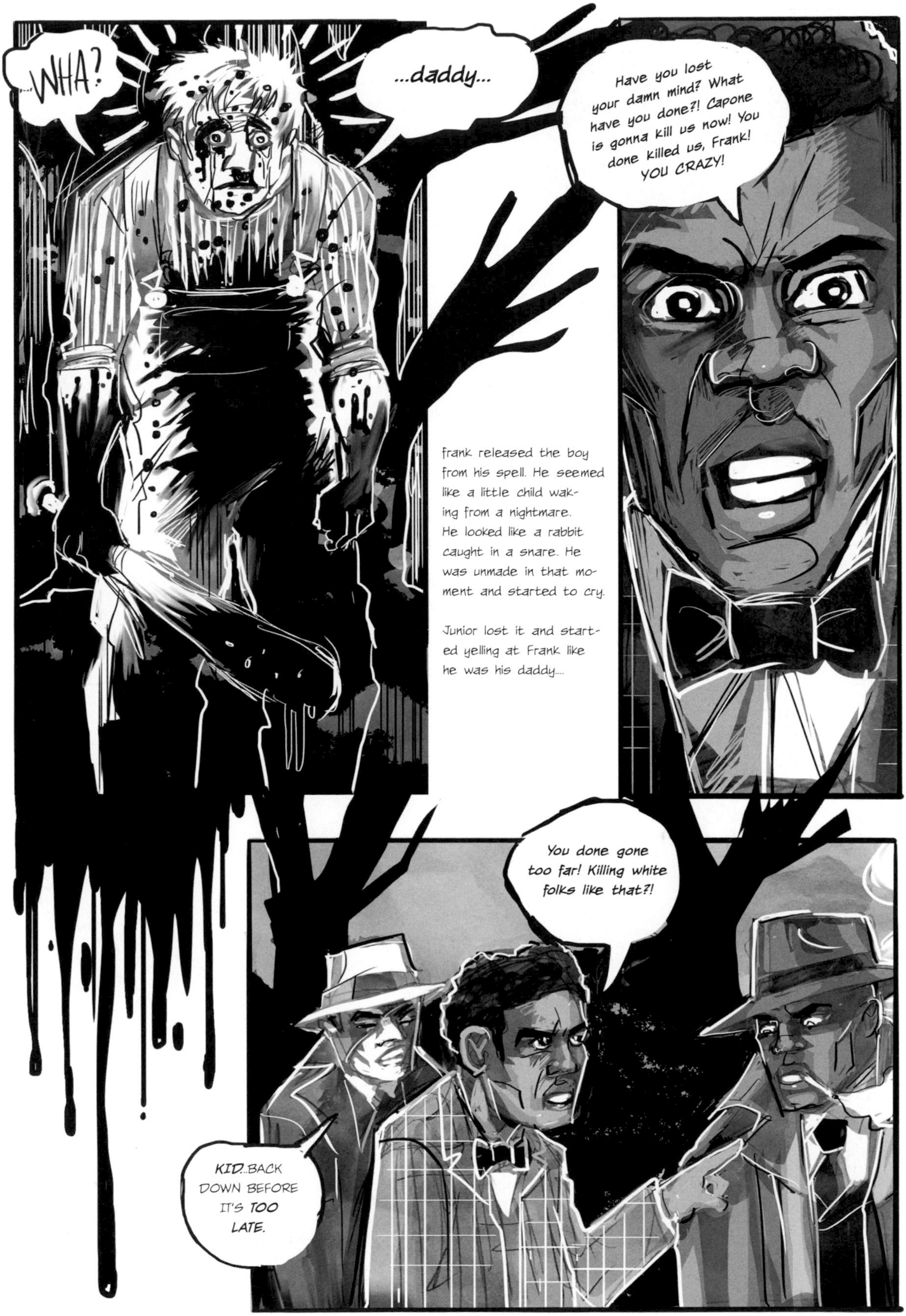
...WHA?
...daddy...
Have you lost your damn mind? What have you done?! Capone is gonna kill us now! You done killed us, Frank! YOU CRAZY!
frank released the boy from his spell. He seemed like a little child waking from a nightmare. He looked like a rabbit caught in a snare. He was unmade in that moment and started to cry.
Junior lost it and started yelling at Frank like he was his daddy....
You done gone too far! Killing white folks like that?!
KID...BACK DOWN BEFORE IT'S TOO LATE.

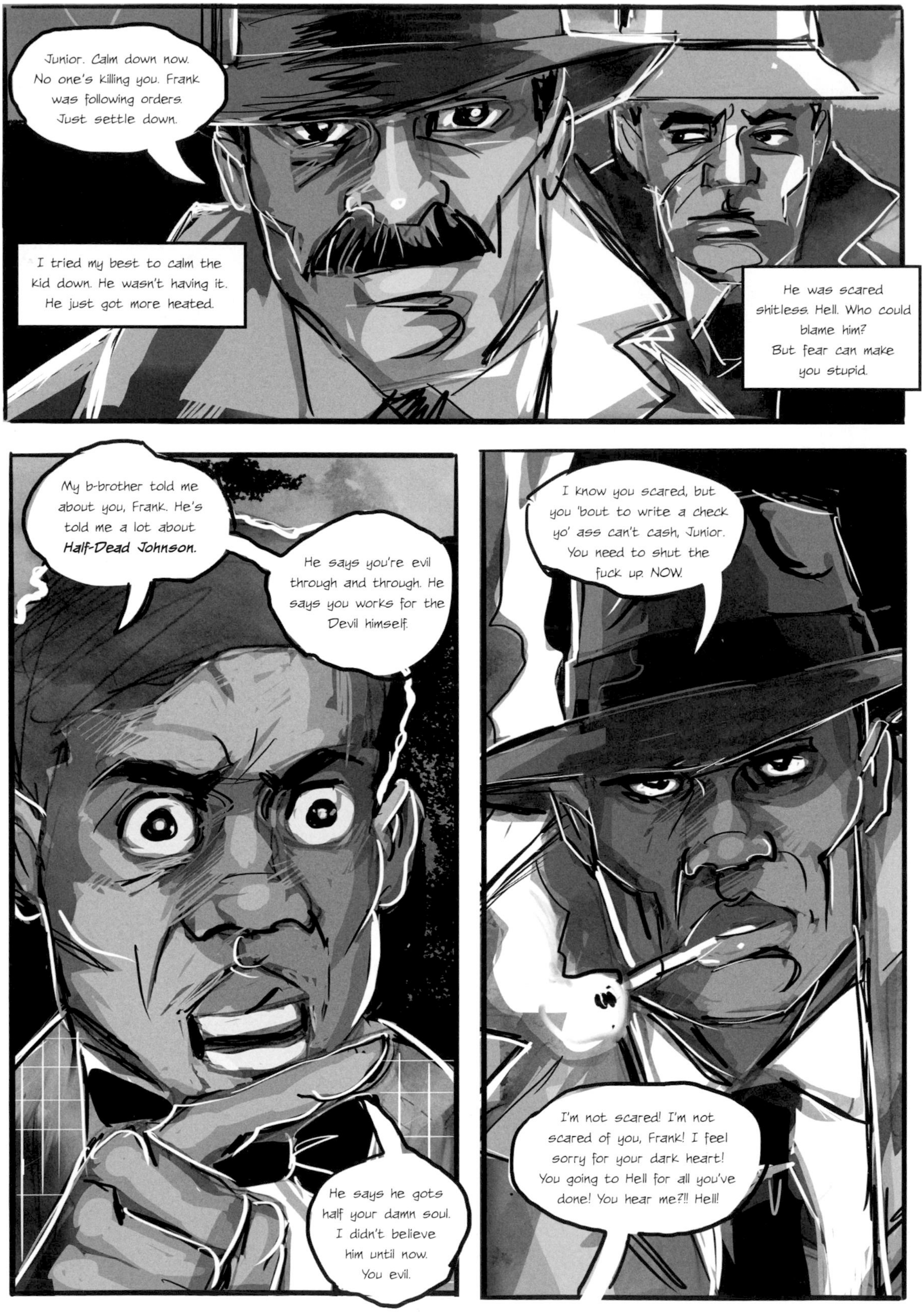
Junior. Calm down now. No one's killing you. Frank was following orders. Just settle down.
I tried my best to calm the kid down. He wasn't having it. He just got more heated.
He was scared shitless. Hell. Who could blame him? But fear can make you stupid.
My b-brother told me about you, Frank. He's told me a lot about Half-Dead Johnson.
He says you're evil through and through. He says you works for the Devil himself.
He says he gots half your damn soul. I didn't believe him until now. You evil.
I know you scared, but you 'bout to write a check yo' ass can't cash, Junior. You need to shut the fuck up. NOW.
I'm not scared! I'm not scared of you, Frank! I feel sorry for your dark heart! You going to Hell for all you've done! You hear me?!! Hell!

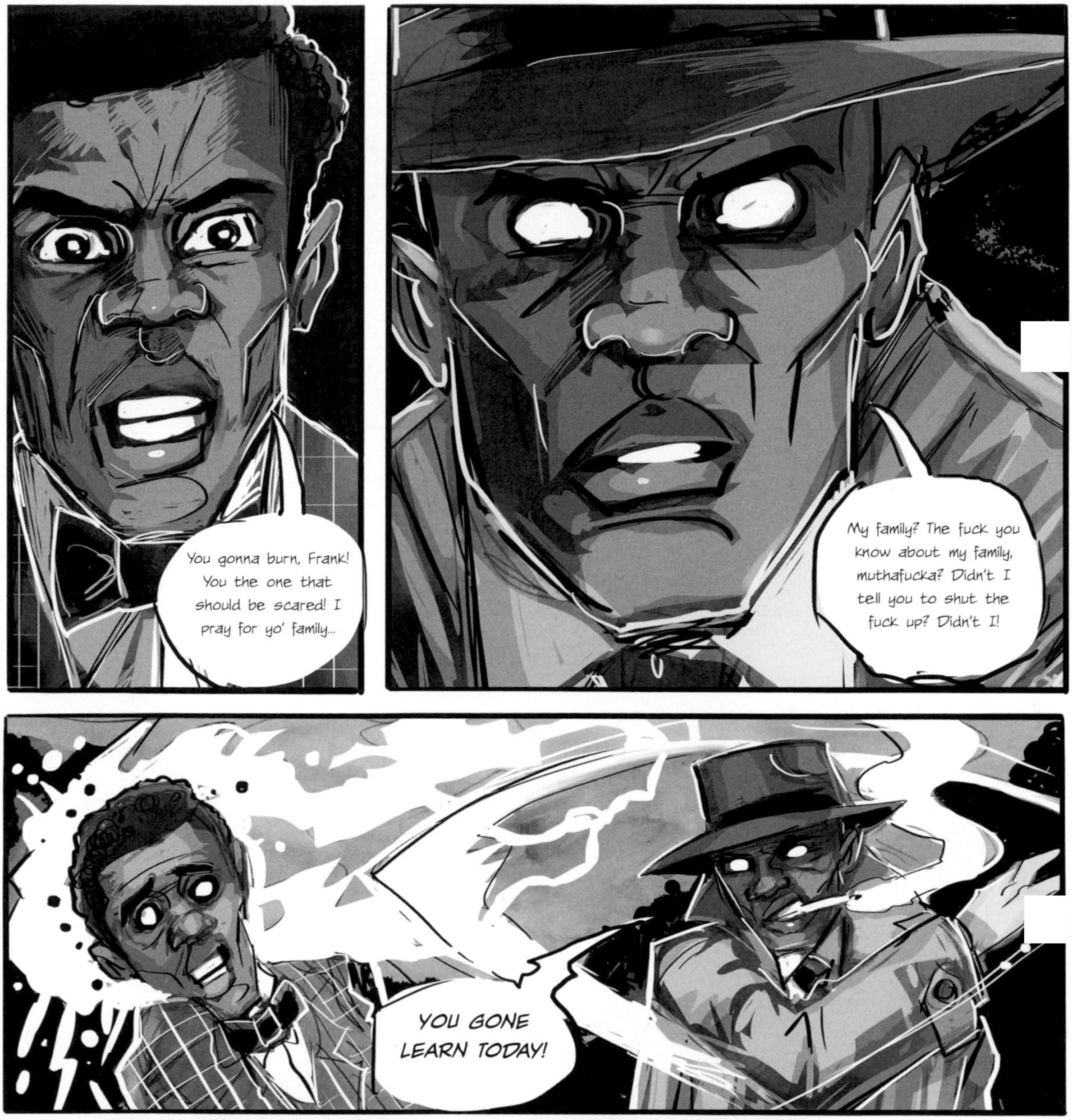
You gonna burn, Frank! You the one that should be scared! I pray for yo' family...
My family? The fuck you know about my family, muthafucka? Didn't I tell you to shut the fuck up? Didn't I!
YOU GONE LEARN TODAY!

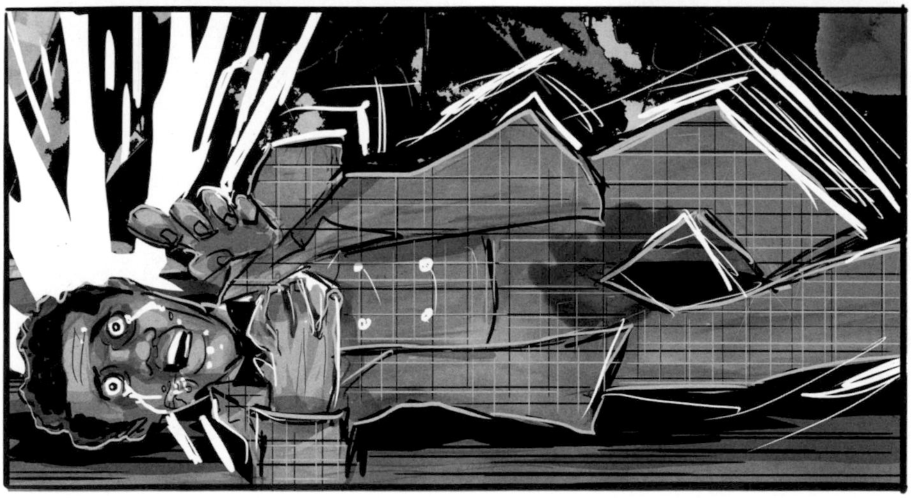

Frank lost his cool then. No one, but no one mentions his family. Junior didn't know that shit either.

Hot light flew from Frank's blue hand and hit Junior square in the puss. He went down screaming, pissing, and shitting himself. He lost his mind in an instant. He never found it again. He died in the looney bin from what I hear.

Damn shame.

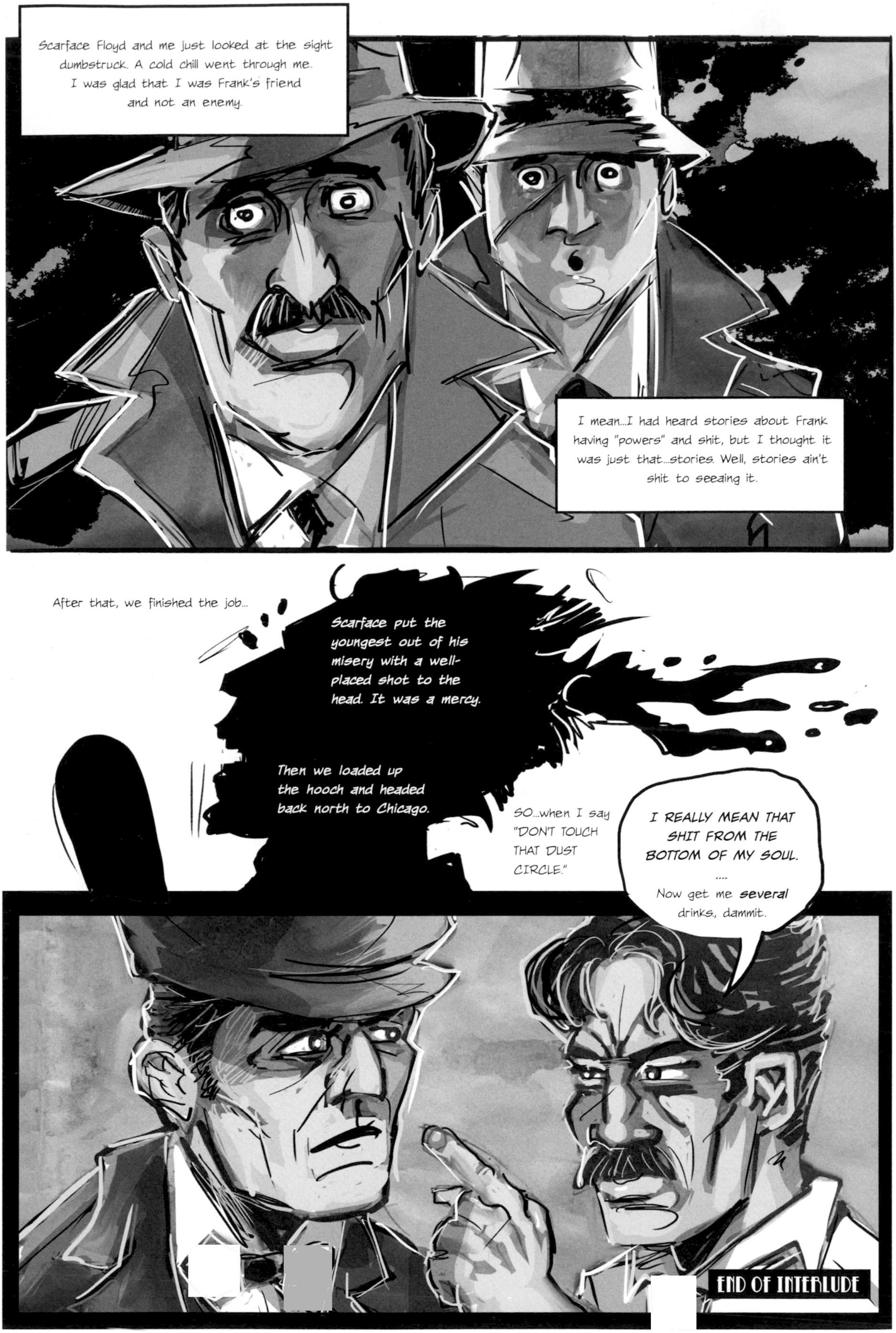
Scarface Floyd and me just looked at the sight dumbstruck. A cold chill went through me. I was glad that I was Frank's friend and not an enemy.
I mean...I had heard stories about Frank having "powers" and shit, but I thought it was just that...stories. Well, stories ain't shit to seeaing it.
After that, we finished the job...
Scarface put the youngest out of his misery with a well-placed shot to the head. It was a mercy.
Then we loaded up the hooch and headed back north to Chicago.
SO...when I say "DON'T TOUCH THAT DUST CIRCLE."
I REALLY MEAN THAT SHIT FROM THE BOTTOM OF MY SOUL.
....
Now get me several drinks., dammit.
END OF INTERLUDE

CHAPTER 6

The Conjure Man Lies

I put the Shark up in one of his safe houses up North and put a goofer dust cricle of protection around him. If that circle gets broken he will just how unsafe that house can get.

I go back to the South Side on the El to see Papa John Gooden. He's the local root doctor.

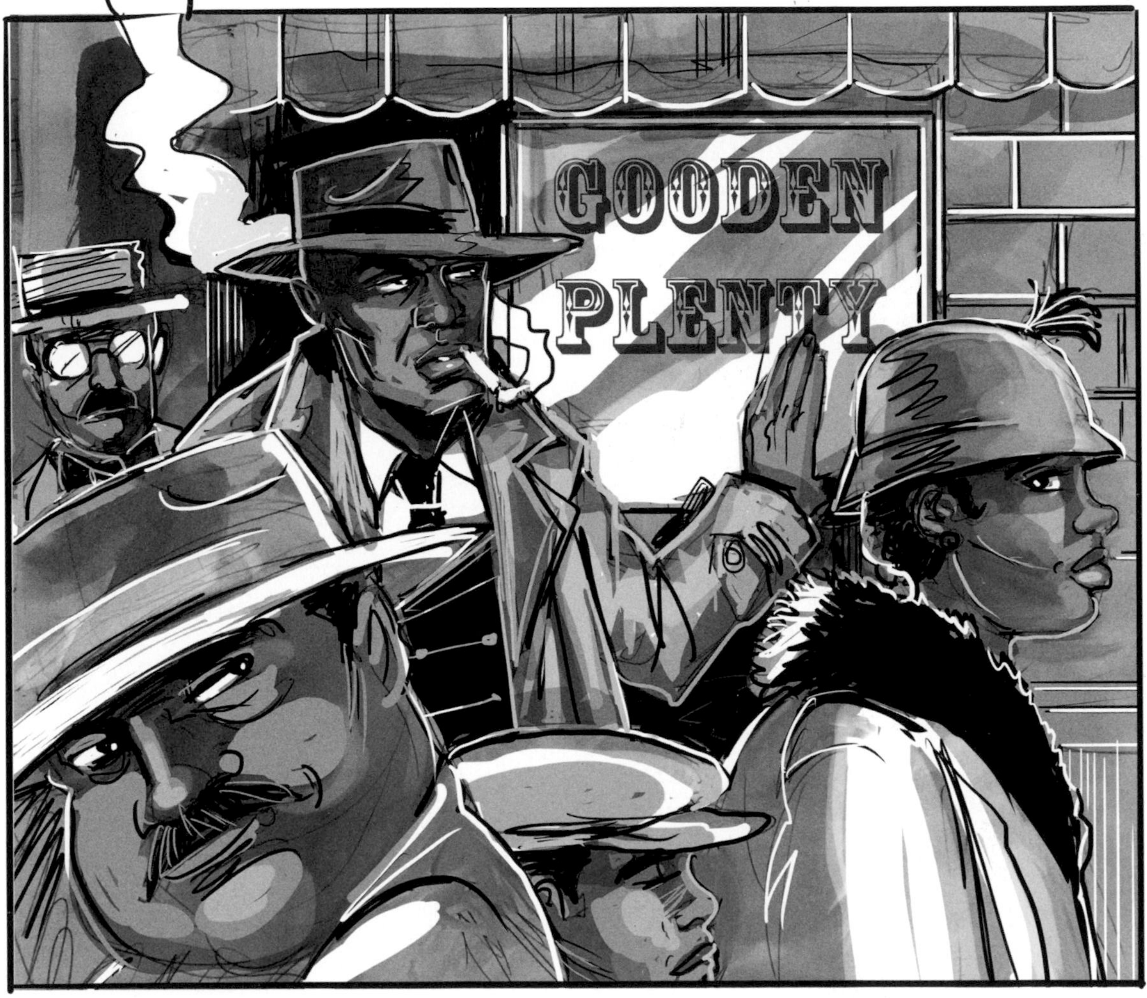
GOODEN
PLENTY

His place is called ***The Gooden Plenty.***

Stupid fucking name.

I hate his ass. He's an underhanded, double-dealing, arrogant, snake.

He also has the absolute best roots, herbs, and conjuring supplies around. He gets the freshest ingredients directly from the source. So, a lot of times, I have to deal with him. The bastard. Papa John hates my ass too.

Because he knows who the best two-headed doctor in town is.

Damn right.

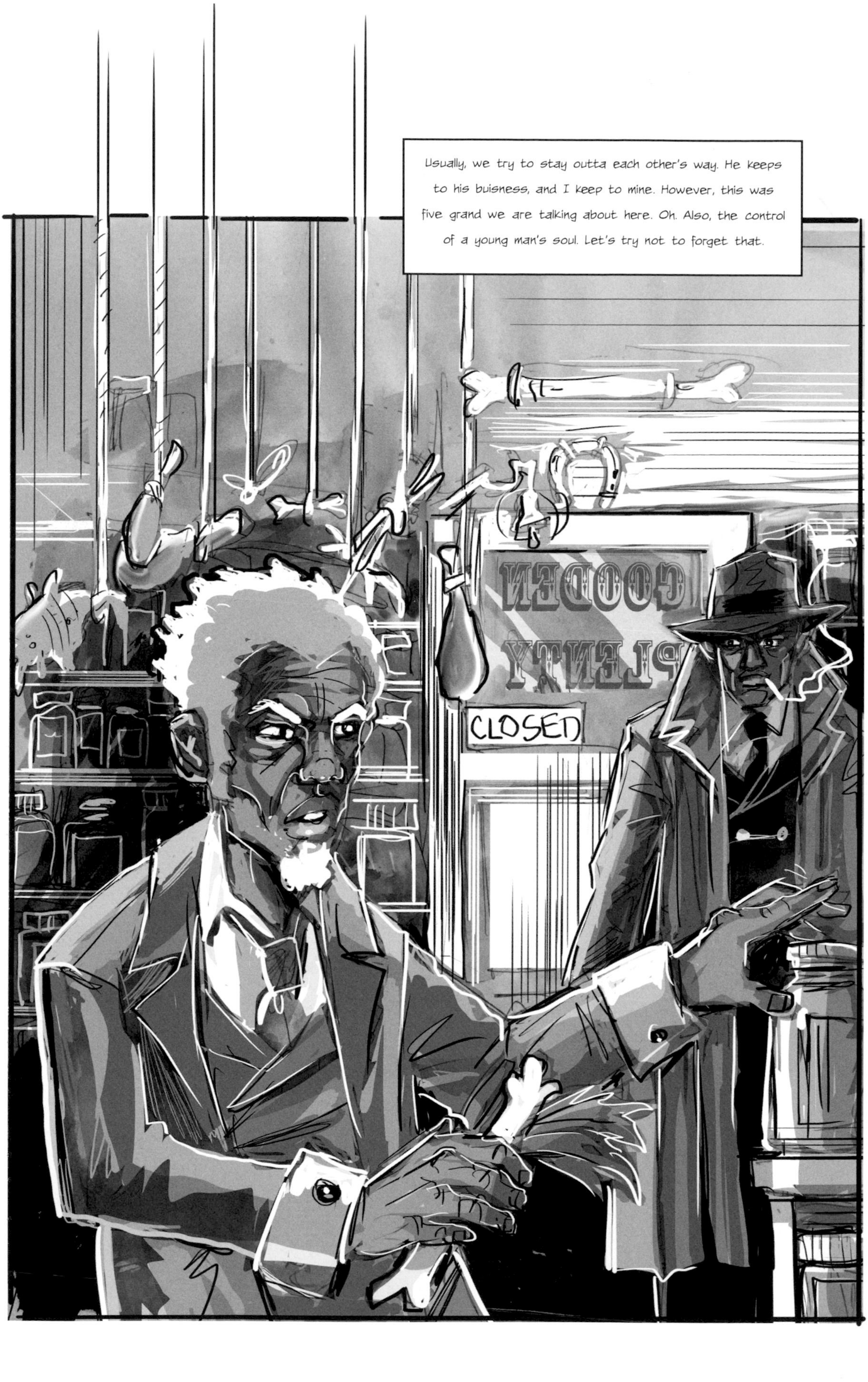
Usually, we try to stay outta each other's way. He keeps to his buisness, and I keep to mine. However, this was five grand we are talking about here. Oh. Also, the control of a young man's soul. Let's try not to forget that.
GOODEN PLENTY
CLOSED

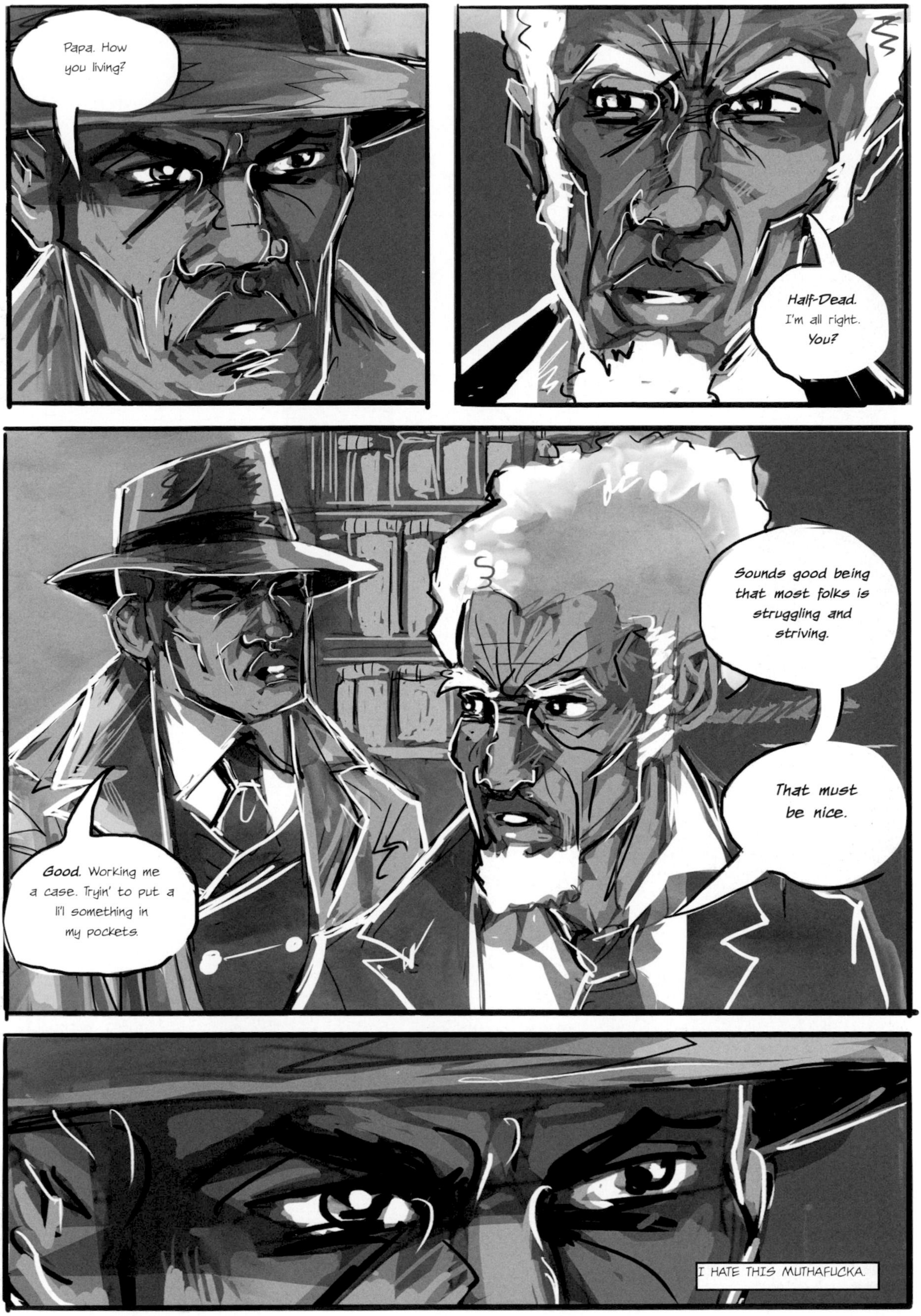
Papa. How you living?
Half-Dead. I'm all right. You?
Good. Working me a case. Tryin' to put a li'l something in my pockets.
Sounds good being that most folks is struggling and striving.
That must be nice.
I HATE THIS MUTHAFUCKA.

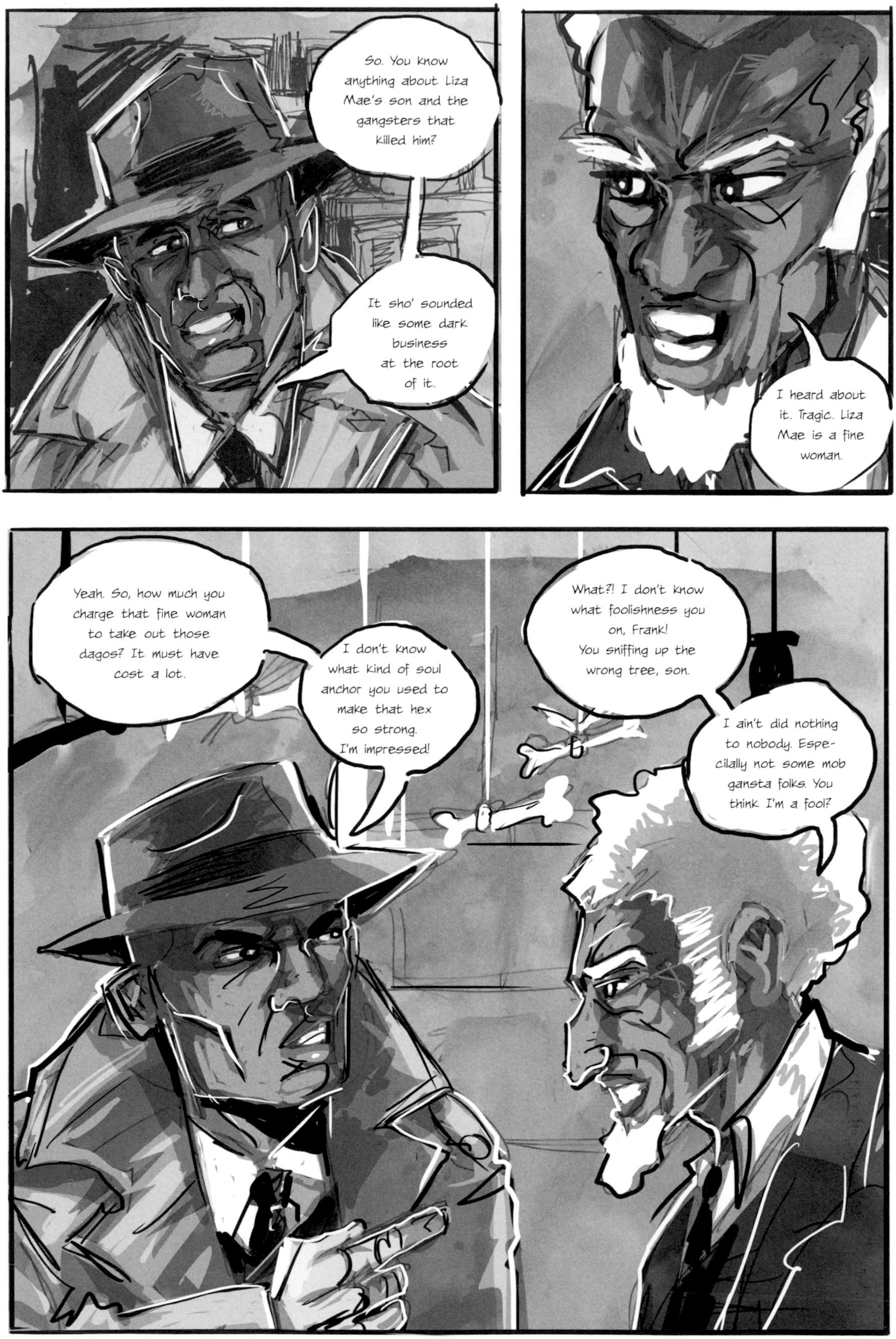
So. You know anything about Liza Mae's son and the gangsters that killed him?
It sho' sounded like some dark business at the root of it.
I heard about it. Tragic. Liza Mae is a fine woman.
Yeah. So, how much you charge that fine woman to take out those dagos? It must have cost a lot.
I don't know what kind of soul anchor you used to make that hex so strong. I'm impressed!
What?! I don't know what foolishness you on, Frank! You sniffing up the wrong tree, son.
I ain't did nothing to nobody. Espe-cilally not some mob gansta folks. You think I'm a fool?

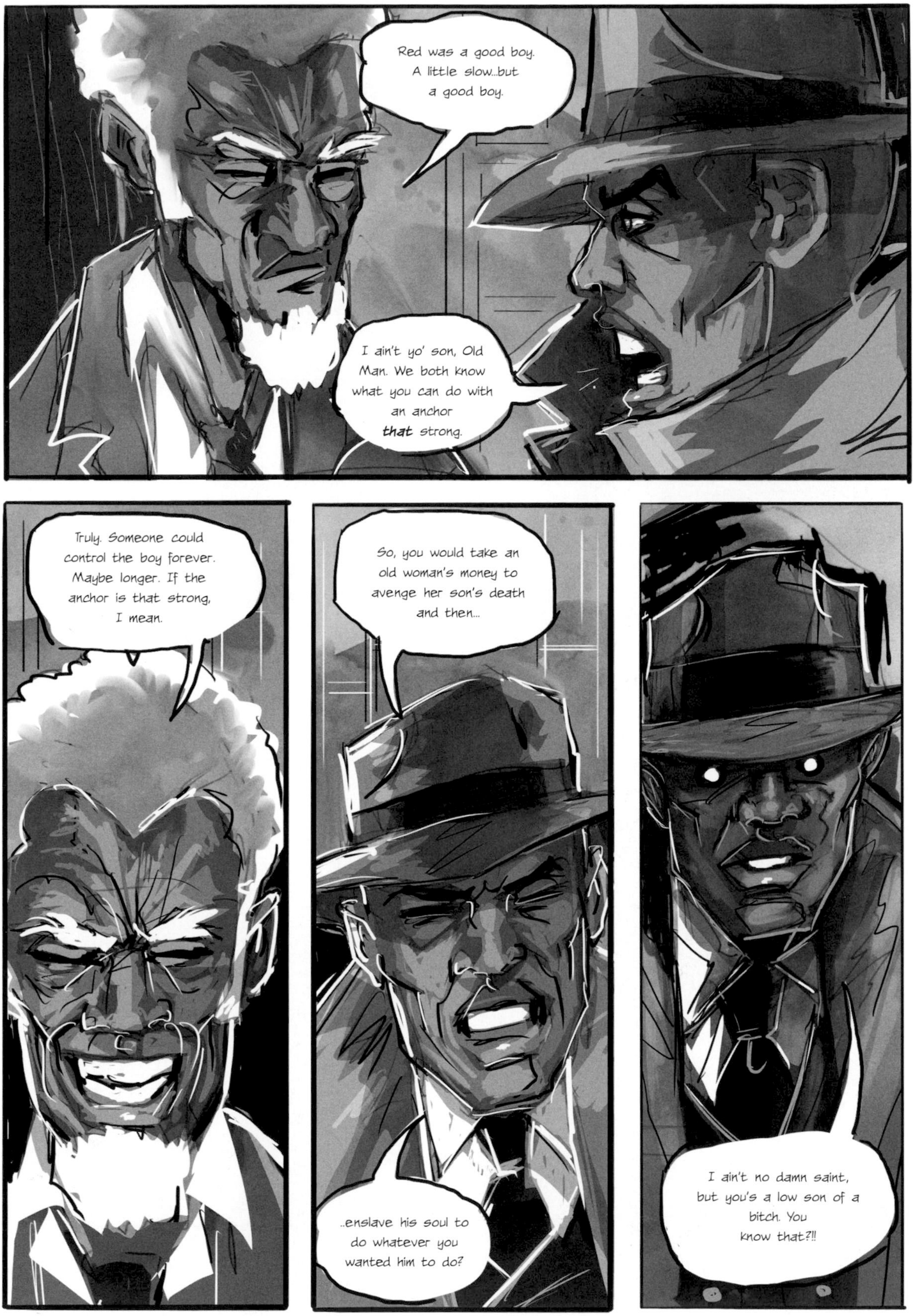
Red was a good boy. A little slow...but a good boy.
I ain't yo' son, Old Man. We both know what you can do with an anchor **that** strong.
Truly. Someone could control the boy forever. Maybe longer. If the anchor is that strong, I mean.
So, you would take an old woman's money to avenge her son's death and then...
...enslave his soul to do whatever you wanted him to do?
I ain't no damn saint, but you's a low son of a bitch. You know that?!!

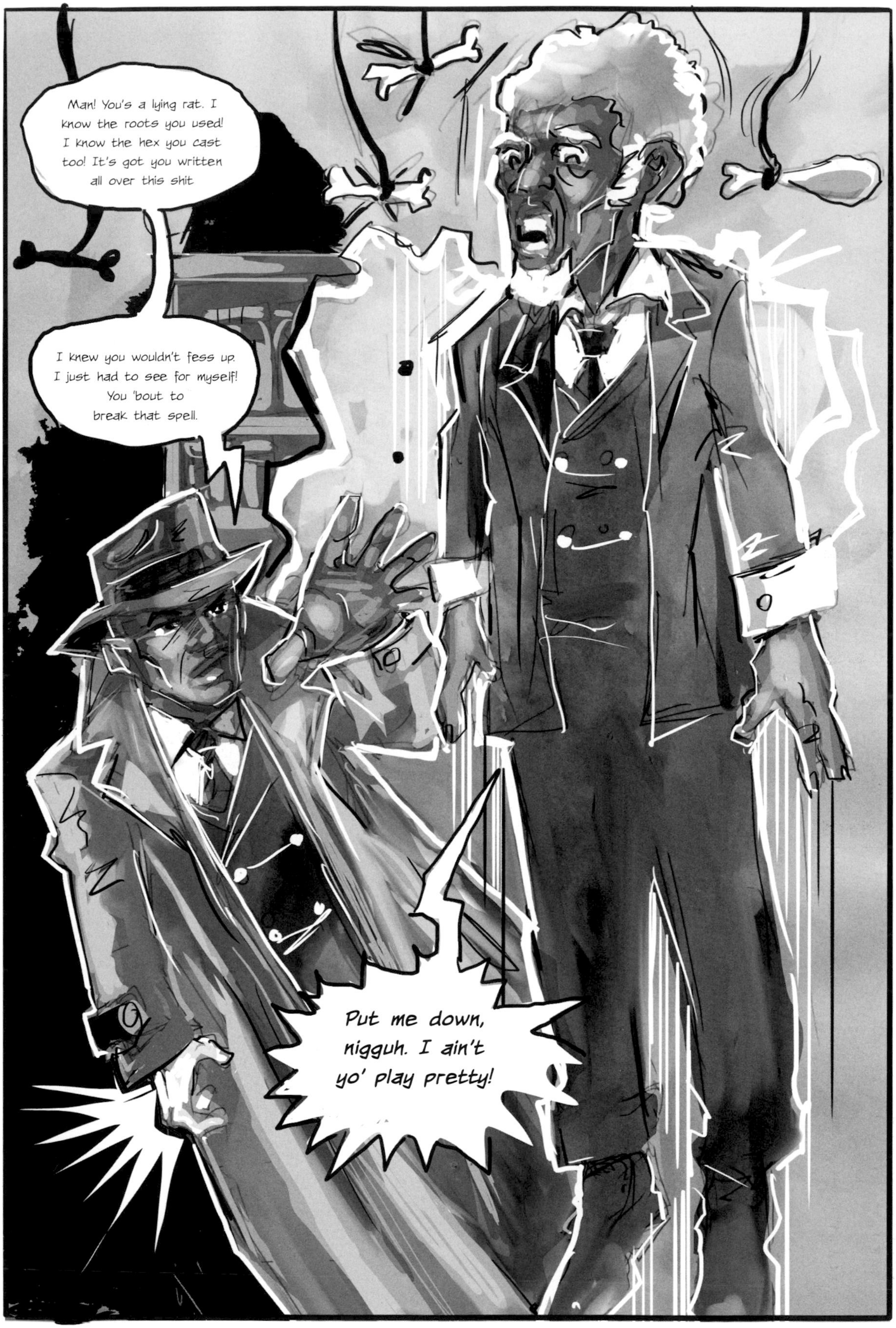
Man! You's a lying rat. I know the roots you used! I know the hex you cast too! It's got you written all over this shit
I knew you wouldn't fess up. I just had to see for myself! You 'bout to break that spell.
Put me down, nigguh. I ain't yo' play pretty!

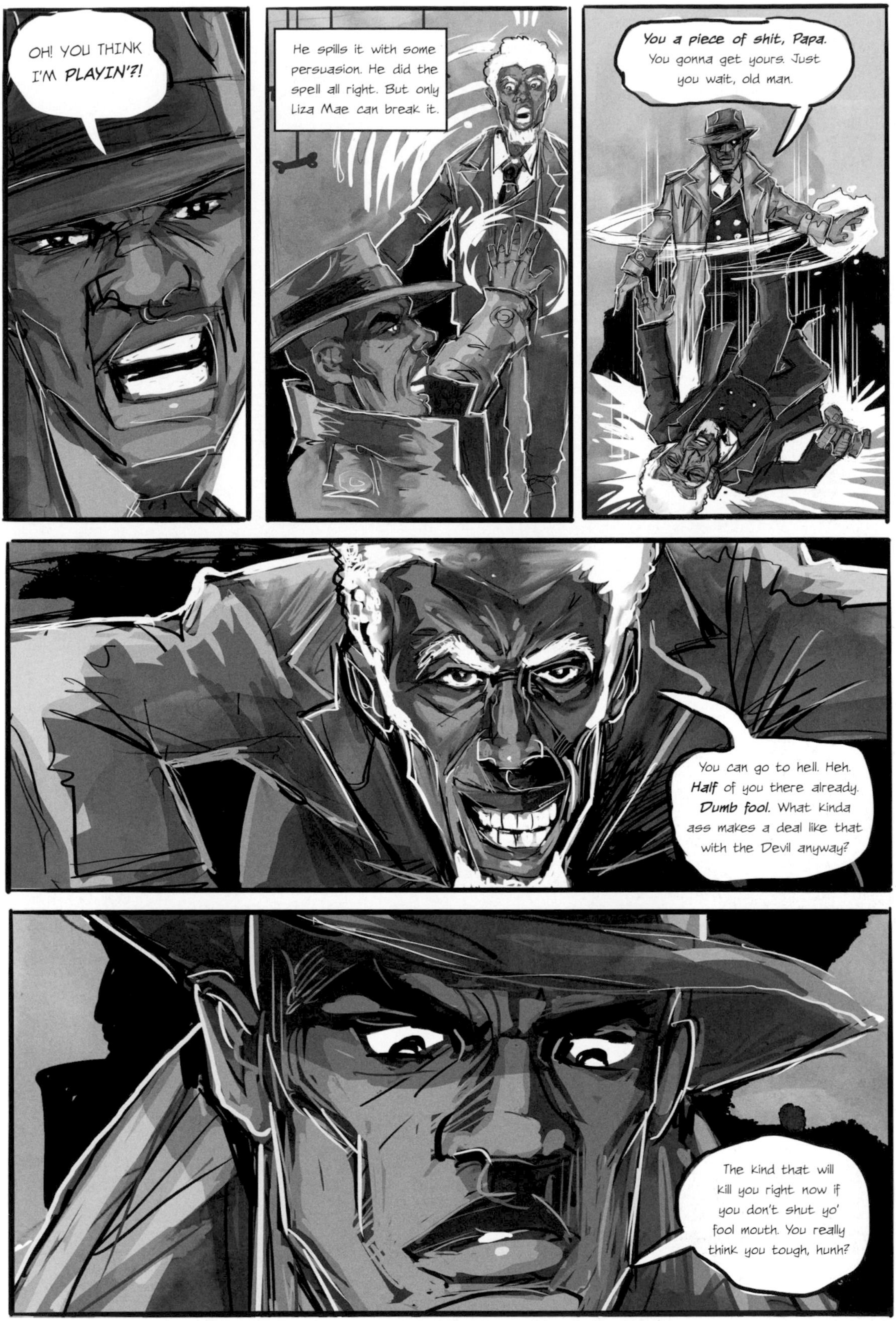
OH! YOU THINK I'M PLAYIN'?!
He spills it with some persuasion. He did the spell all right. But only Liza Mae can break it.
You a piece of shit, Papa. You gonna get yours. Just you wait, old man.
You can go to hell. Heh. Half of you there already. Dumb fool. What kinda ass makes a deal like that with the Devil anyway?
The kind that will kill you right now if you don't shut yo' fool mouth. You really think you tough, hunh?

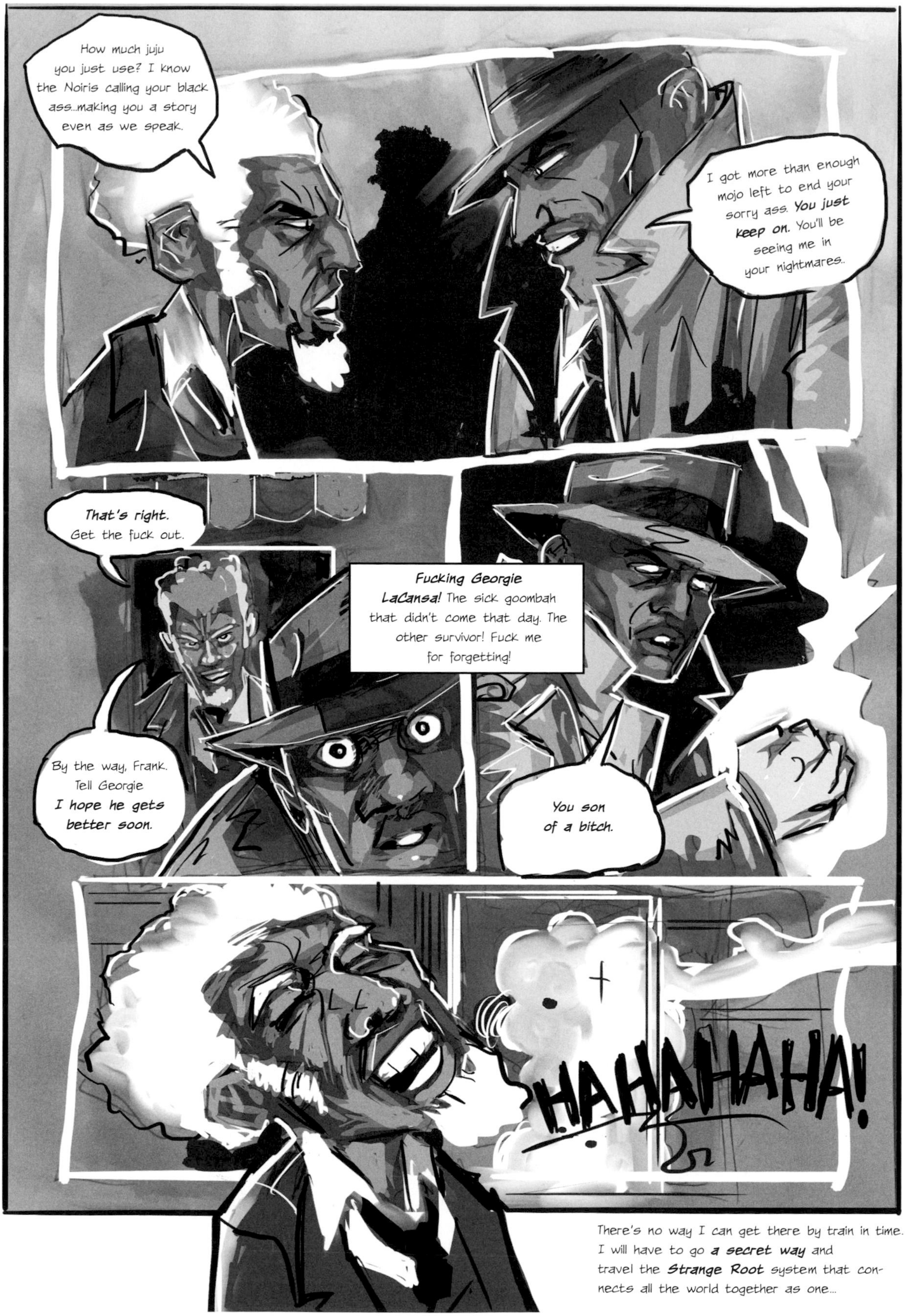
How much juju you just use? I know the Noiris calling your black ass...making you a story even as we speak.
I got more than enough mojo left to end your sorry ass. You just keep on. You'll be seeing me in your nightmares..
That's right. Get the fuck out.
Fucking Georgie LaCansa! The sick goombah that didn't come that day. The other survivor! Fuck me for forgetting!
By the way, Frank. Tell Georgie I hope he gets better soon.
You son of a bitch.
HAHAHAHA!

There's no way I can get there by train in time. I will have to go ***a secret way*** and travel the ***Strange Root*** system that connects all the world together as one...

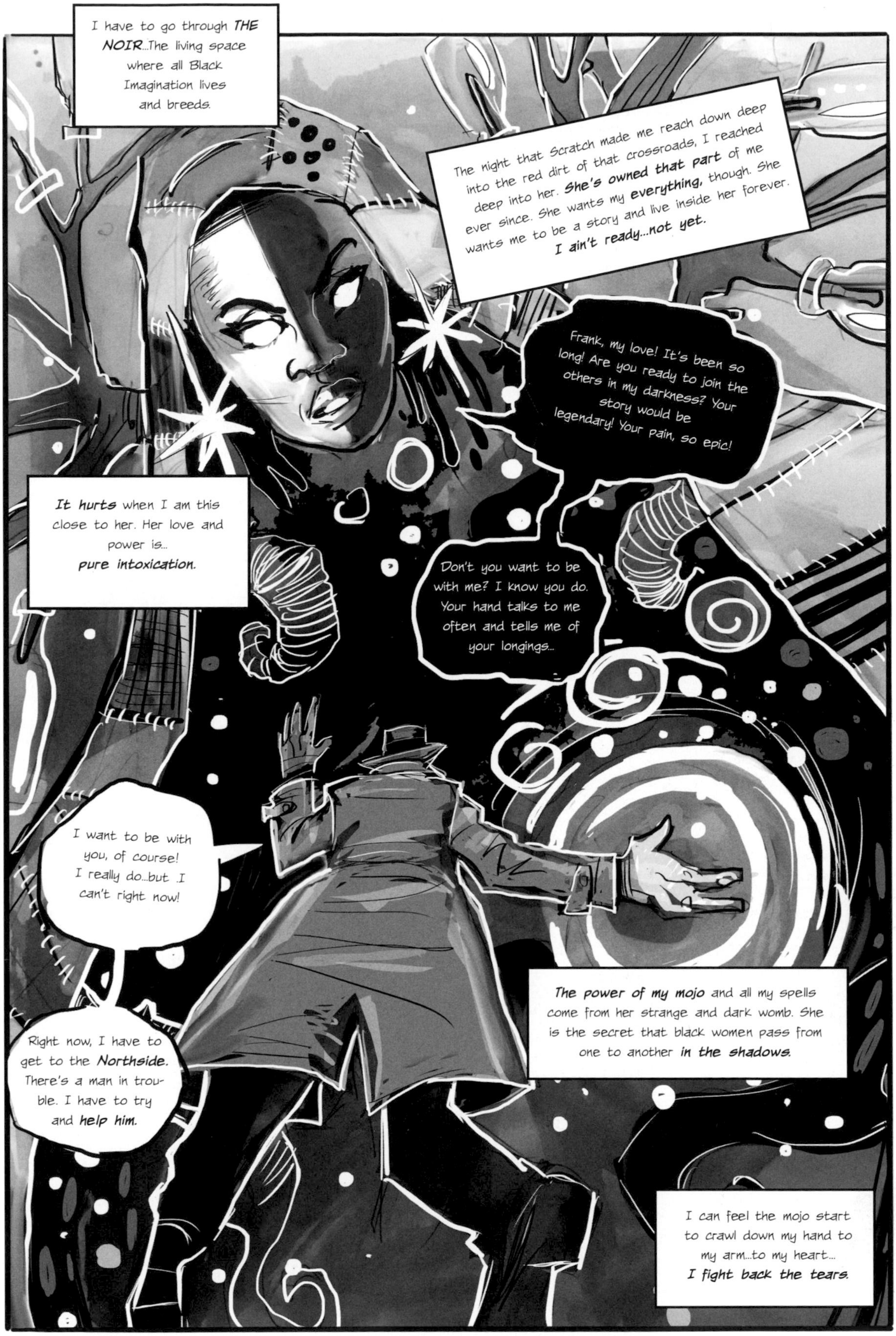
I have to go through **THE NOIR**...The living space where all Black Imagination lives and breeds.
The night that Scratch made me reach down deep into the red dirt of that crossroads, I reached deep into her. **She's owned that part** of me ever since. She wants my **everything**, though. She wants me to be a story and live inside her forever. **I ain't ready...not yet.**
Frank, my love! It's been so long! Are you ready to join the others in my darkness? Your story would be legendary! Your pain, so epic!
It hurts when I am this close to her. Her love and power is... **pure intoxication.**
Don't you want to be with me? I know you do. Your hand talks to me often and tells me of your longings...
I want to be with you, of course! I really do...but .I can't right now!
Right now, I have to get to the **Northside.** There's a man in trouble. I have to try and **help him.**
The power of my mojo and all my spells come from her strange and dark womb. She is the secret that black women pass from one to another **in the shadows.**
I can feel the mojo start to crawl down my hand to my arm...to my heart... **I fight back the tears.**

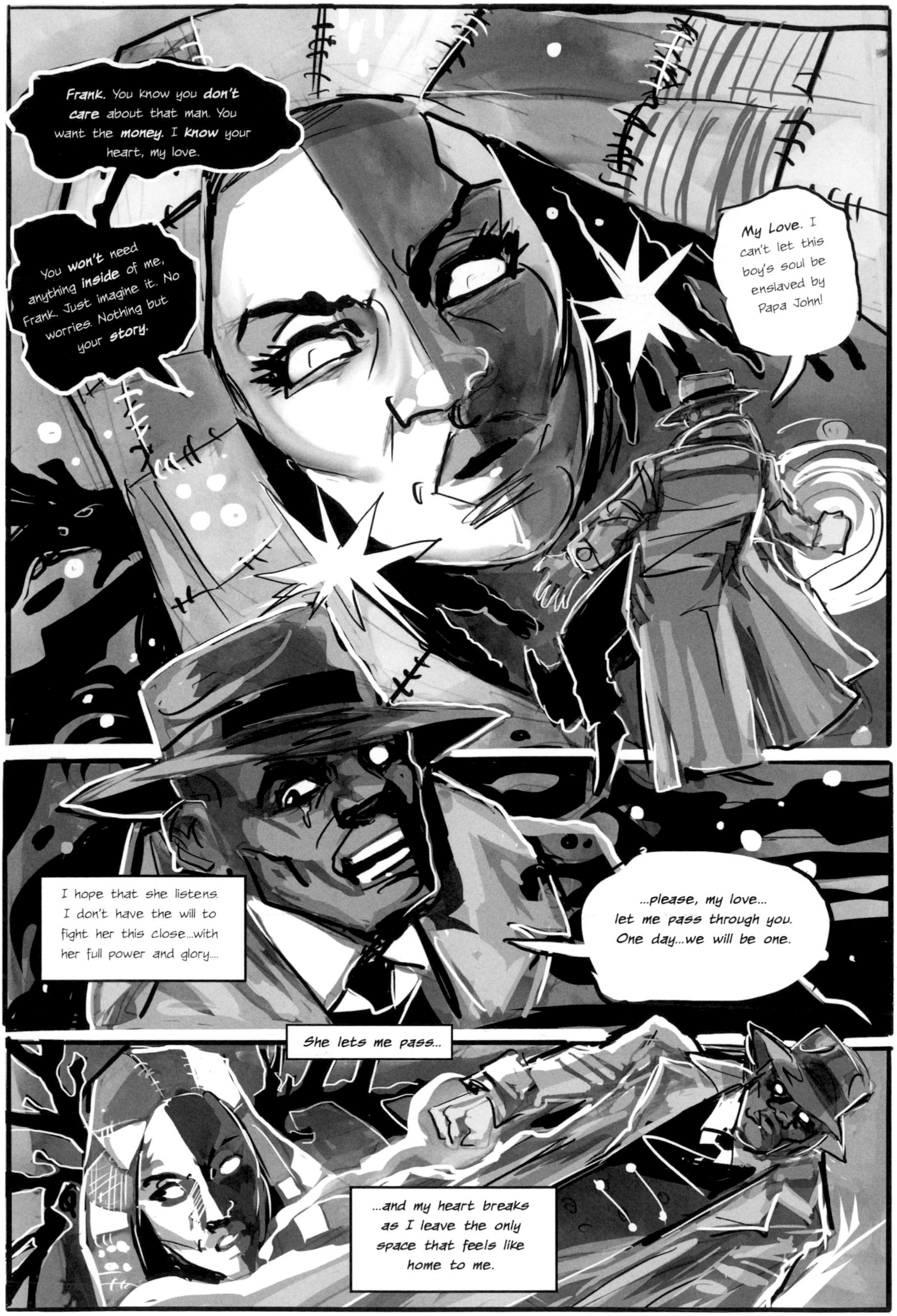

Frank. You know you don't care about that man. You want the money. I know your heart, my love.
You won't need anything inside of me, Frank. Just imagine it. No worries. Nothing but your story.
My Love. I can't let this boy's soul be enslaved by Papa John!
I hope that she listens. I don't have the will to fight her this close...with her full power and glory....
...please, my love... let me pass through you. One day...we will be one.
She lets me pass...
...and my heart breaks as I leave the only space that feels like home to me.

CHAPTER 7

A SOMBER MERCY

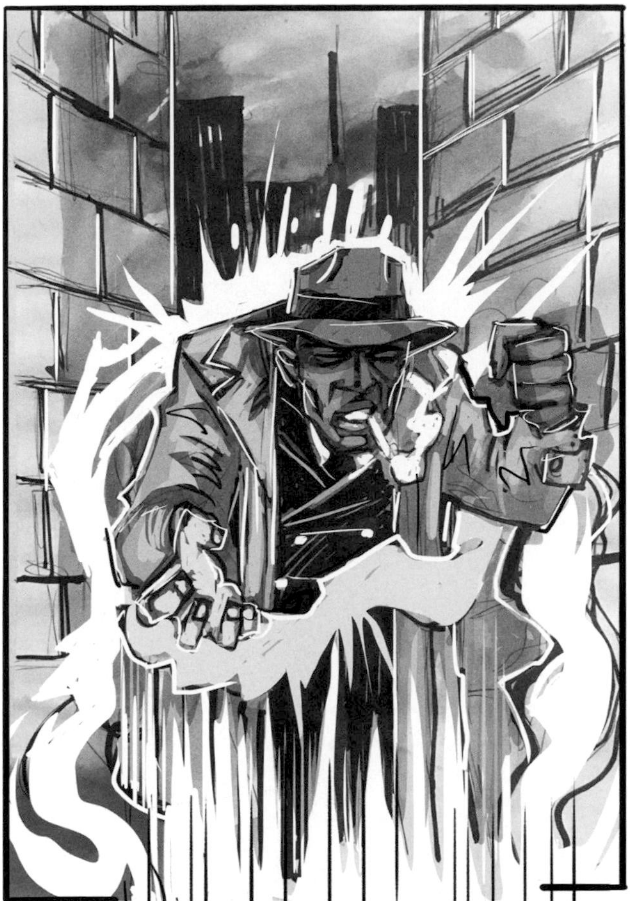

I enter back into this world pretty close to my intended stop. I choose a nearby alleyway, so I won't alert the good white folks in this neihgborhood to my arrival. I wonder which part of me would scare them the most. That I a hoodoo man, or that I'm a black hoodoo man?

After all, I am still a strange spook in the wrong part of town.

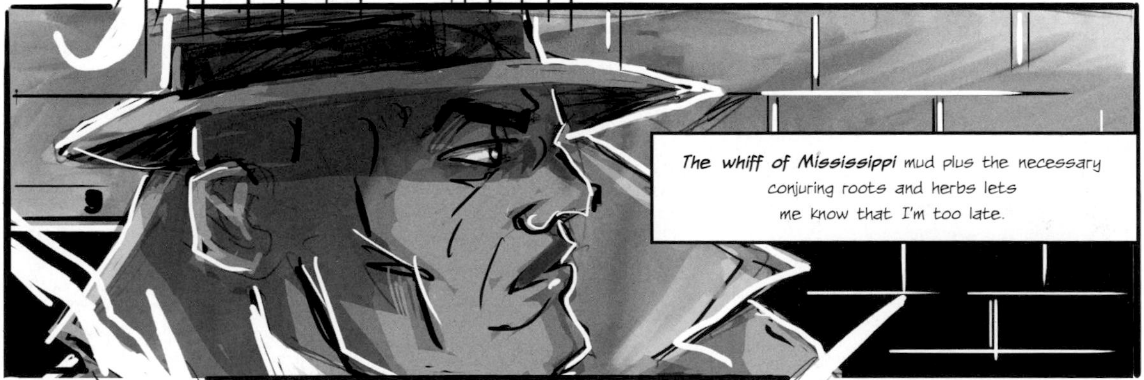
The whiff of Mississippi mud plus the necessary conjuring roots and herbs lets me know that I'm too late.

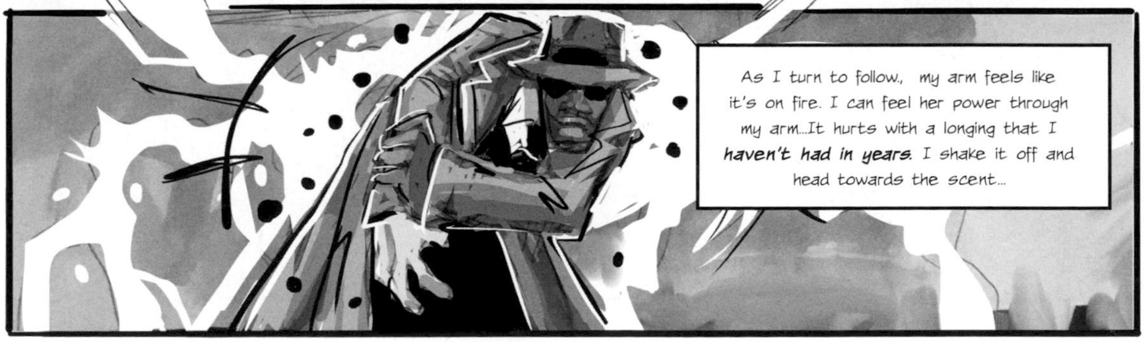
As I turn to follow., my arm feels like it's on fire. I can feel her power through my arm...It hurts with a longing that I ***haven't had in years.*** I shake it off and head towards the scent...

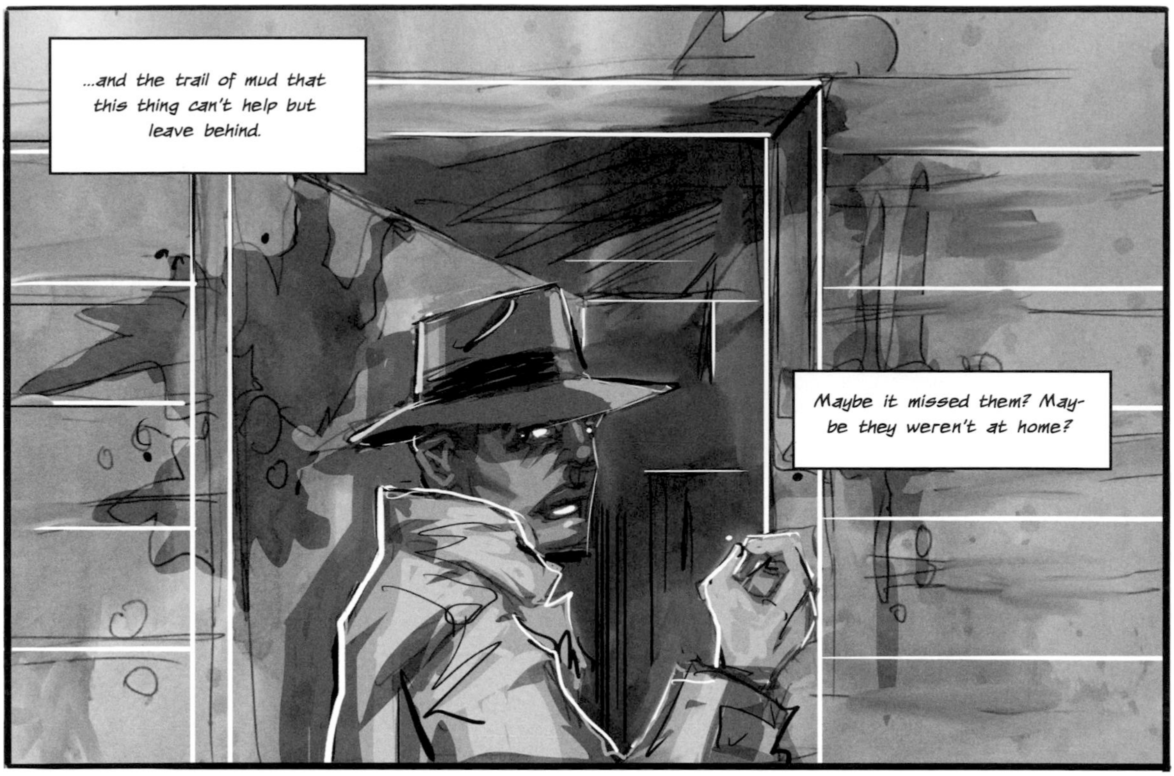
...and the trail of mud that this thing can't help but leave behind.
Maybe it missed them? Maybe they weren't at home?

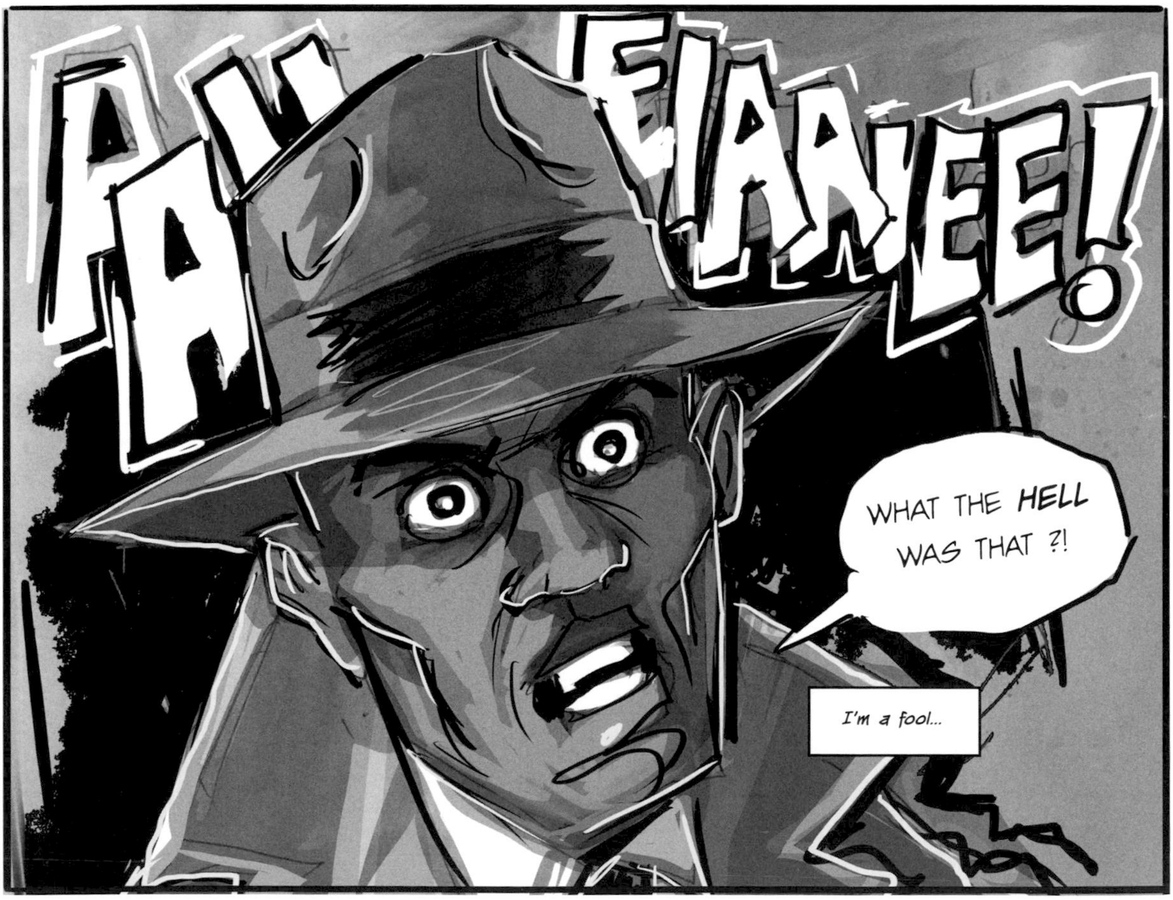
AAIEIAAIEE!
WHAT THE HELL WAS THAT ?!
I'm a fool...

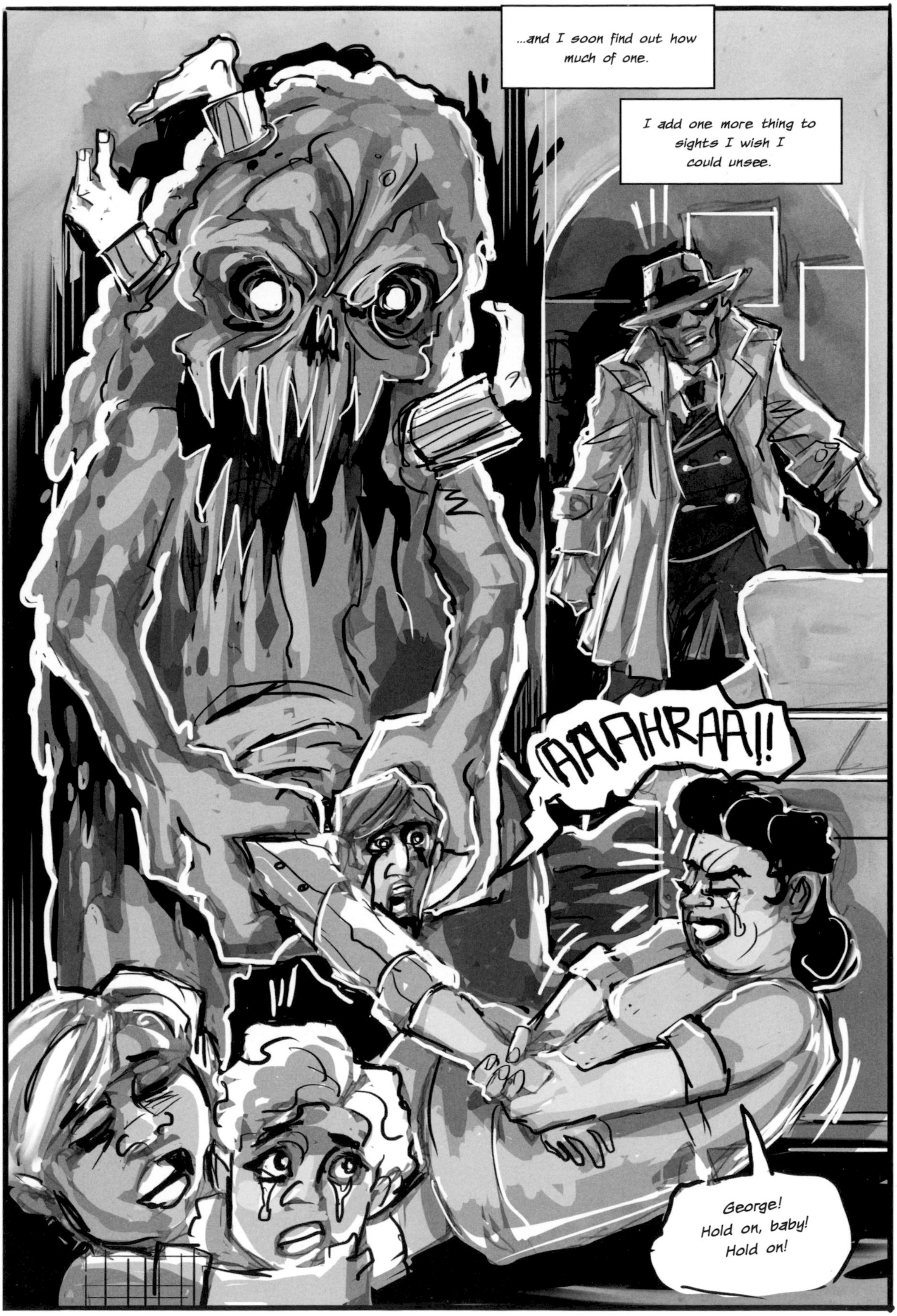

...and I soon find out how much of one.
I add one more thing to sights I wish I could unsee.
AAAHRAA!!
George! Hold on, baby! Hold on!

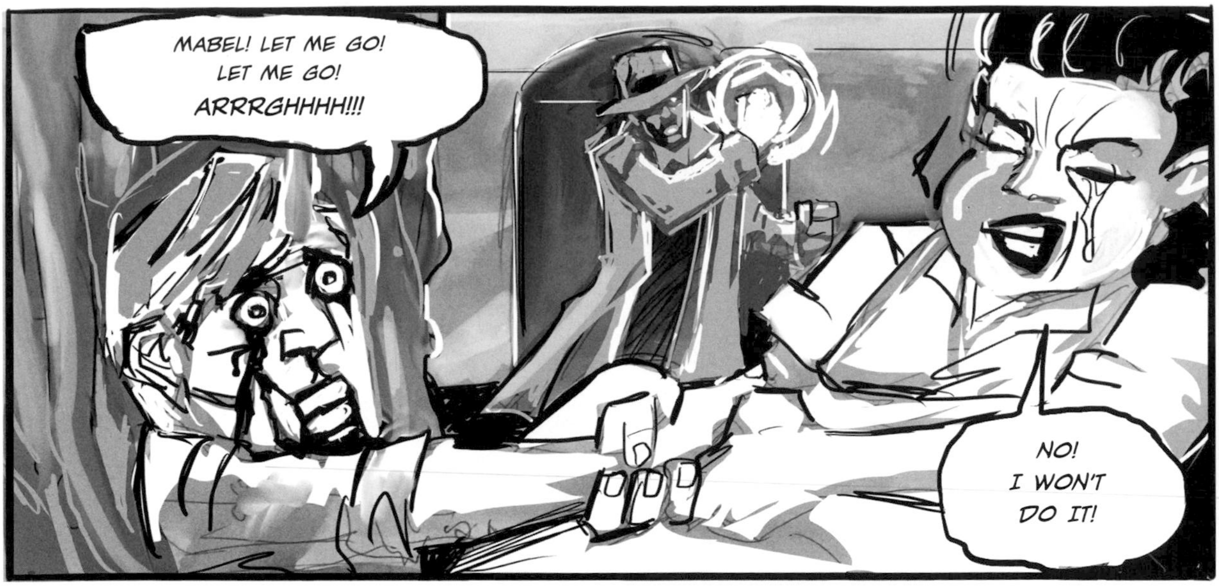
MABEL! LET ME GO!
LET ME GO!
ARRRGHHHH!!!
NO!
I WON'T
DO IT!

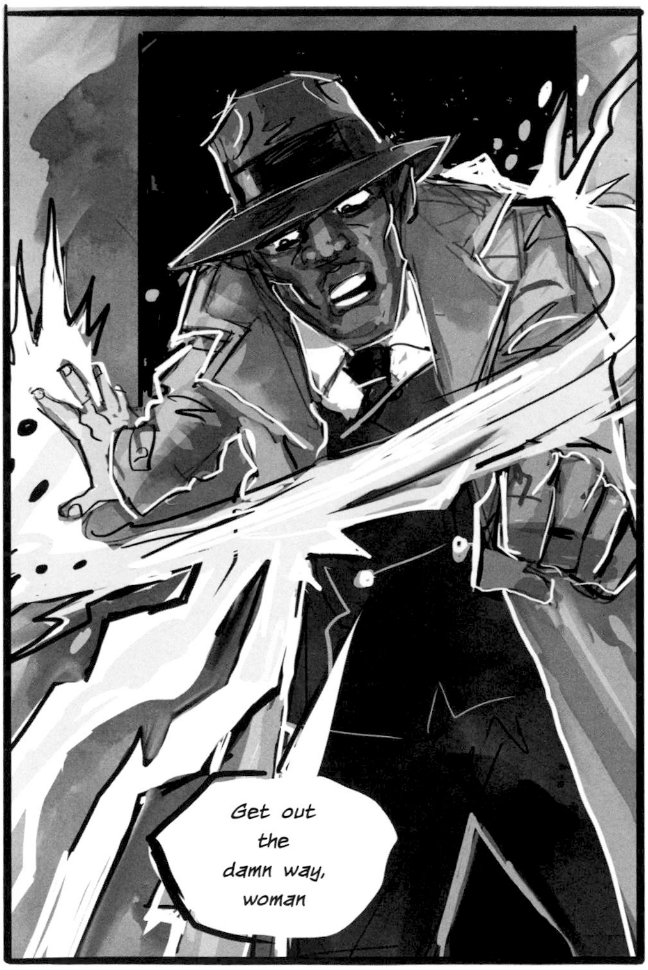
Get out
the
damn way,
woman

There was no way she was letting go. There was no way she could save him. She was the Queen of Lost Causes and I admired her for that title for all of a split second.

He knows he's already dead, and there's no coming back from what that thing did to him. Its hold was too strong on the man. The only thing I could do was put him out of his misery. So, that's what I do...

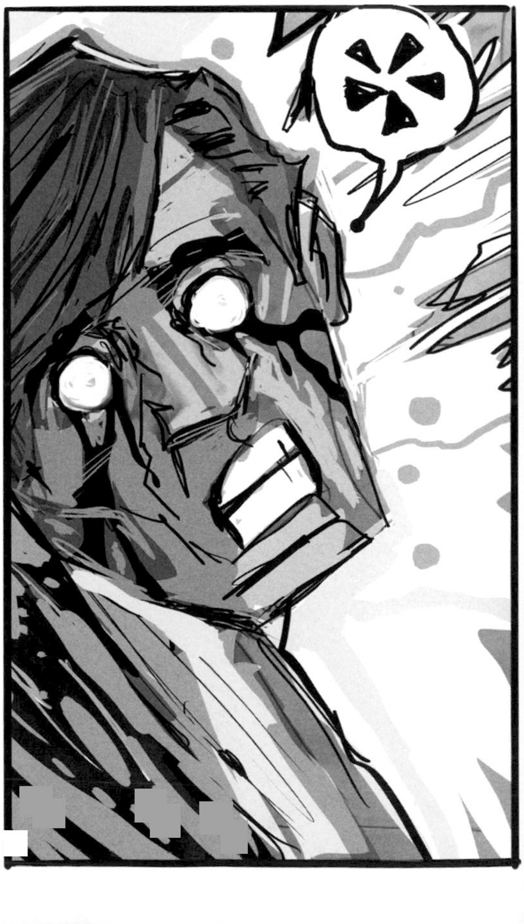

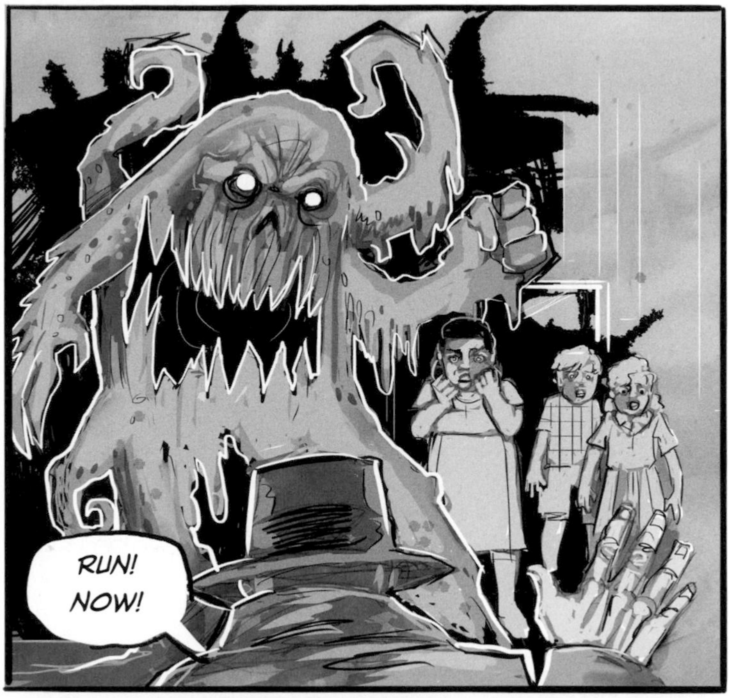
RUN! NOW!

LOOK AT THESE FOOLS!

They stand there dumbfounded by what they thought was impossible.

Mabel and her kids try to figure out which they are more afraid of: a crazed mud monster or the black man who just killed their loved one.

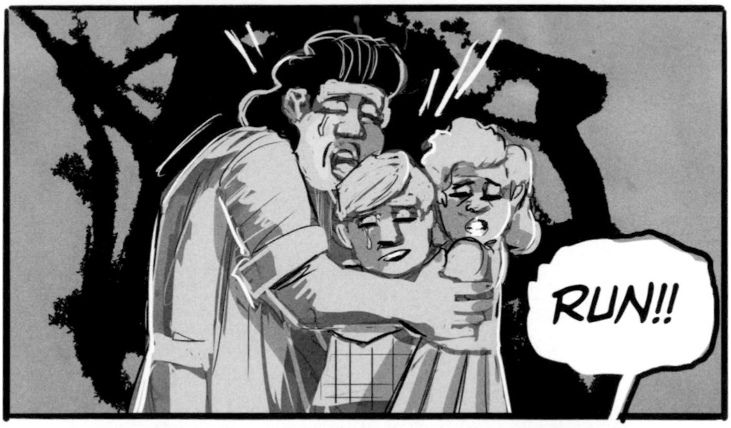
RUN!!

Black. White. The shit's all a sham. Nothing more than an illusion.

This whole family's about to die because of their fear of
dark skin.

Uncle Sam is the best conjure man of them all.

Damn right.

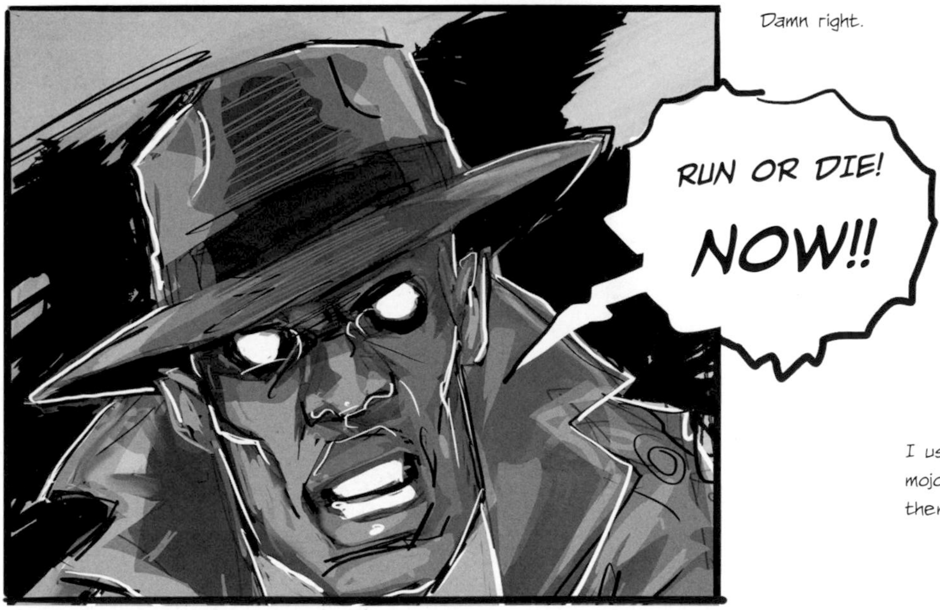
RUN OR DIE!
NOW!!

I use a little mojo to get them moving.

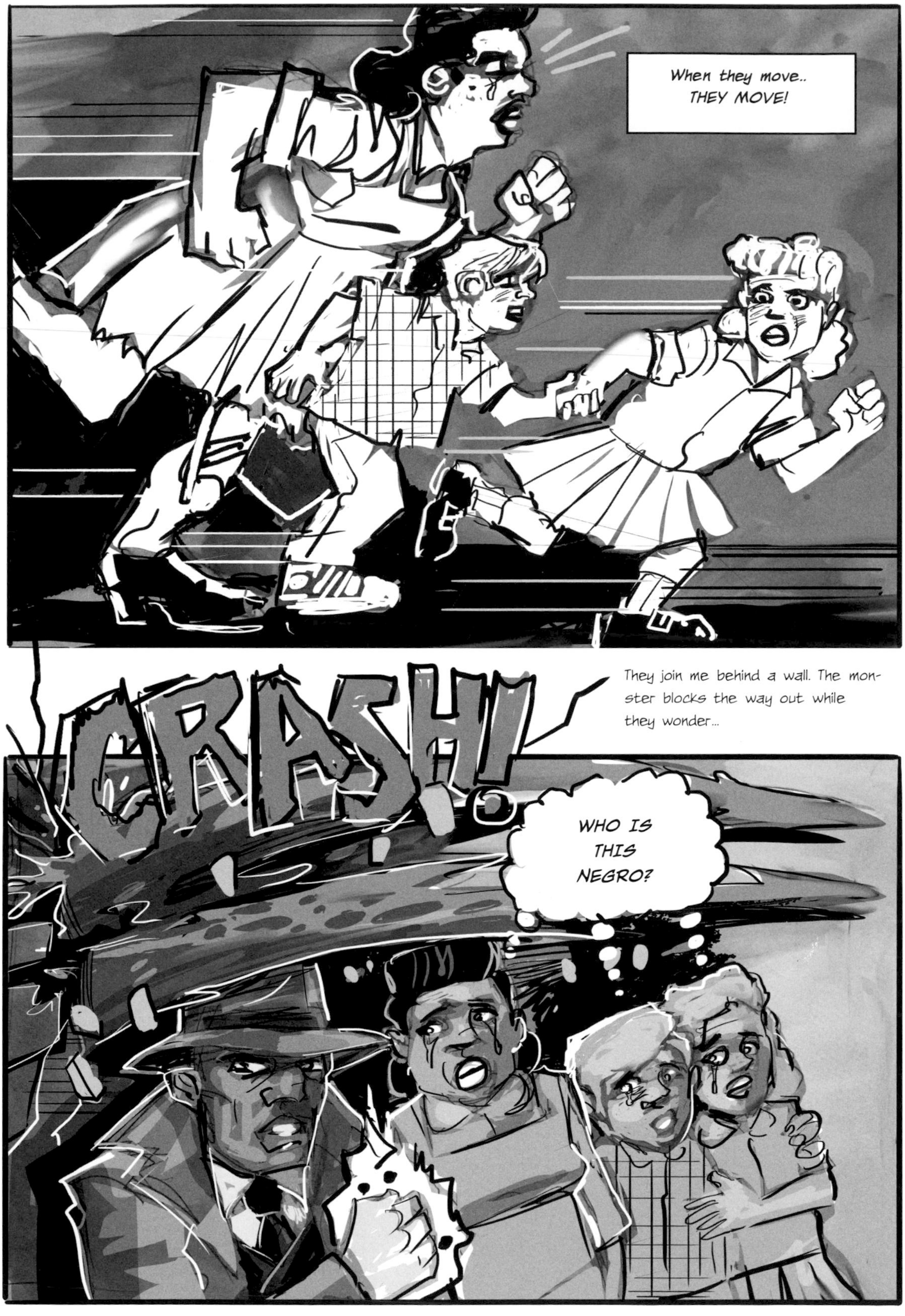
When they move.. THEY MOVE!
They join me behind a wall. The monster blocks the way out while they wonder...
CRASH!
WHO IS THIS NEGRO?

The thing sees us, and is about to make its move. I can feel the mojo hand talking to me...it wants me to use it. I have no choice but to do so. ***I know that it drags me closer to Her...to The Noir.***

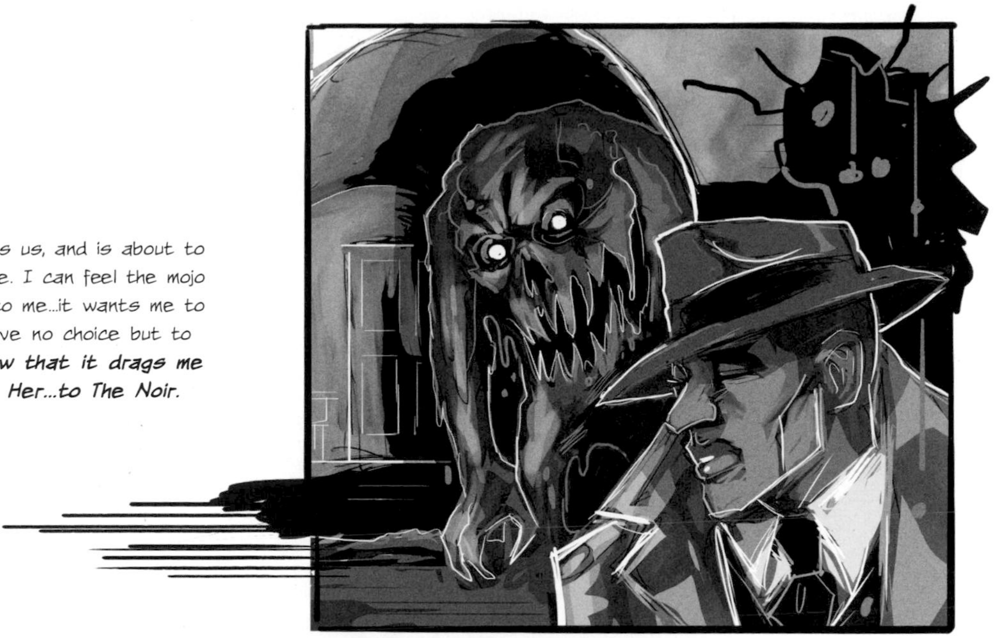

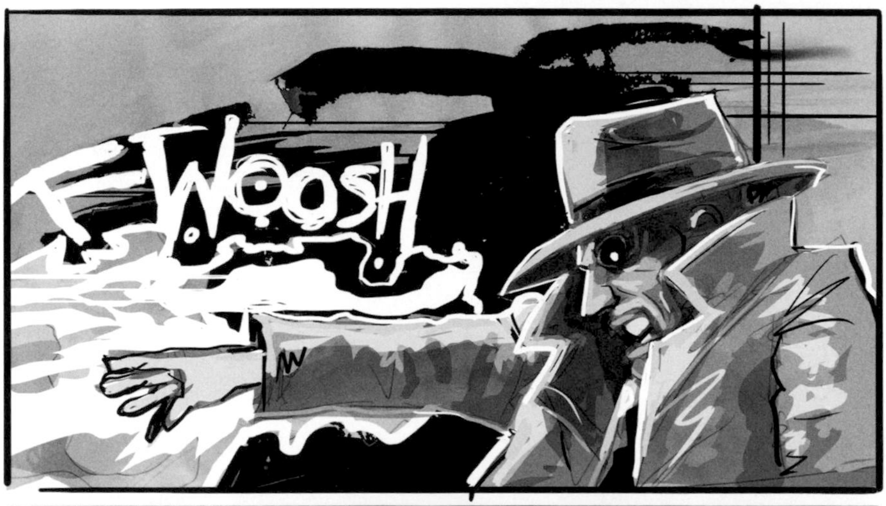
WOOSH

The only thing I could think of was that we were all going to die with our lungs filled with mud and stinkin' river water.

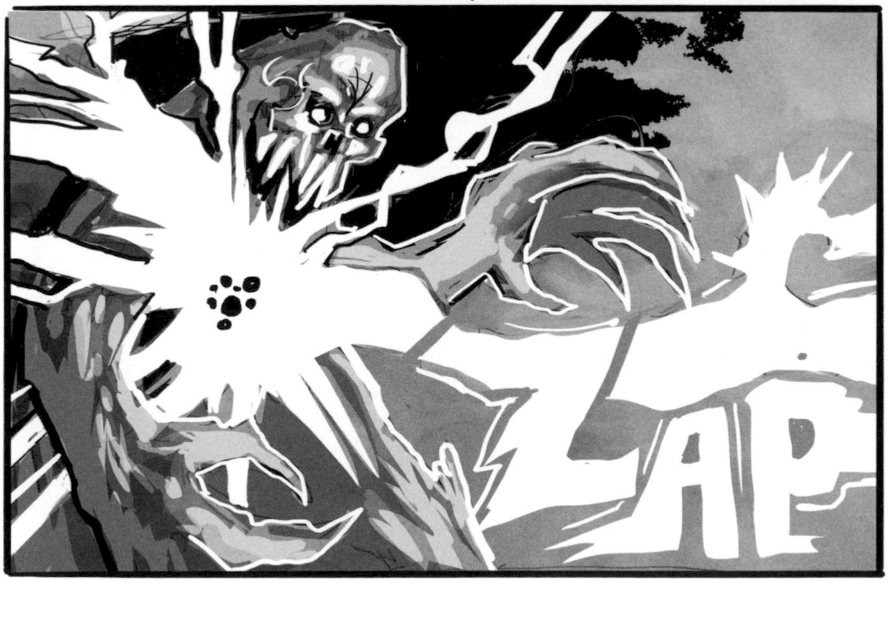

Well. At least I wouldn't have to worry about shipping my body home to buried in my native soil.

I give it all that I have in one big-ass all-or-be-damned hex. I give it all.

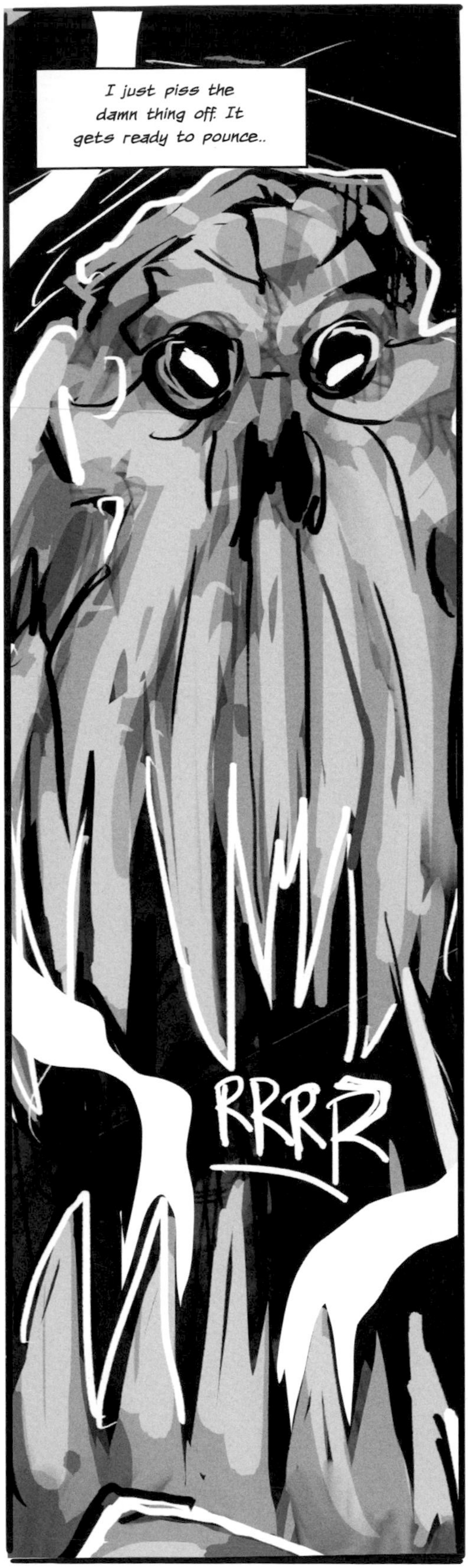
I just piss the damn thing off. It gets ready to pounce..
RRRR

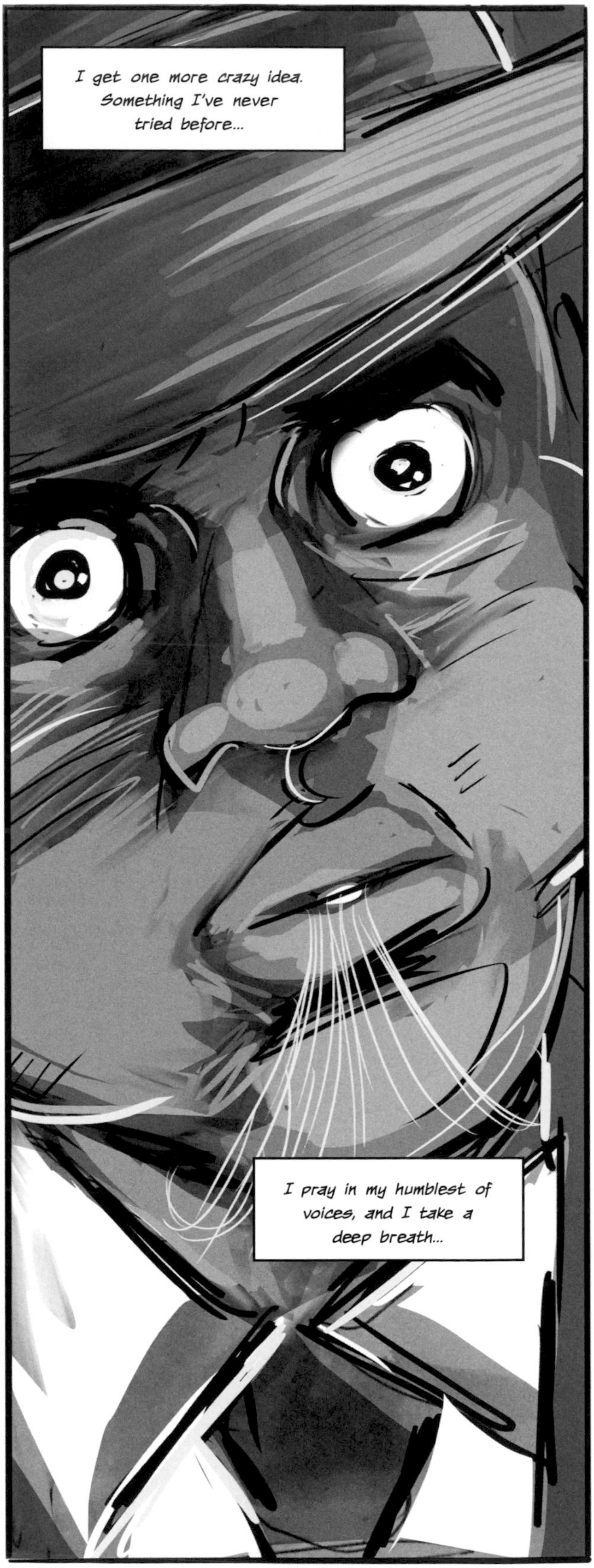
I get one more crazy idea. Something I've never tried before...
I pray in my humblest of voices, and I take a deep breath...

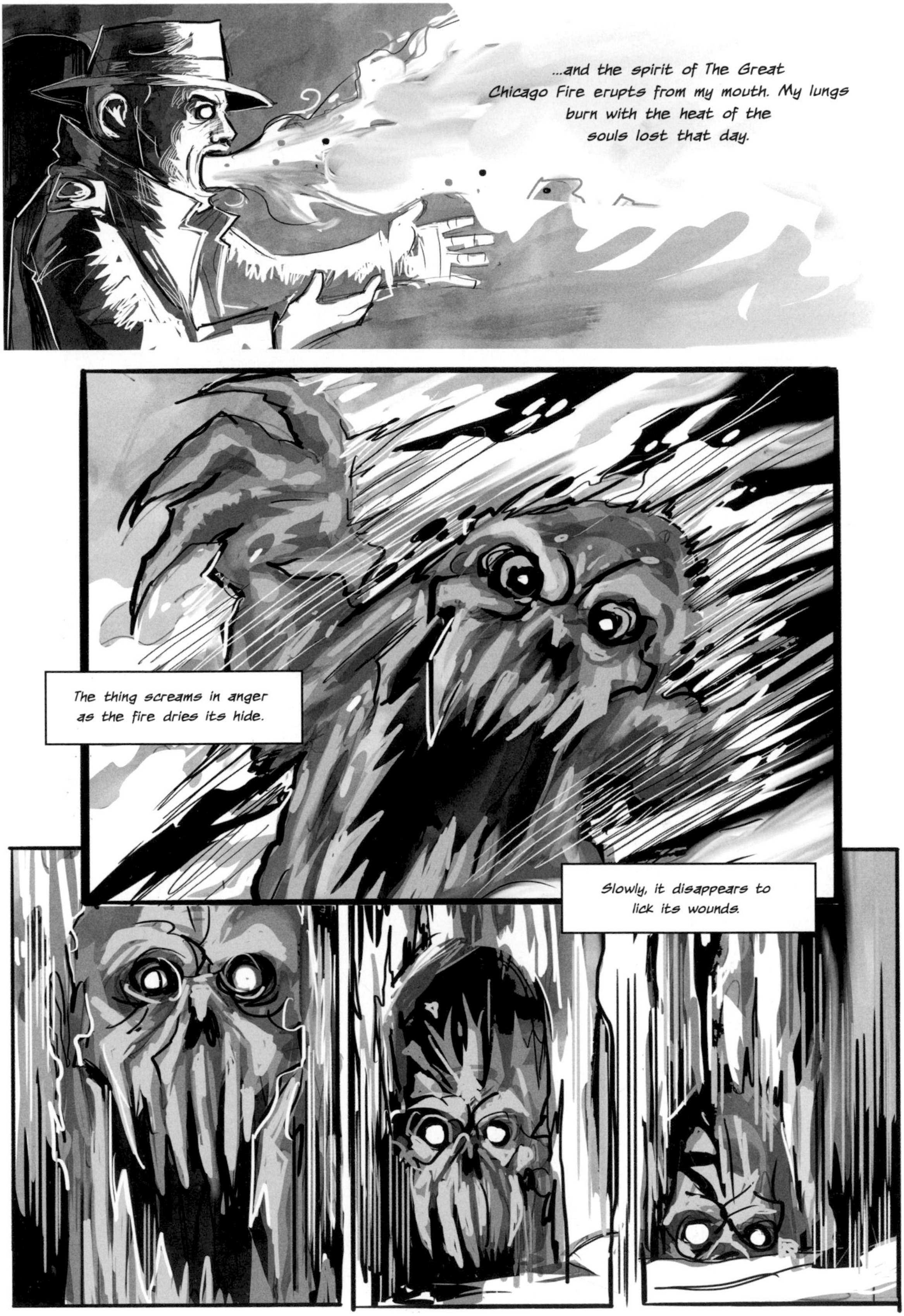
...and the spirit of The Great Chicago Fire erupts from my mouth. My lungs burn with the heat of the souls lost that day.
The thing screams in anger as the fire dries its hide.
Slowly, it disappears to lick its wounds.

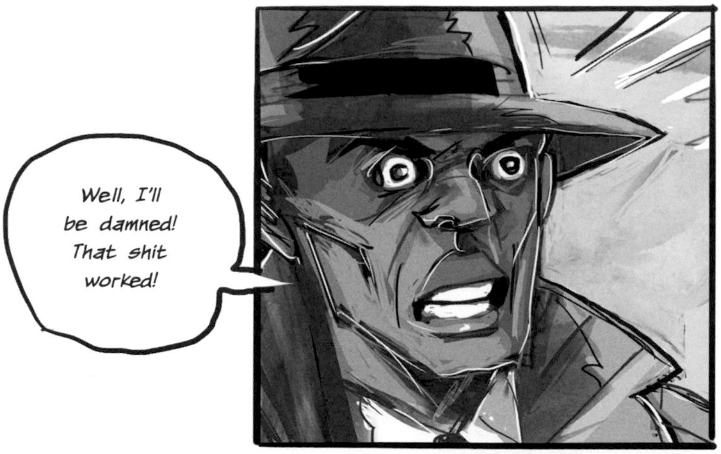
Well, I'll be damned! That shit worked!

I stand there dumbstruck that my gamble paid off. My body feels like it's been ridden by the universe.
The angry burning ghosts will haunt my dreams tonight.

But,

we're alive,
and they ain't.

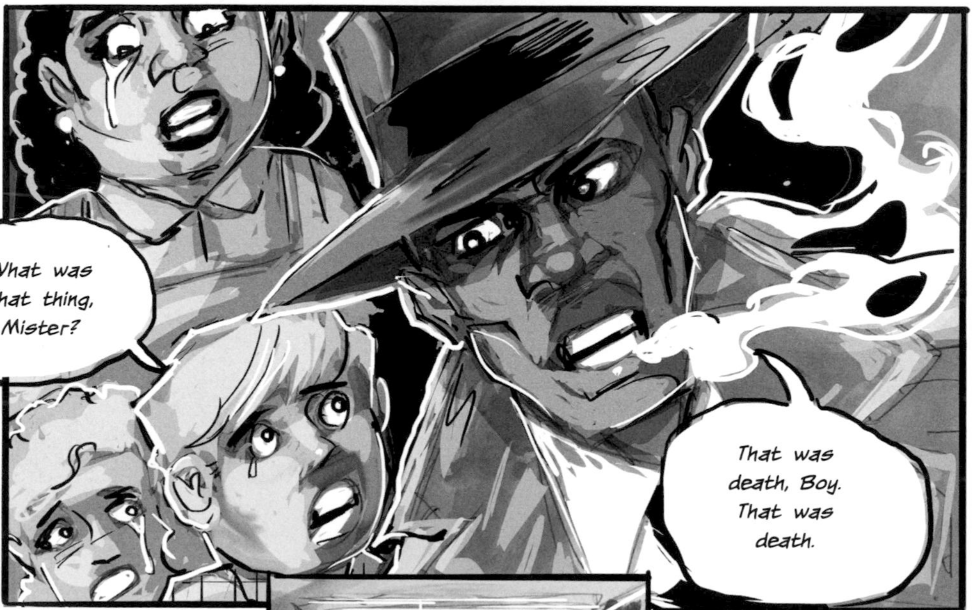
What was that thing, Mister?
That was death, Boy. That was death.

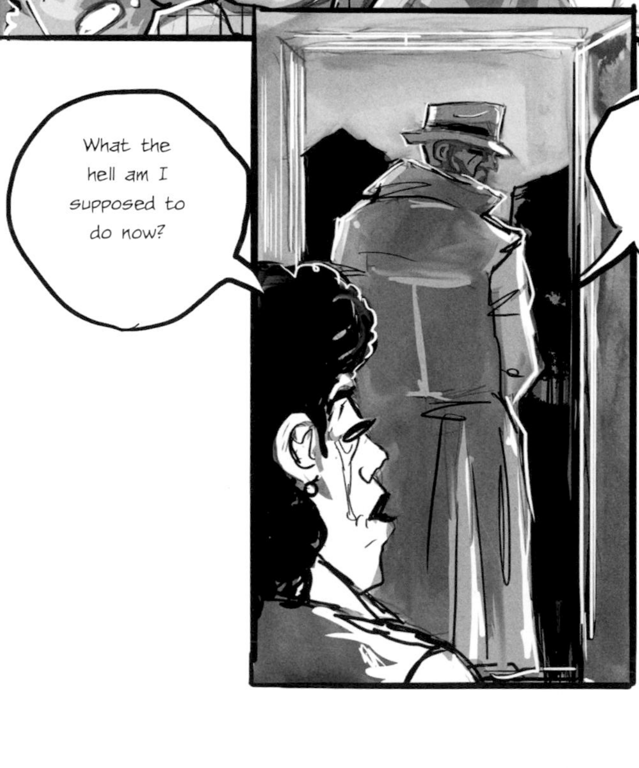
What the hell am I supposed to do now?
Thank the God you pray to and go pick a coffin.

What's left of Georgie lies crumpled on the floor like a twisted-up doll.

Closed casket for sure.

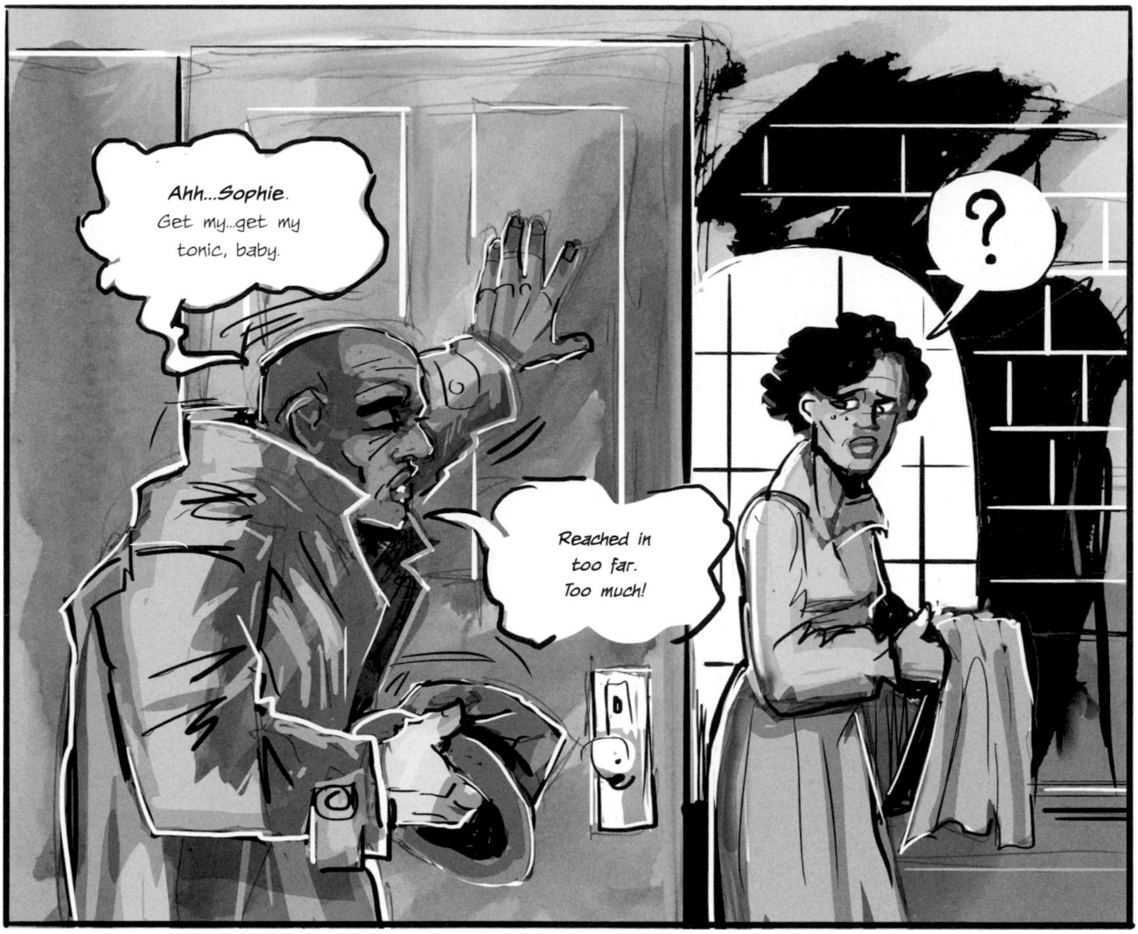
Ahh...Sophie. Get my...get my tonic, baby.
?
Reached in too far. Too much!

I take the El back to **Sophie's Place.** It was too risky to travel the roots again. I can feel **the Noir** in my head.

She's near.

The curse of the Noir Lock is on my tail. The curse of **losing yourself** to the story that she says you are. Forever. Locked in that one story. No escape.

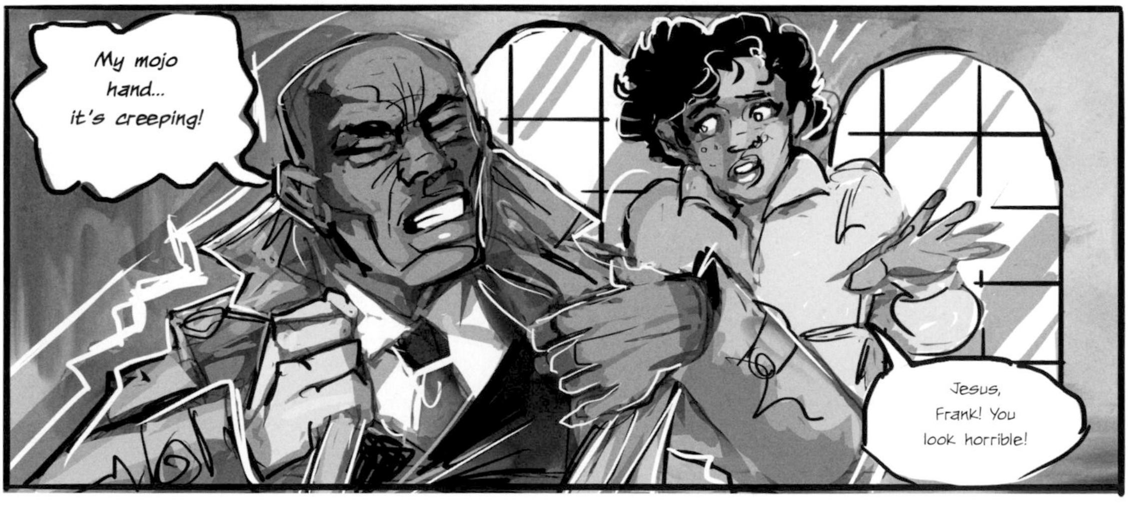
My mojo hand... it's creeping!
Jesus, Frank! You look horrible!

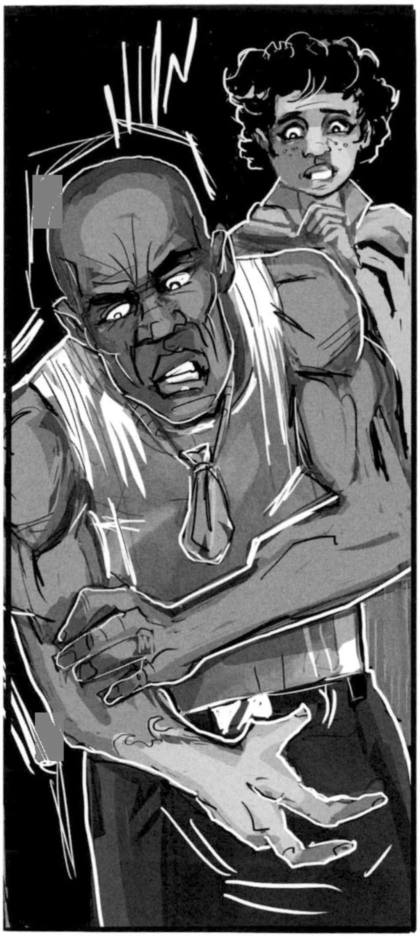

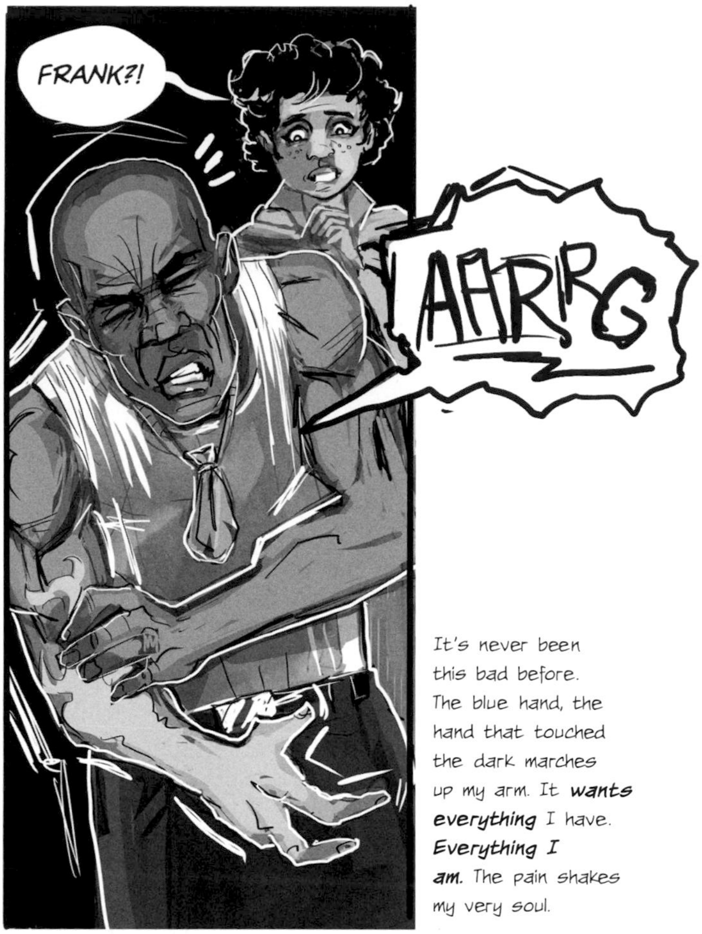
FRANK?!
AHRRG

It's never been this bad before. The blue hand, the hand that touched the dark marches up my arm. It ***wants everything*** I have. ***Everything I am.*** The pain shakes my very soul.

I guzzle the tonic Sophie made for me. It burns as the arm tries to fight against it. ***The inevitable*** and the ***stubborness*** of being human collide in my ***very core.*** I ain't ready, and I mean that shit!

Gottdammit! NOT. YET.

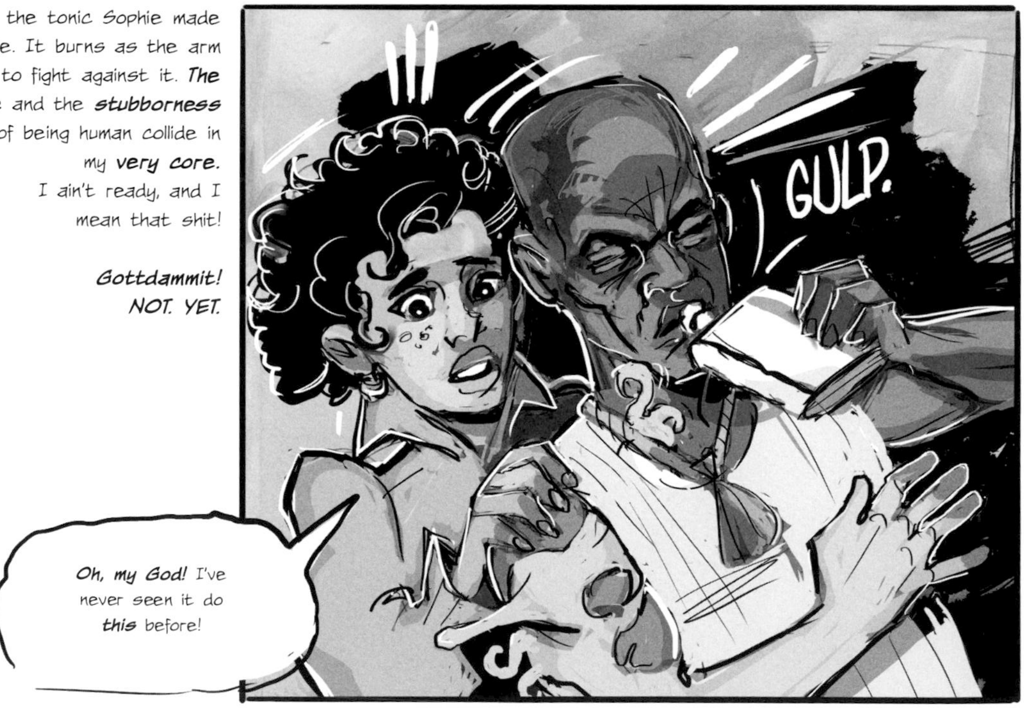
GULP.
Oh, my God! I've never seen it do *this* before!

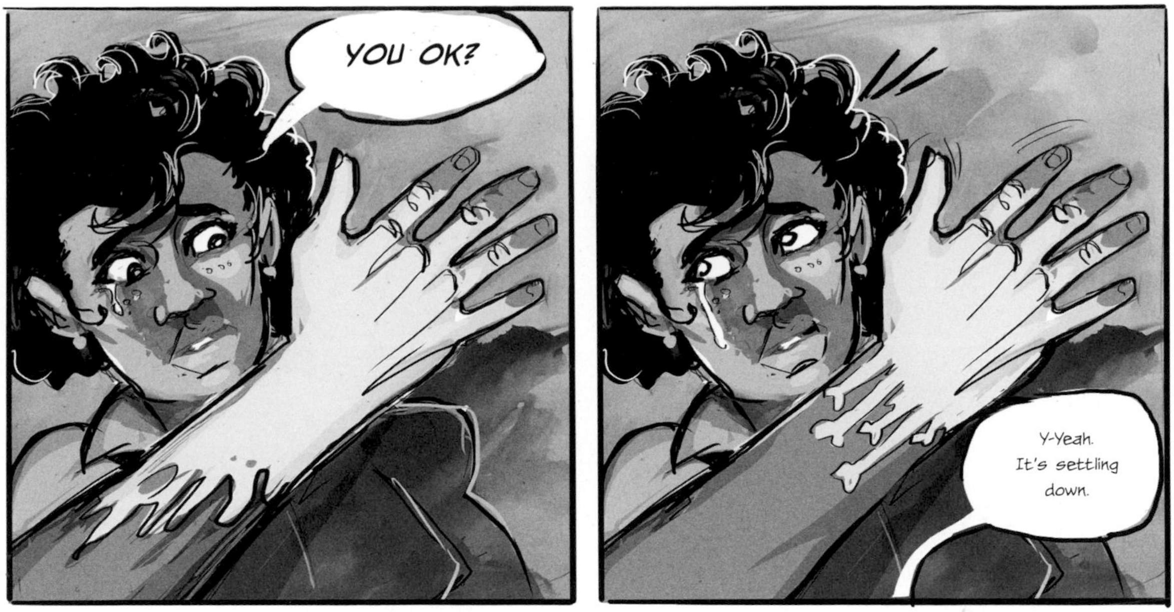
YOU OK?
Y-Yeah. It's settling down.

My sweet **Sophie**. She saved my black ass once again. We have a really sweet deal. The tonic has to be made by the hands of someone who cares for you. Can't make it yourself. ***Them's the rules.***

She makes it for me and in return she takes a little of my blood for her ***passing potion.*** A conjure man's blood and little rootwork, and she can look as ***white as snow.*** Damn ***high price*** to pay for a gig.

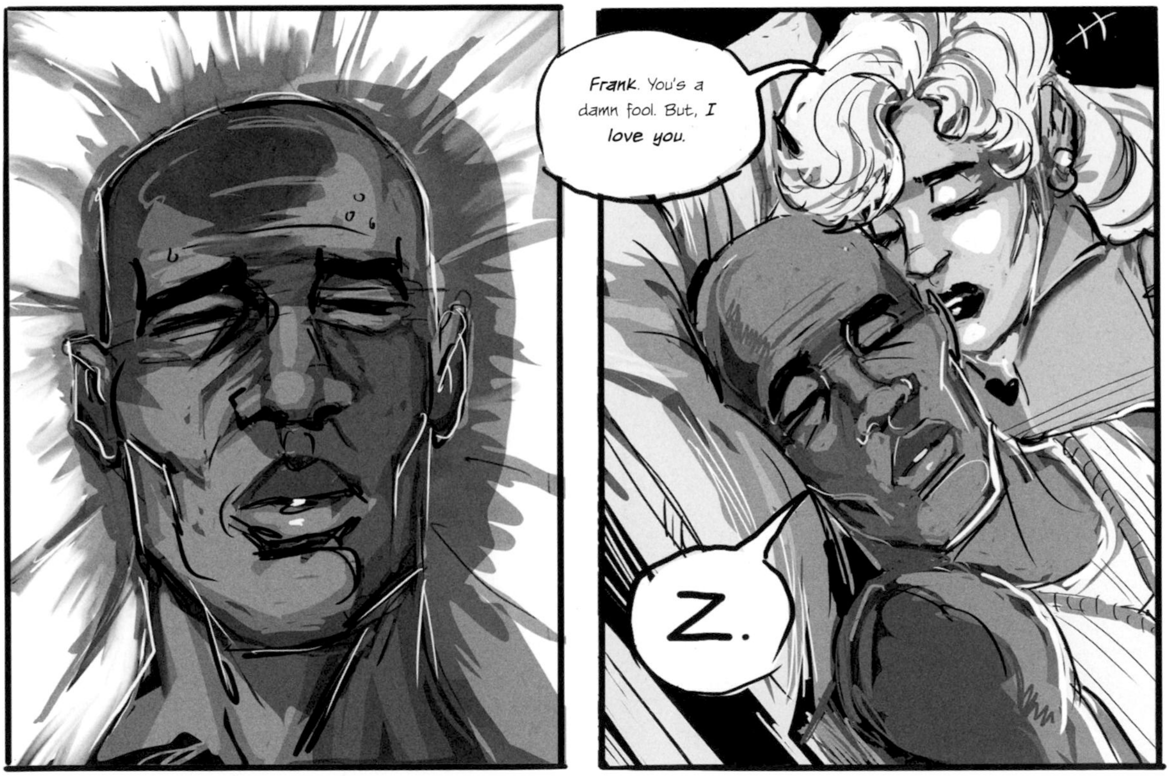
Frank. You's a damn fool. But, I love you.
Z.

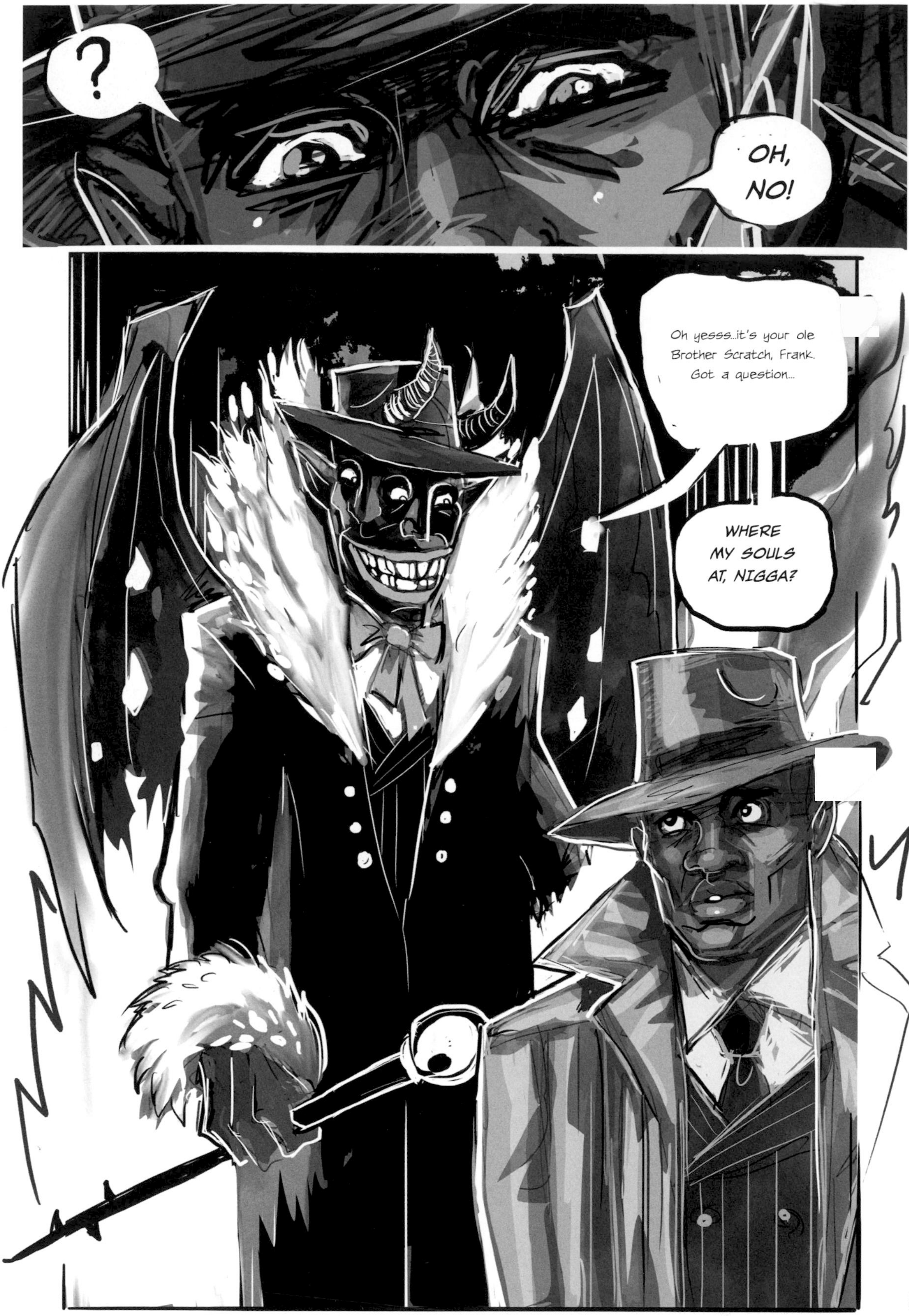
?
OH, NO!
Oh yesss...it's your ole Brother Scratch, Frank. Got a question...
WHERE MY SOULS AT, NIGGA?

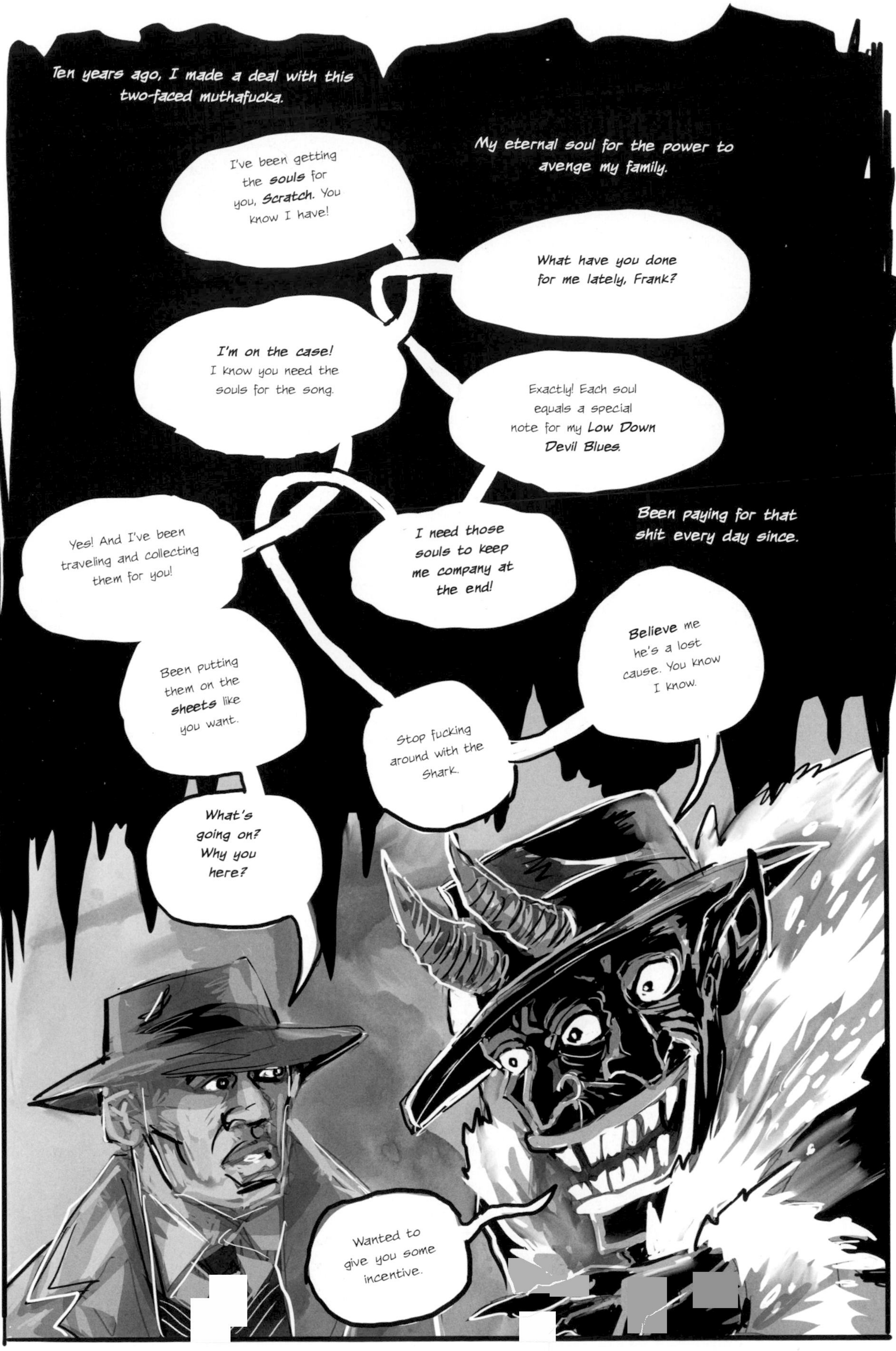
Ten years ago, I made a deal with this two-faced muthafucka.
My eternal soul for the power to avenge my family.
I've been getting the souls for you, Scratch. You know I have!
What have you done for me lately, Frank?
I'm on the case! I know you need the souls for the song.
Exactly! Each soul equals a special note for my Low Down Devil Blues.
Yes! And I've been traveling and collecting them for you!
I need those souls to keep me company at the end!
Been putting them on the sheets like you want.
Stop fucking around with the Shark.
Been paying for that shit every day since.
Believe me he's a lost cause. You know I know.
What's going on? Why you here?
Wanted to give you some incentive.

I managed to work a different deal.
He kept half my soul in return
for my help finding the right souls.

Souls that resonate with the right tone for
his ultimate blues song for the end times....

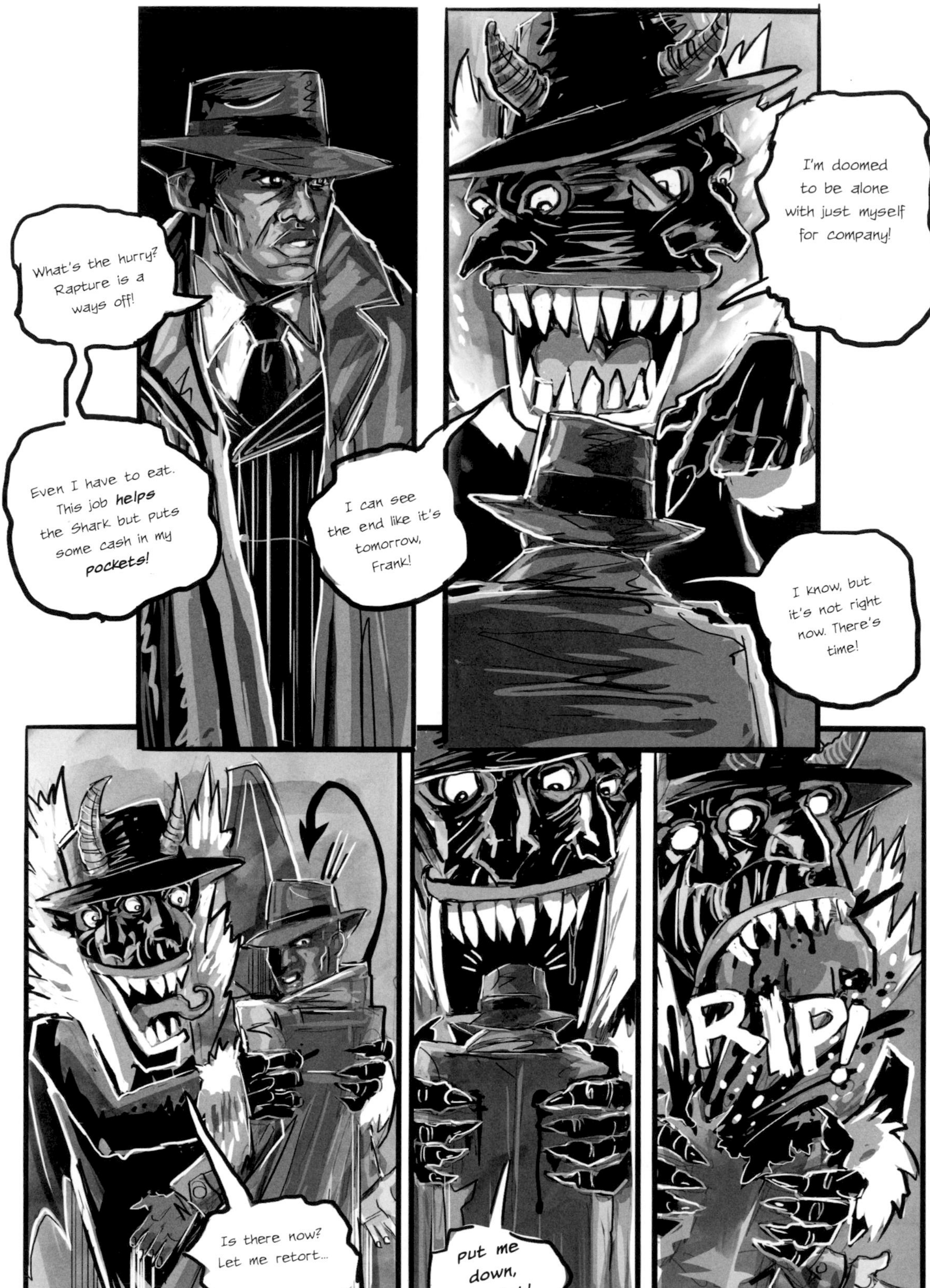
What's the hurry? Rapture is a ways off!
Even I have to eat. This job **helps** the Shark but puts some cash in my **pockets!**
I'm doomed to be alone with just myself for company!
I can see the end like it's tomorrow, Frank!
I know, but it's not right now. There's time!
Is there now? Let me retort...
Put me down, Scratch!
RIP!

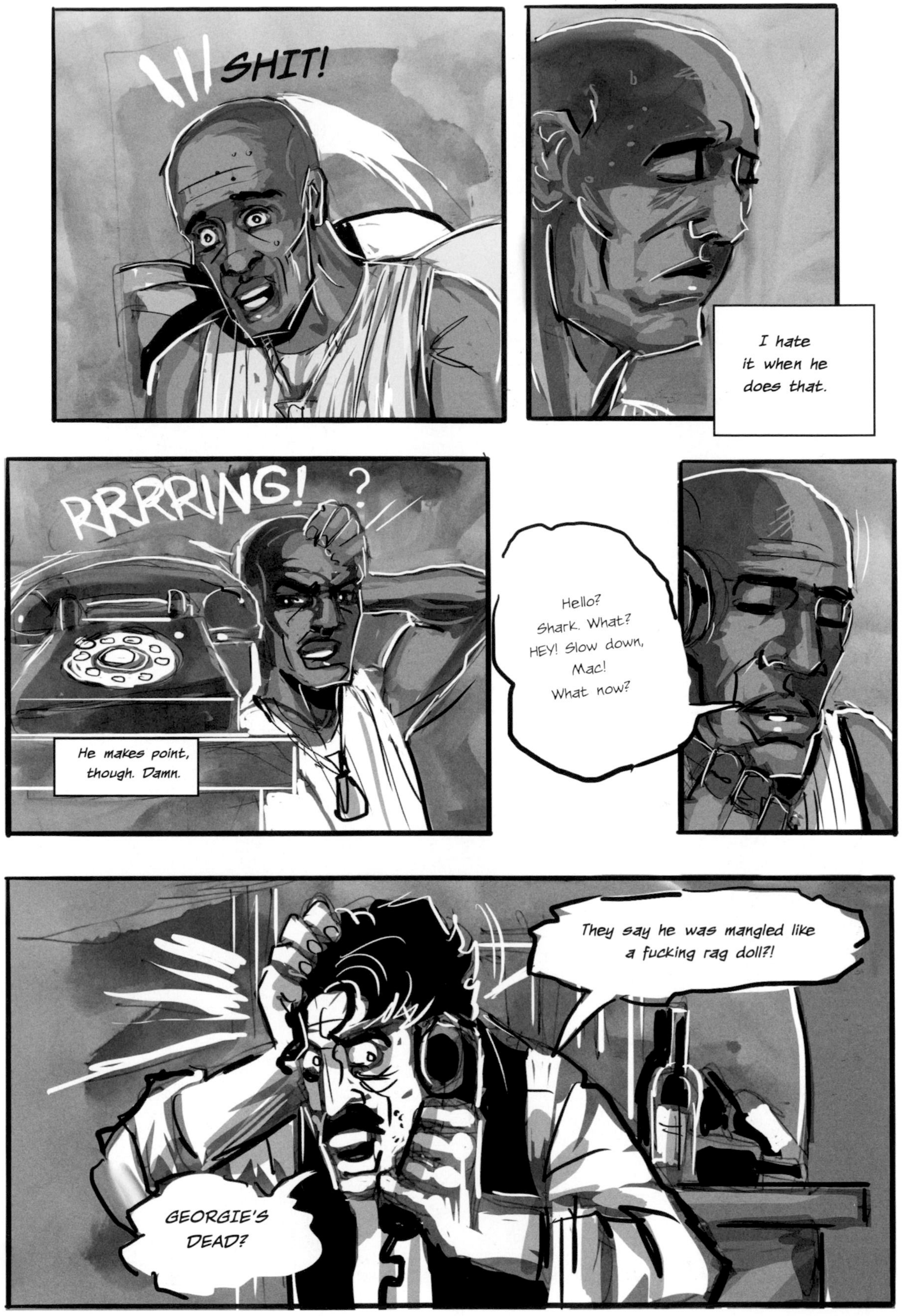
SHIT!
I hate it when he does that.
RRRRING! ?
He makes point, though. Damn.
Hello? Shark. What? HEY! Slow down, Mac! What now?
They say he was mangled like a fucking rag doll?!
GEORGIE'S DEAD?

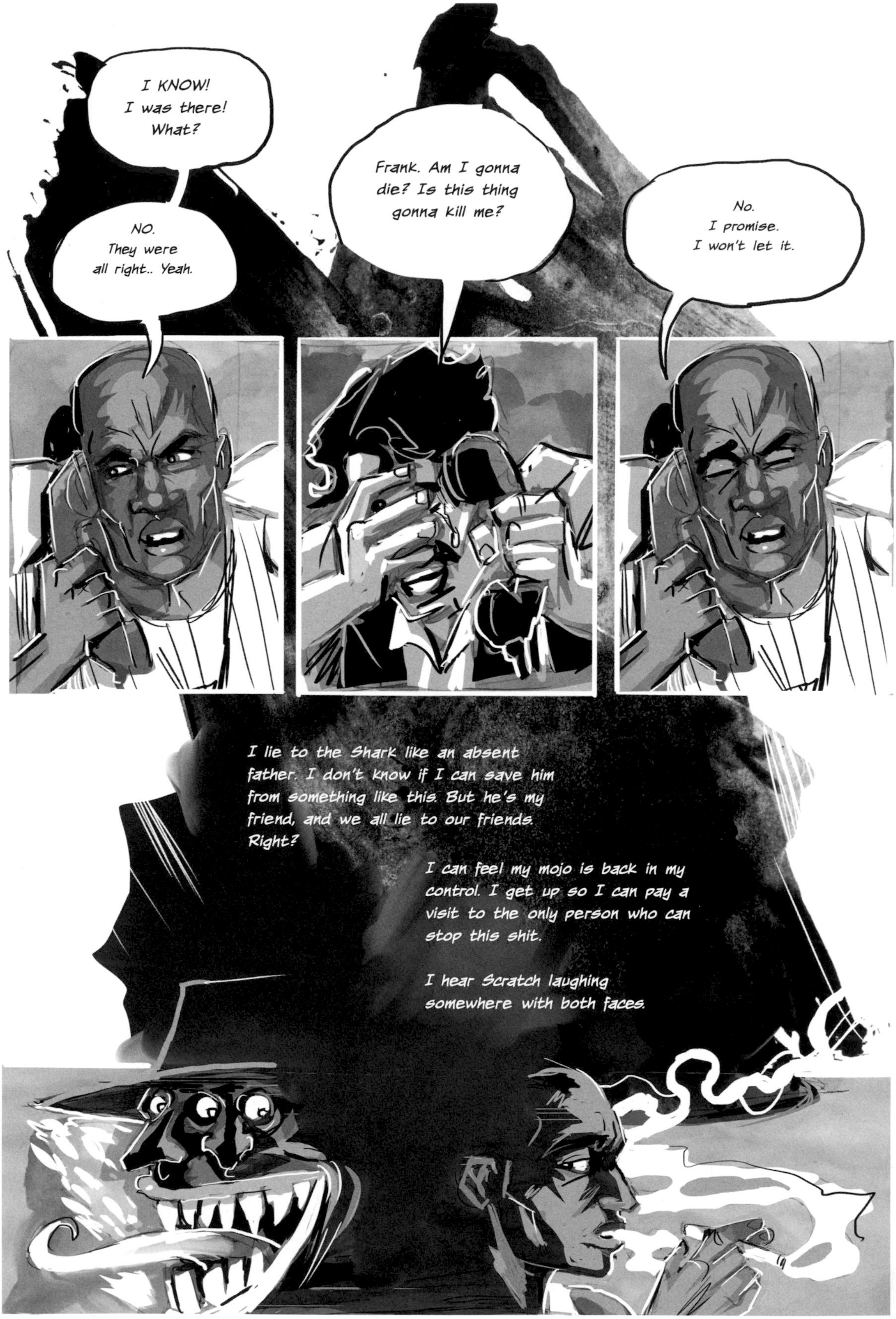
I KNOW! I was there! What?
NO. They were all right.. Yeah.
Frank. Am I gonna die? Is this thing gonna kill me?
No. I promise. I won't let it.
I lie to the Shark like an absent father. I don't know if I can save him from something like this. But he's my friend, and we all lie to our friends. Right?
I can feel my mojo is back in my control. I get up so I can pay a visit to the only person who can stop this shit.
I hear Scratch laughing somewhere with both faces.

Chapter 8

A Mother Scorned

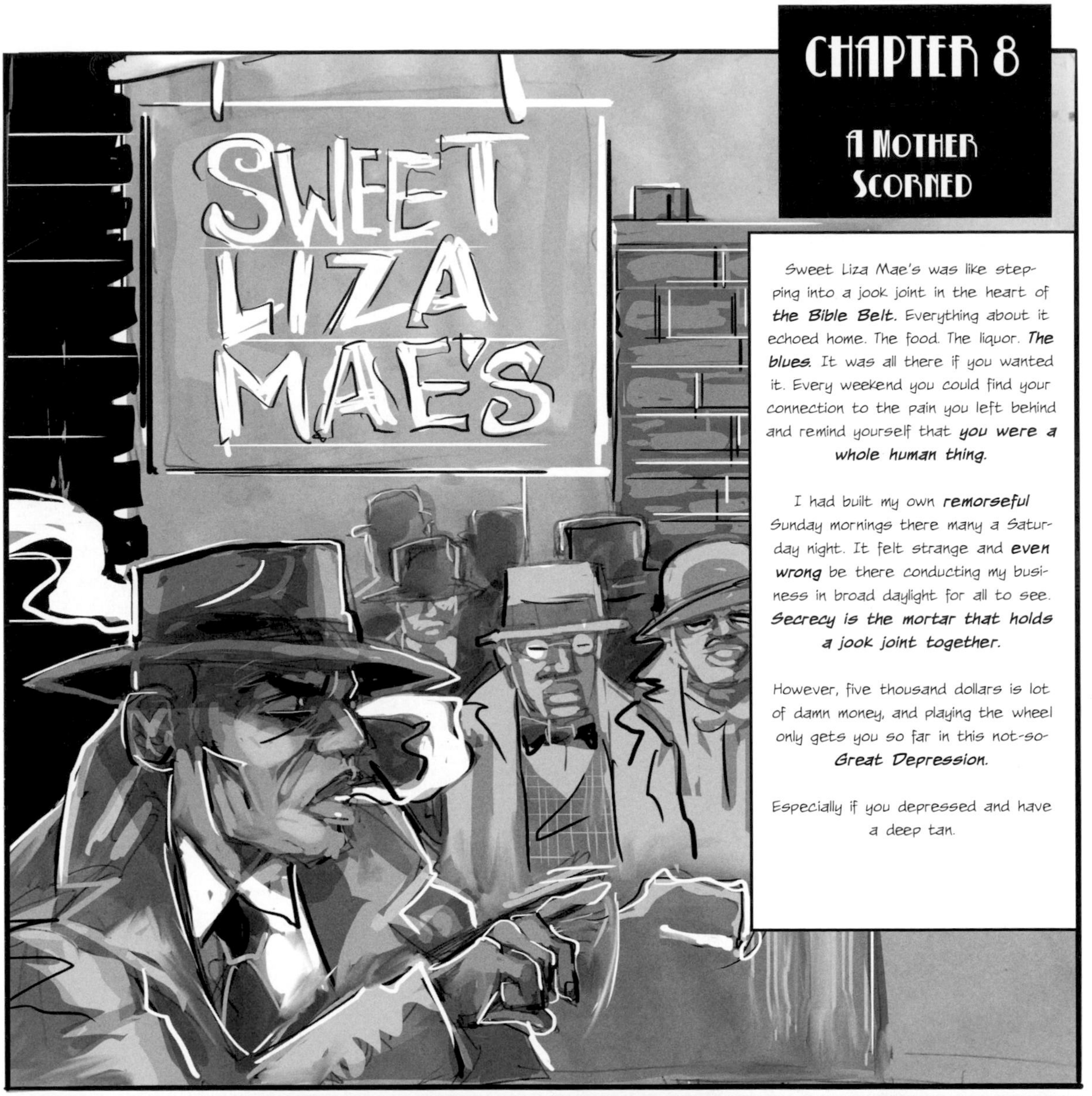
SWEET LIZA MAE'S
Sweet Liza Mae's was like stepping into a jook joint in the heart of **the Bible Belt.** Everything about it echoed home. The food. The liquor. ***The blues.*** It was all there if you wanted it. Every weekend you could find your connection to the pain you left behind and remind yourself that ***you were a whole human thing.***
I had built my own ***remorseful*** Sunday mornings there many a Saturday night. It felt strange and ***even wrong*** be there conducting my business in broad daylight for all to see. ***Secrecy is the mortar that holds a jook joint together.***
However, five thousand dollars is lot of damn money, and playing the wheel only gets you so far in this not-so-***Great Depression.***
Especially if you depressed and have a deep tan.

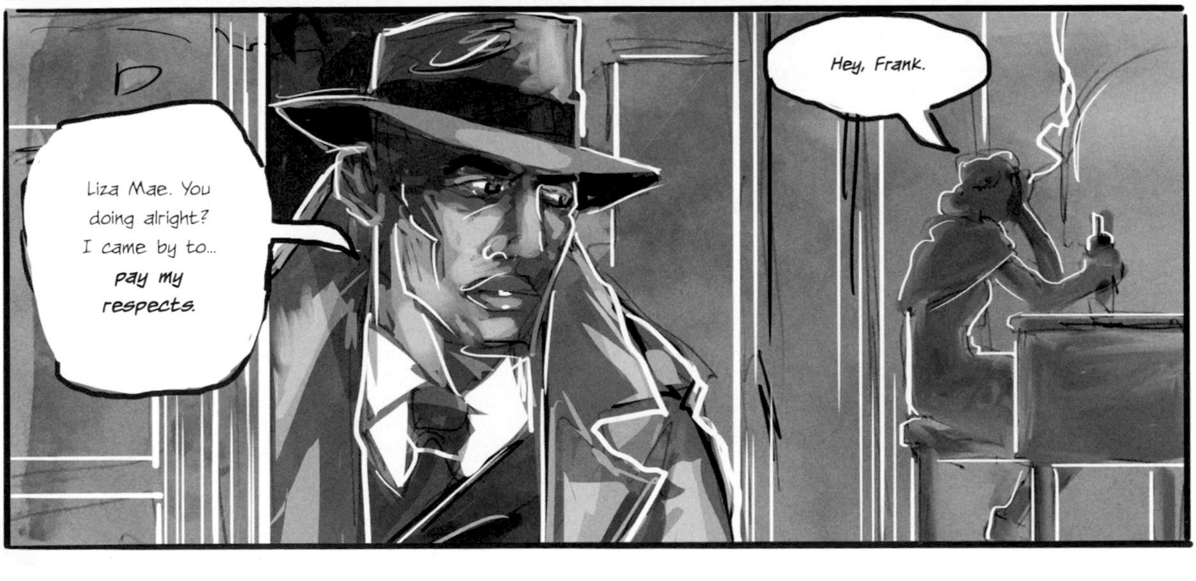
Liza Mae. You doing alright? I came by to... ***pay my respects.***
Hey, Frank.

Liza Mae was a lovely old lady. You could tell that she'd had her share of things. I remember how she'd carry on those weekend nights; laughing, singing, and cussing with the best of them. Now she seemed hollowed out like some old stump in the middle of a lonely thicket.

I entered the joint, which now seemed to have the air of a crypt. Death was in the corner.

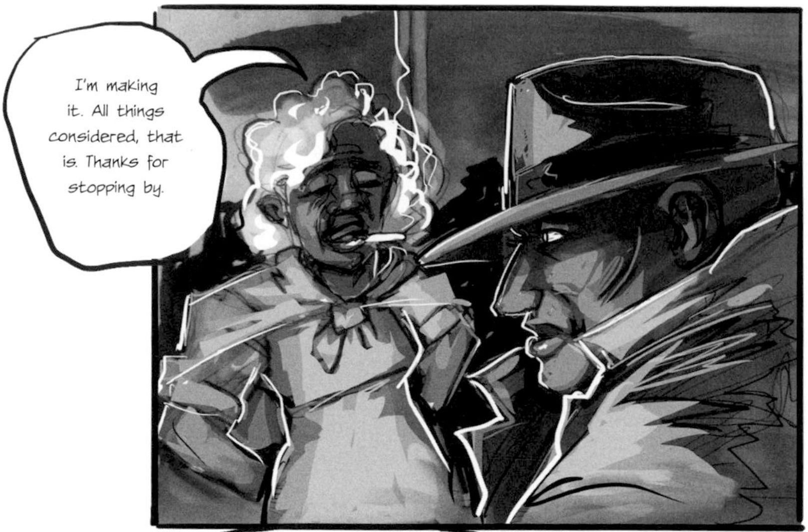
I'm making it. All things considered, that is. Thanks for stopping by.

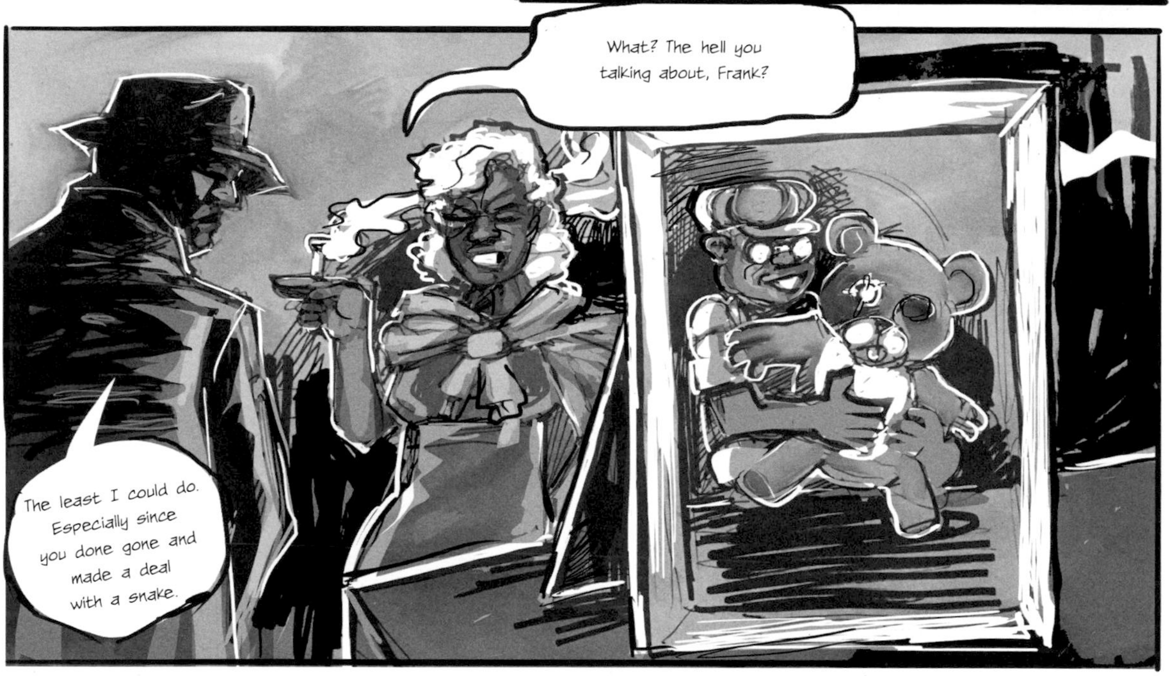
The least I could do. Especially since you done gone and made a deal with a snake.
What? The hell you talking about, Frank?

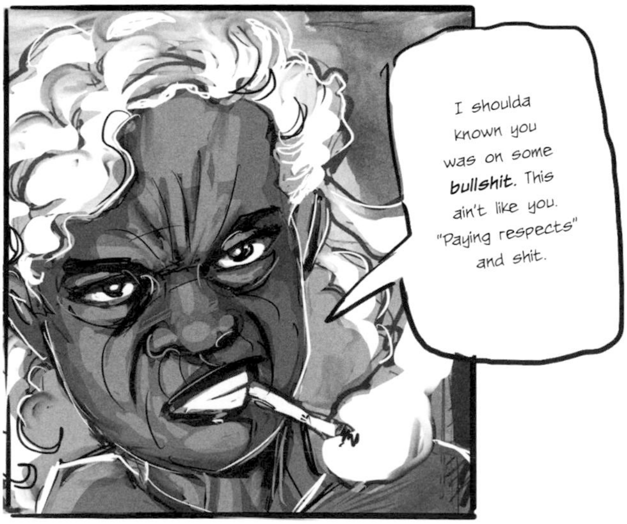
I shoulda known you was on some **bullshit**. This ain't like you. "Paying respects" and shit.

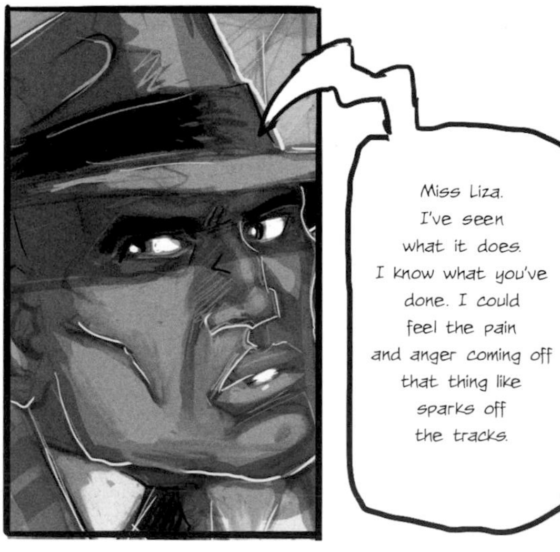
Miss Liza. I've seen what it does. I know what you've done. I could feel the pain and anger coming off that thing like sparks off the tracks.

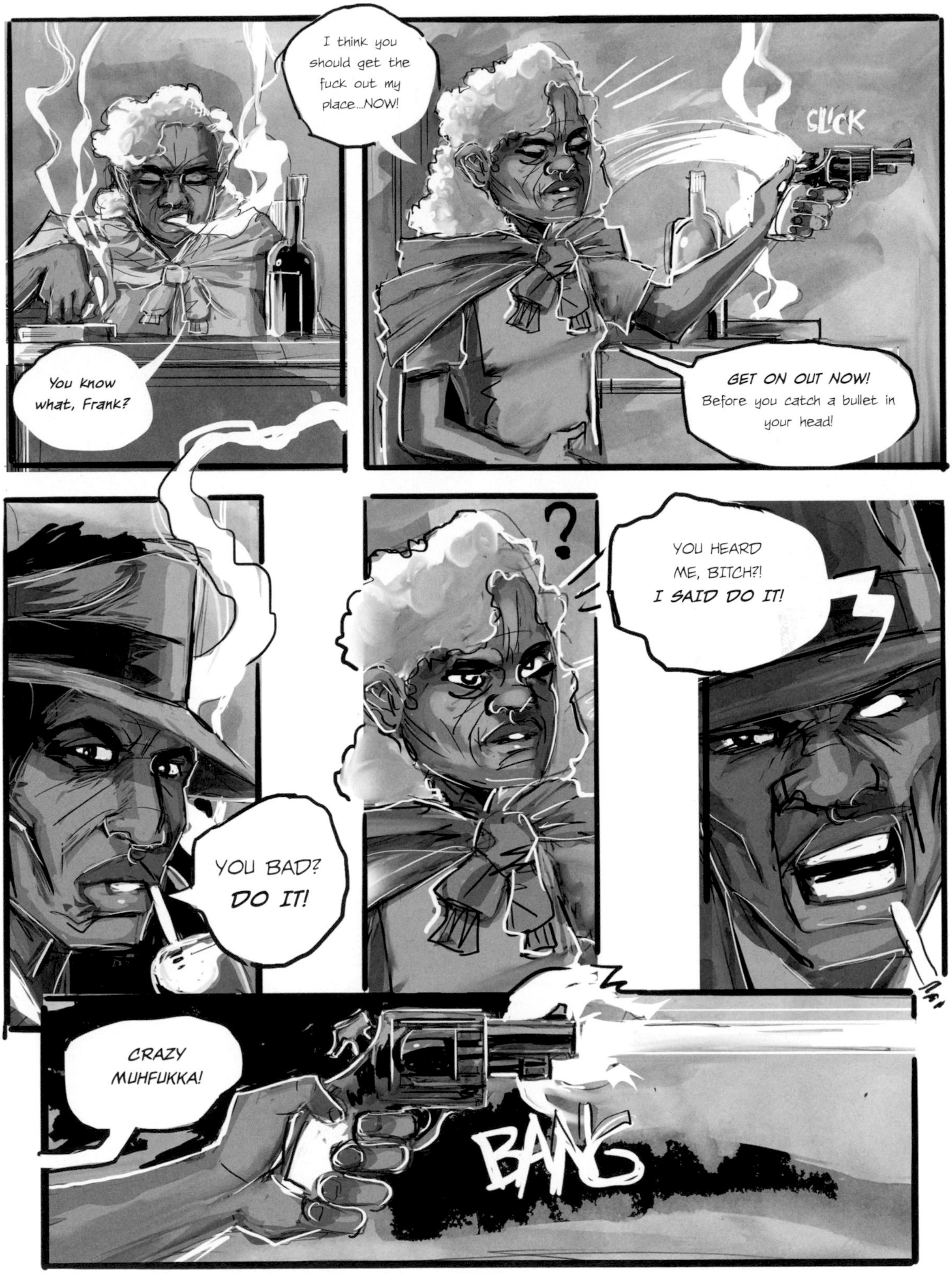
You know what, Frank?
I think you should get the fuck out my place...NOW!
SLICK
GET ON OUT NOW! Before you catch a bullet in your head!
YOU BAD? DO IT!
?
YOU HEARD ME, BITCH?! I SAID DO IT!
CRAZY MUHFUKKA!
BANG

Time slows. I see my life. ***I see the crossroads.*** I see my wife's face.
I see my baby girl's braided hair. ***A wolf howls in the distance.***
I feel the weight of my newborn son in my arms. I close my heart...

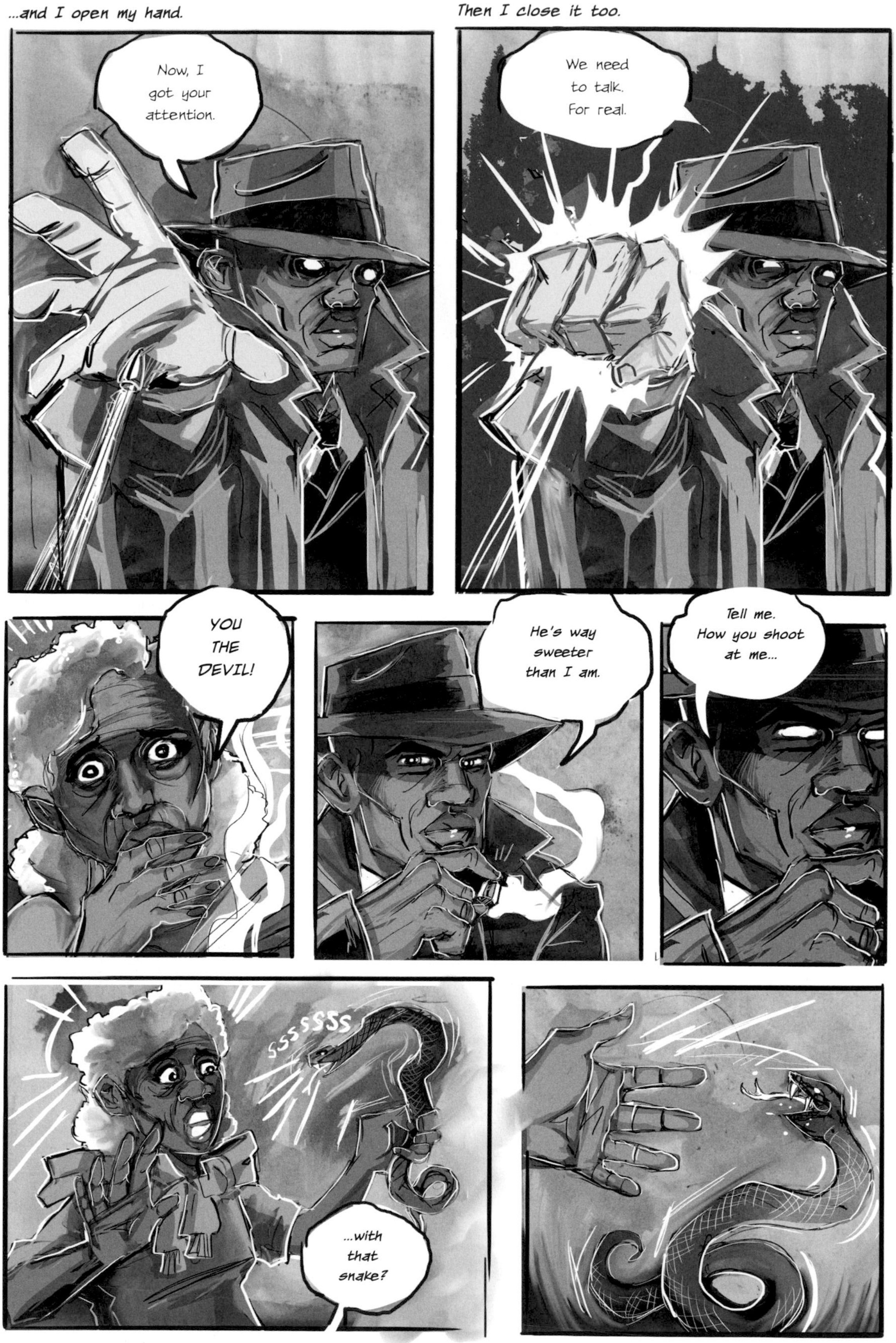
...and I open my hand.
Now, I got your attention.
Then I close it too.
We need to talk. For real.
YOU THE DEVIL!
He's way sweeter than I am.
Tell me. How you shoot at me...
SSSSSSS
...with that snake?

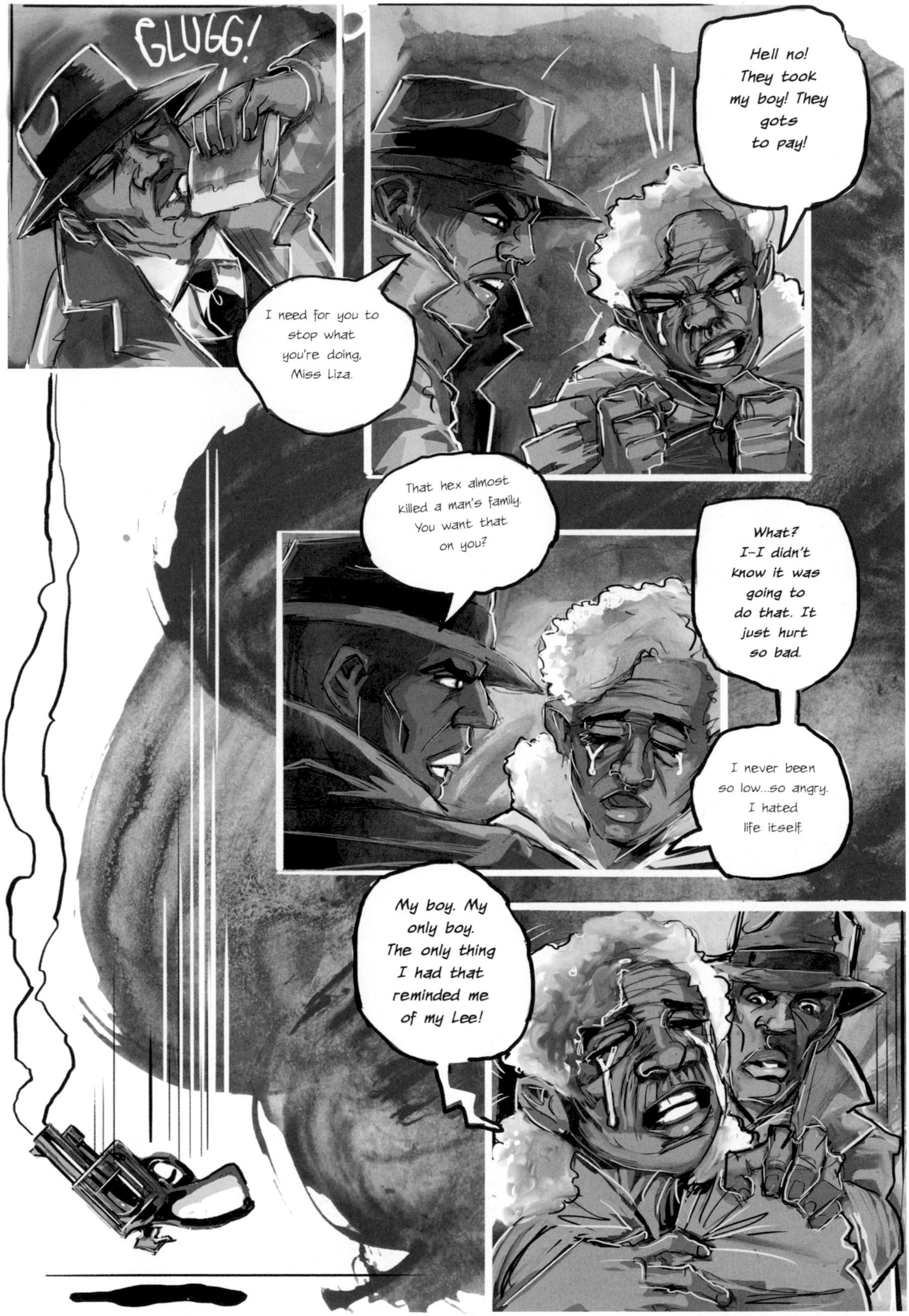
GLUGG!
Hell no! They took my boy! They gots to pay!
I need for you to stop what you're doing, Miss Liza.
That hex almost killed a man's family. You want that on you?
What? I-I didn't know it was going to do that. It just hurt so bad.
I never been so low...so angry. I hated life itself.
My boy. My only boy. The only thing I had that reminded me of my Lee!

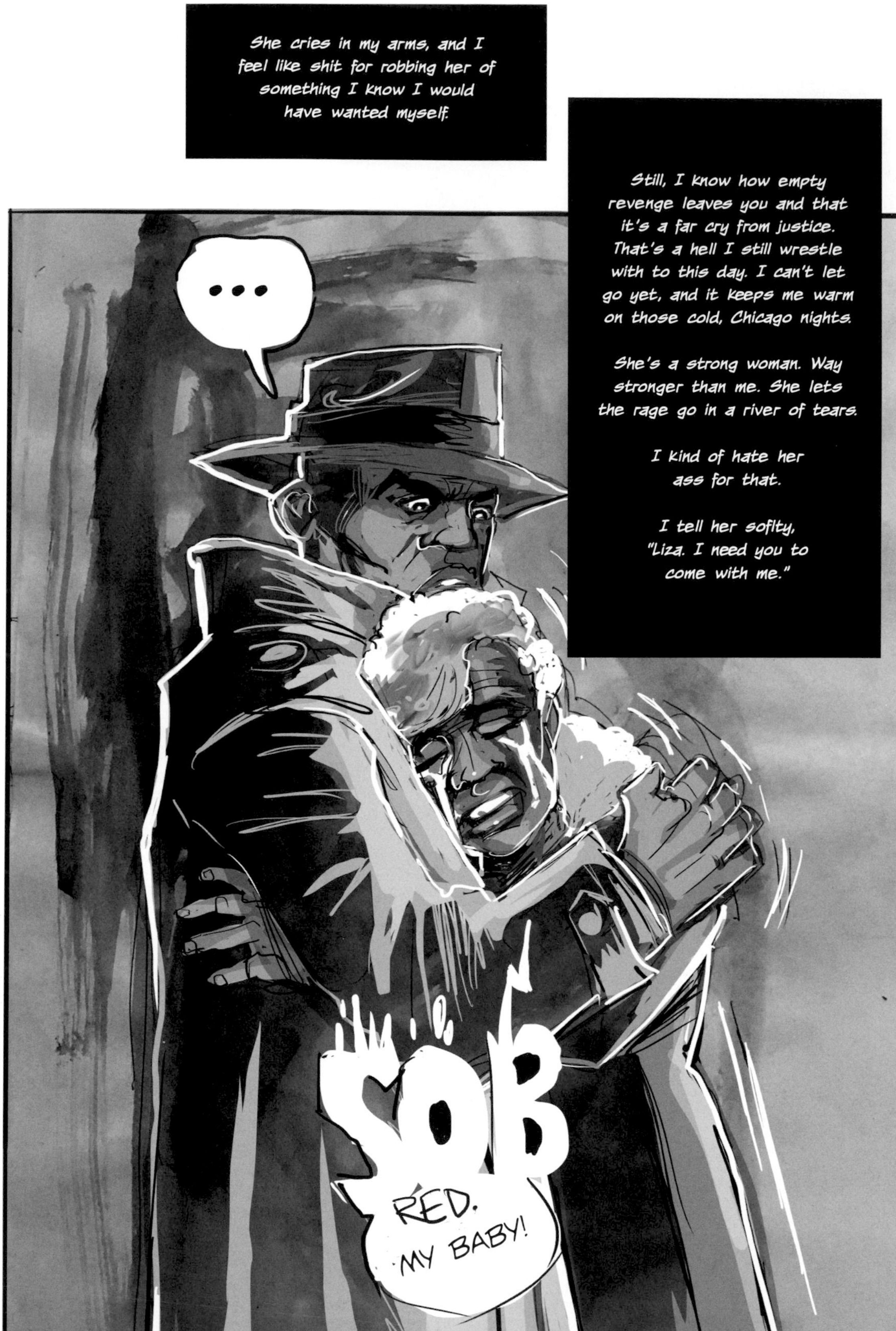
She cries in my arms, and I feel like shit for robbing her of something I know I would have wanted myself.
Still, I know how empty revenge leaves you and that it's a far cry from justice. That's a hell I still wrestle with to this day. I can't let go yet, and it keeps me warm on those cold, Chicago nights.
She's a strong woman. Way stronger than me. She lets the rage go in a river of tears.
I kind of hate her ass for that.
I tell her sofitly, "Liza. I need you to come with me."
...
SOB
RED. MY BABY!

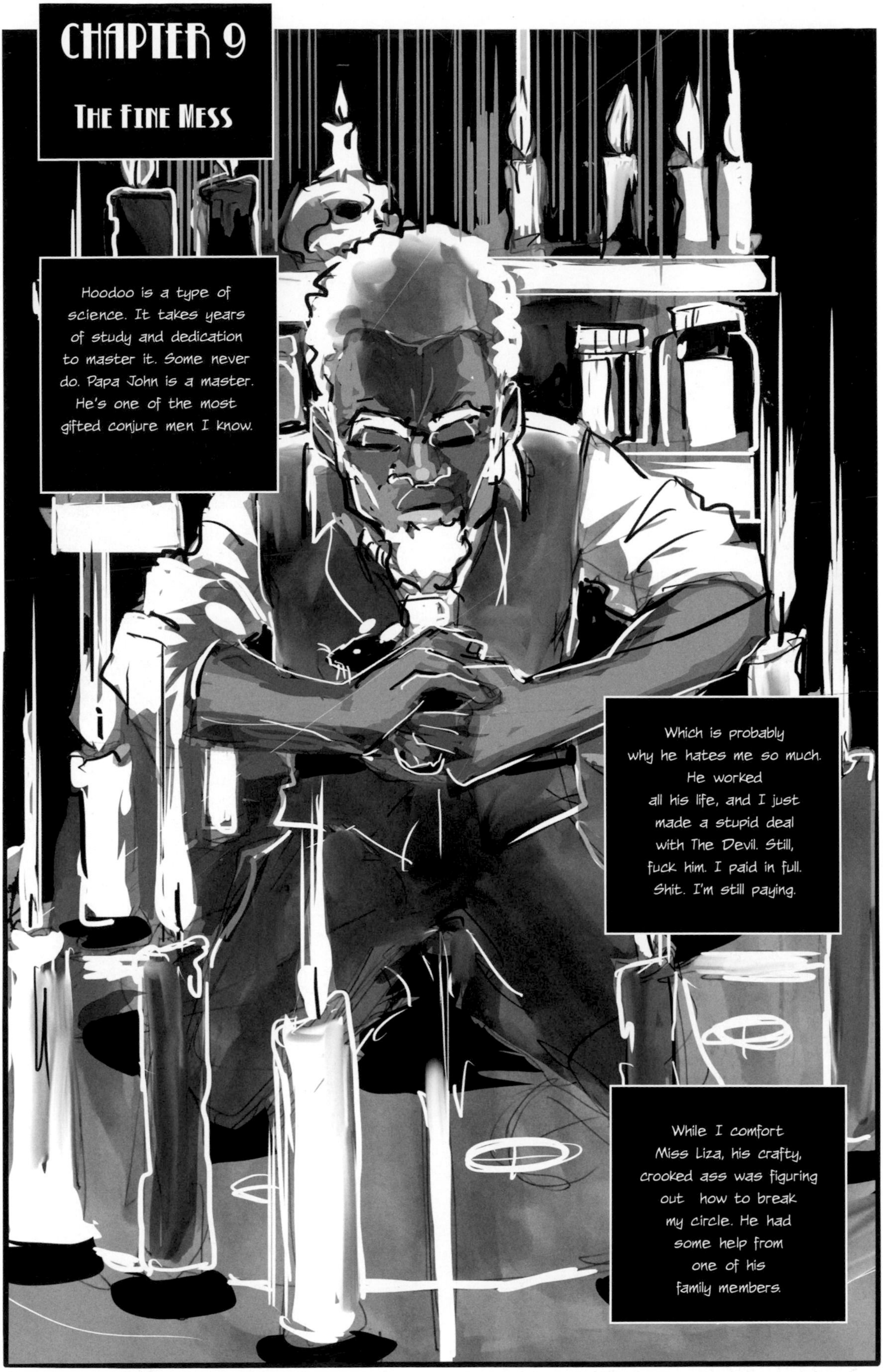
CHAPTER 9
THE FINE MESS
Hoodoo is a type of science. It takes years of study and dedication to master it. Some never do. Papa John is a master. He's one of the most gifted conjure men I know.
Which is probably why he hates me so much. He worked all his life, and I just made a stupid deal with The Devil. Still, fuck him. I paid in full. Shit. I'm still paying.
While I comfort Miss Liza, his crafty, crooked ass was figuring out how to break my circle. He had some help from one of his family members.

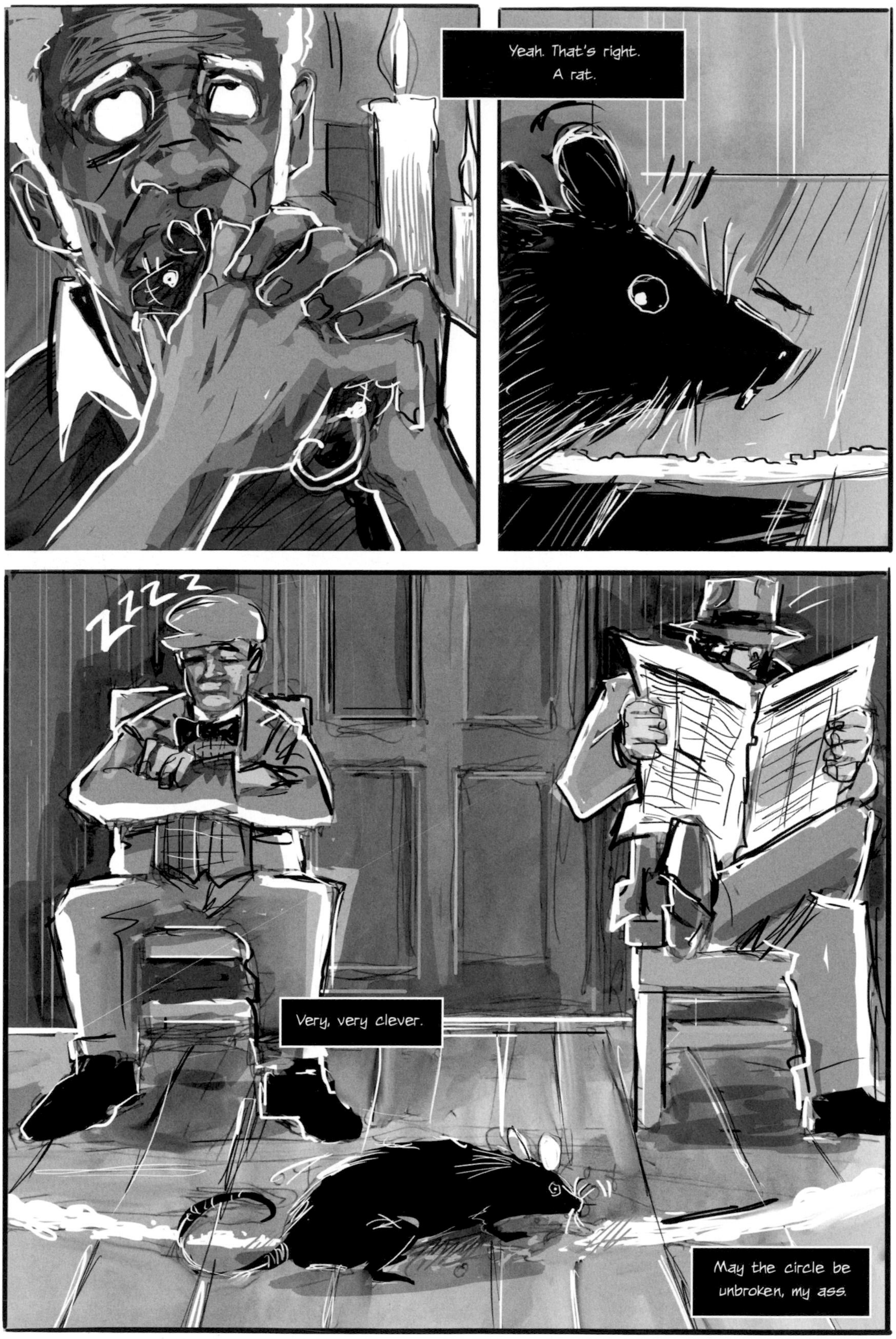
Yeah. That's right.
A rat.
ZZZZ
Very, very clever.
May the circle be
unbroken, my ass.

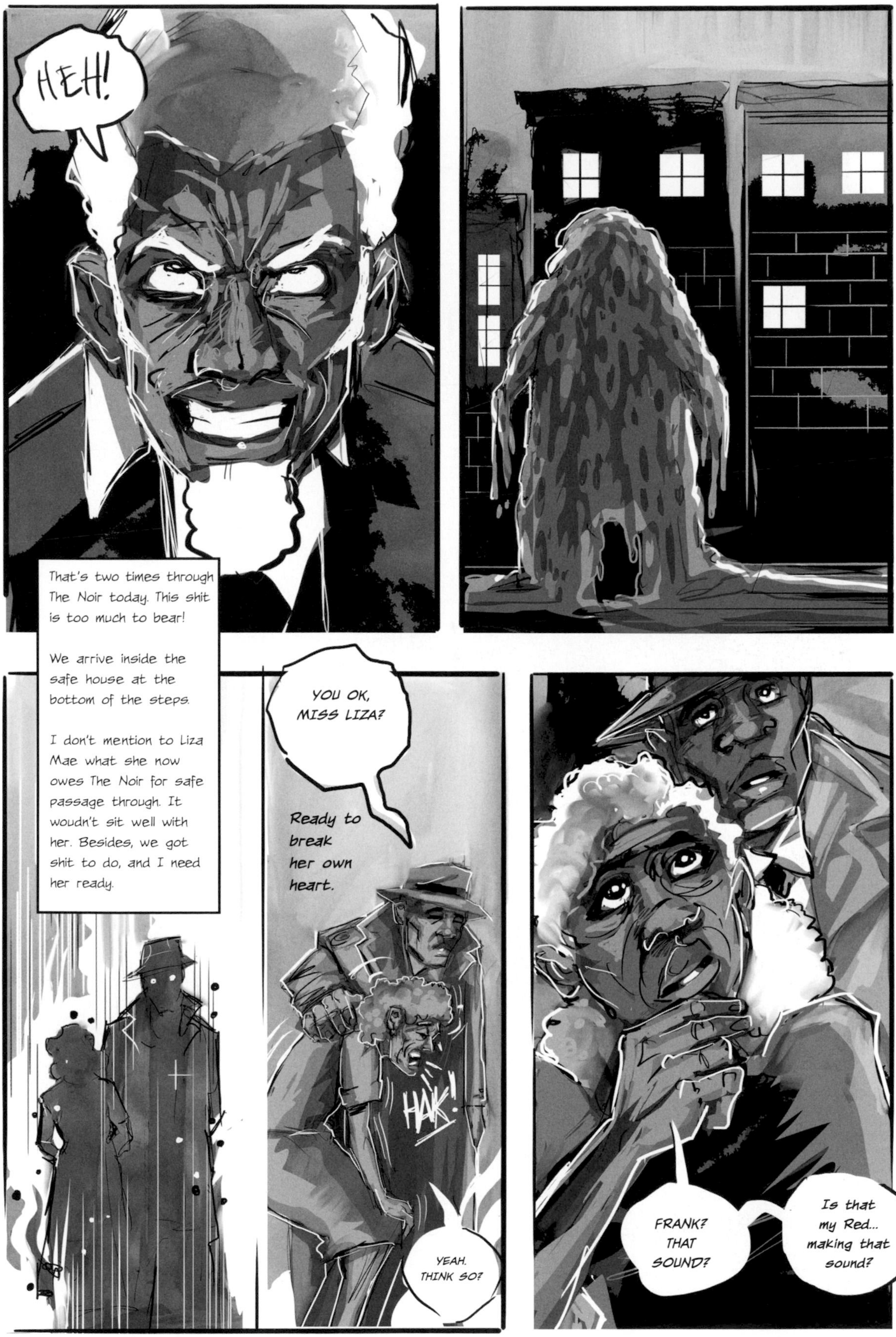
HEH!
That's two times through The Noir today. This shit is too much to bear!
We arrive inside the safe house at the bottom of the steps.
I don't mention to Liza Mae what she now owes The Noir for safe passage through. It woudn't sit well with her. Besides, we got shit to do, and I need her ready.
YOU OK, MISS LIZA?
Ready to break her own heart.
HAK!
YEAH. THINK SO?
FRANK? THAT SOUND?
Is that my Red... making that sound?

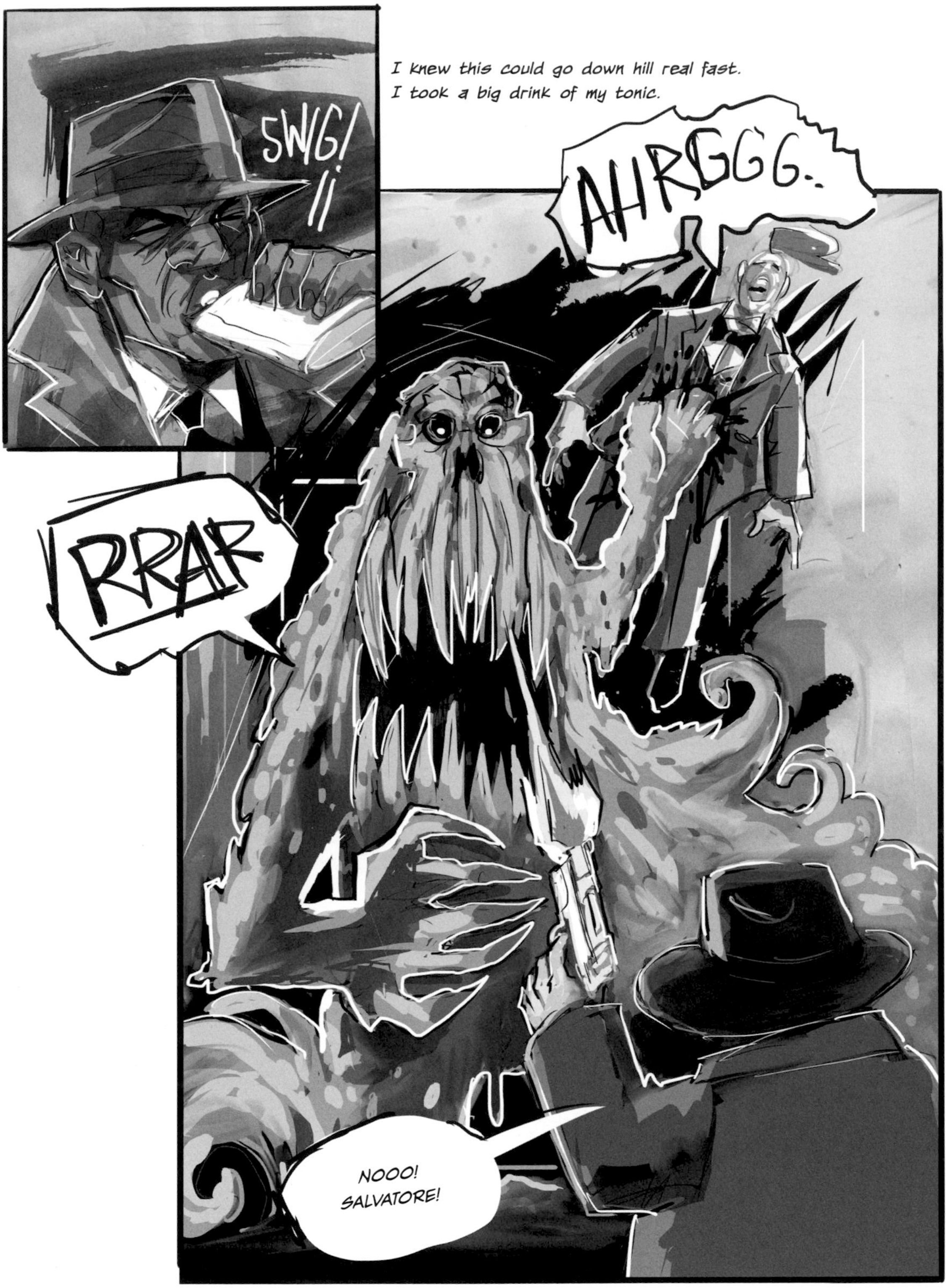
I knew this could go down hill real fast.
I took a big drink of my tonic.
SWIG!
AHRGGG..
RRAR
NOOO! SALVATORE!

The sounds upstairs chill us to the bone. We are both almost knocked off our feet by the scent of rich, wet Mississippi mud. The smell mixed with blood, sweat the cordite from gunfire. My gut tightens as we head up the stairs..

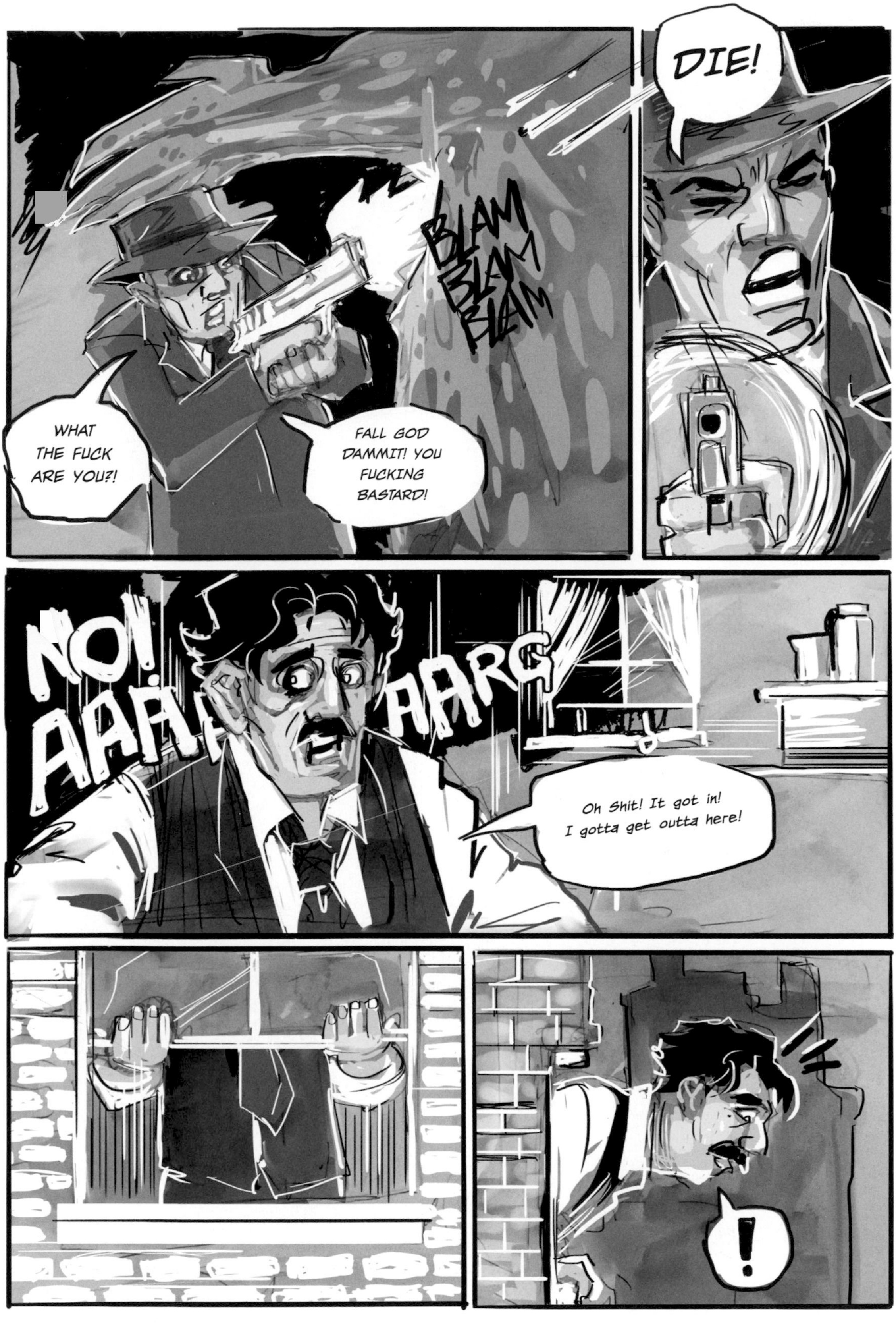
BLAM BLAM BLAM BLAM
WHAT THE FUCK ARE YOU?!
FALL GOD DAMMIT! YOU FUCKING BASTARD!
DIE!
NO! AAAH AARG
Oh Shit! It got in! I gotta get outta here!
!

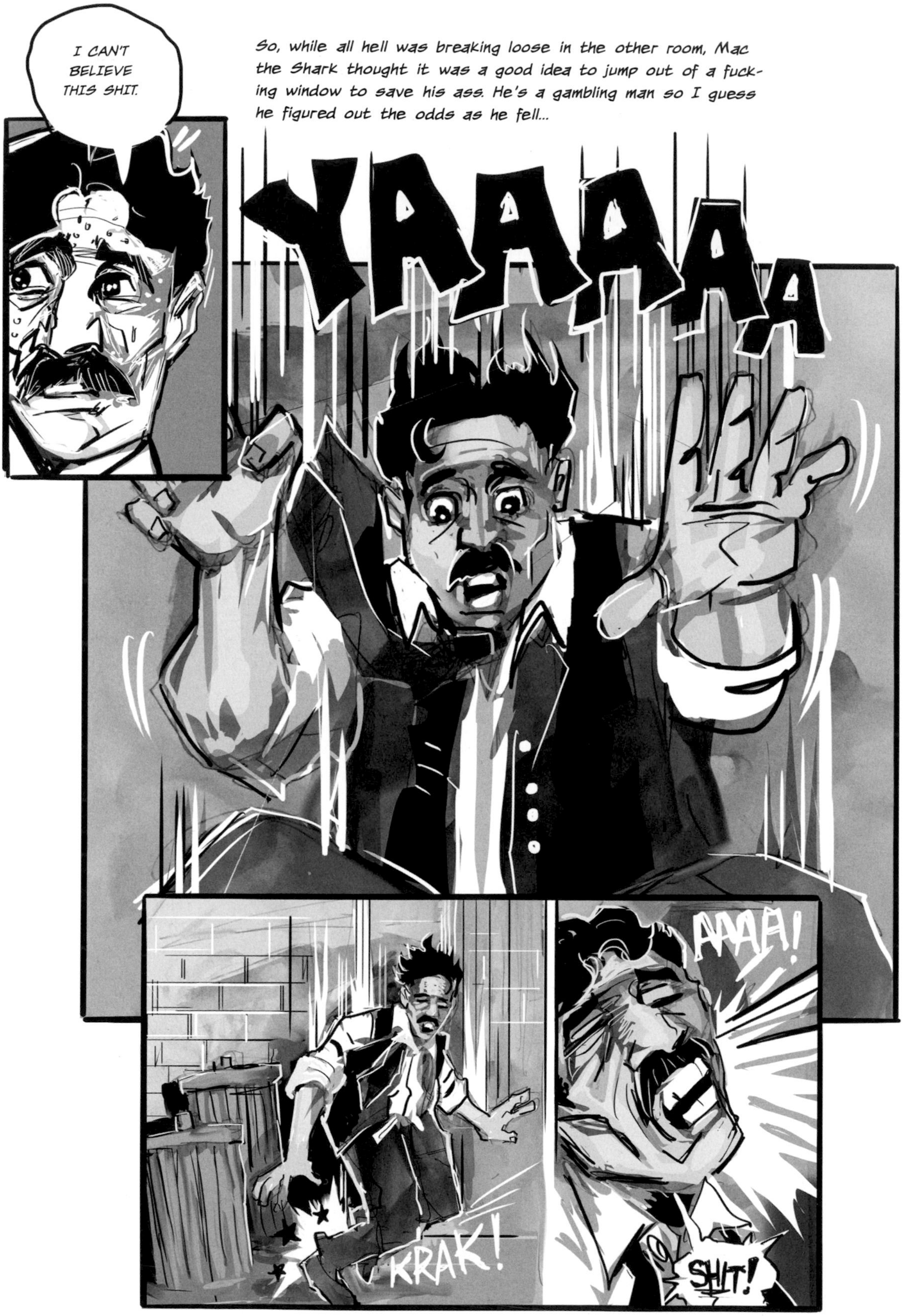
I CAN'T BELIEVE THIS SHIT.
So, while all hell was breaking loose in the other room, Mac the Shark thought it was a good idea to jump out of a fucking window to save his ass. He's a gambling man so I guess he figured out the odds as he fell...
YAAAAAA
KRAK!
AAAA!
SHIT!

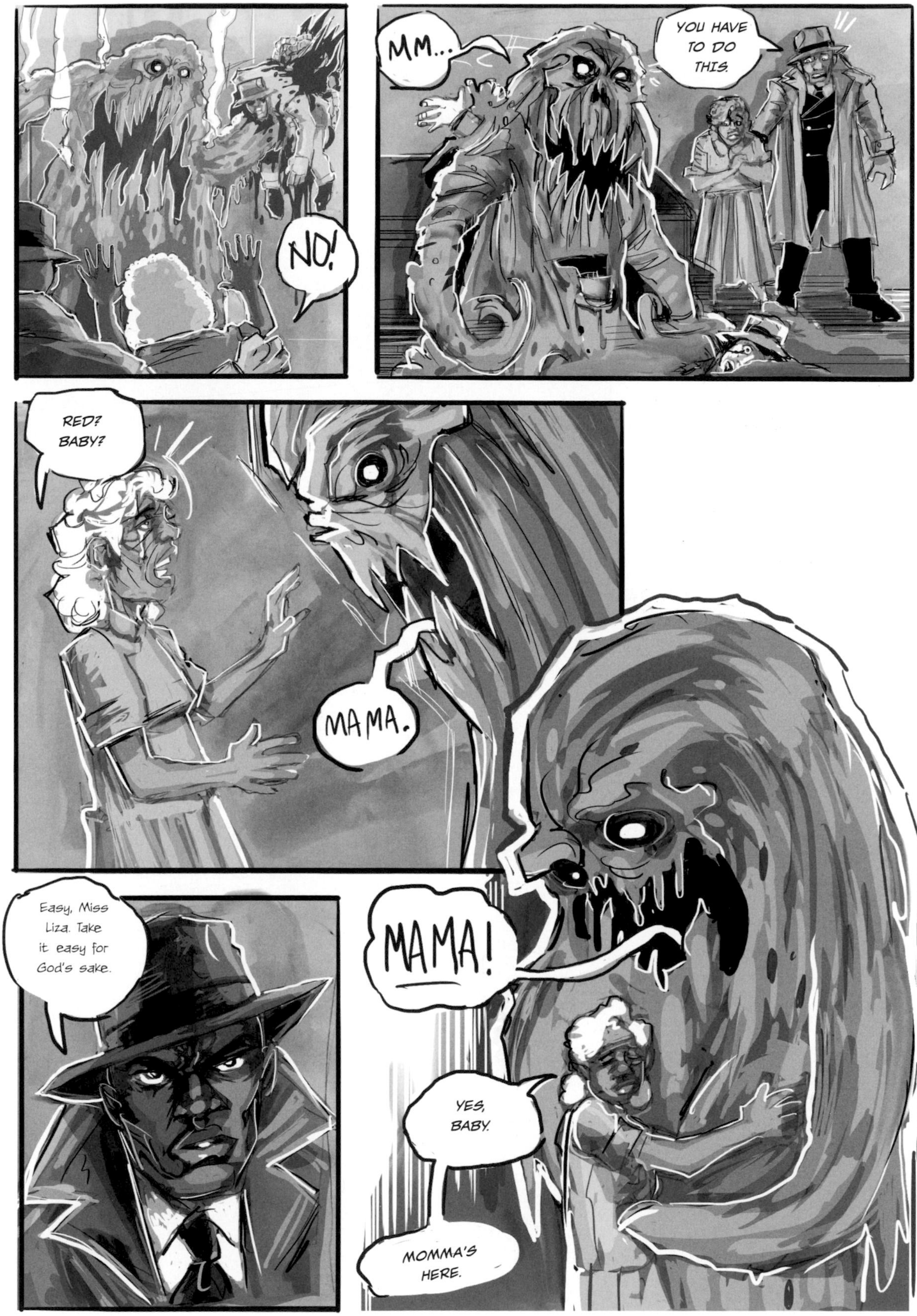
NO!
MM...
YOU HAVE TO DO THIS.
RED? BABY?
MAMA.
Easy, Miss Liza. Take it easy for God's sake.
MAMA!
YES, BABY.
MOMMA'S HERE.

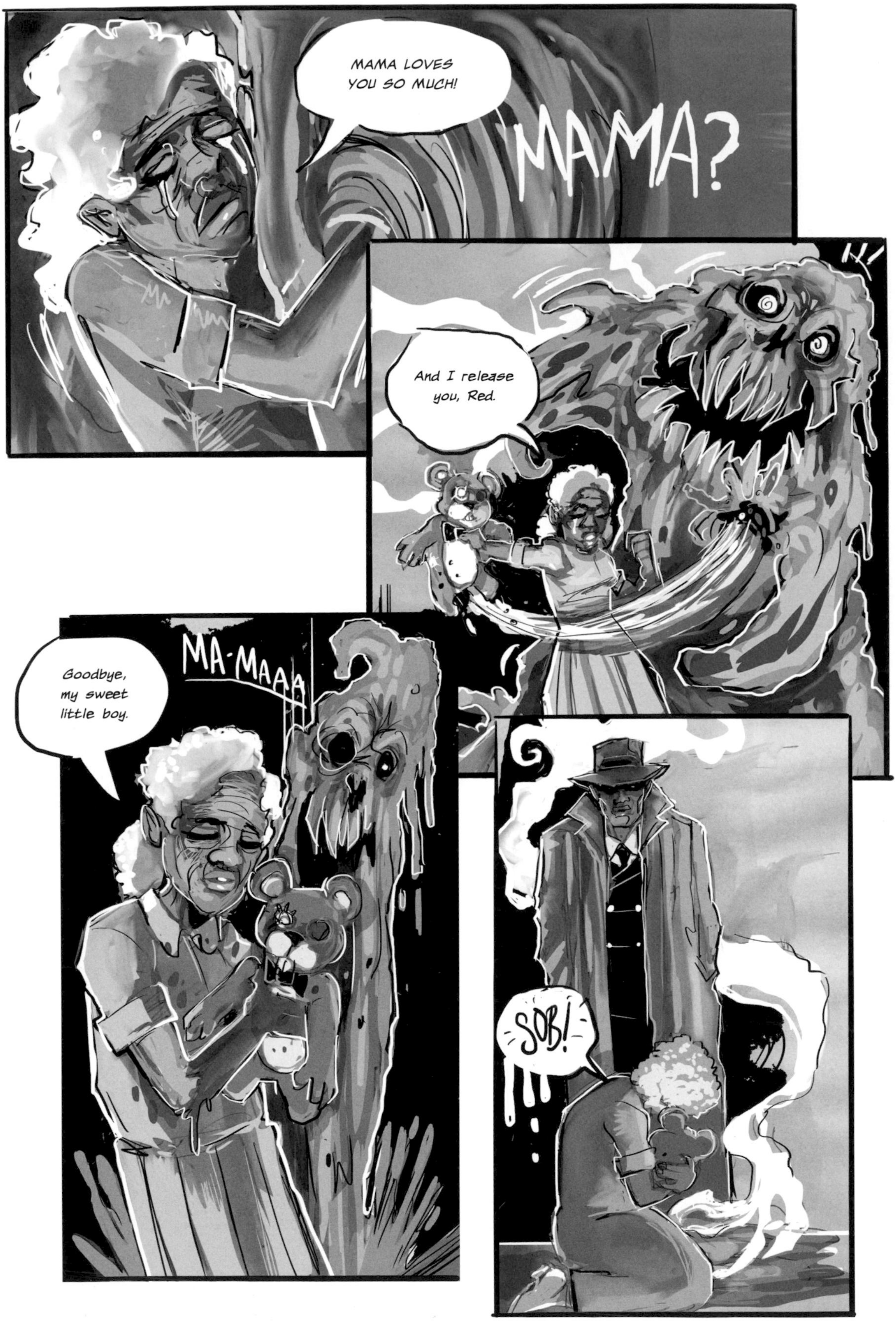
MAMA LOVES YOU SO MUCH!
MAMA?
And I release you, Red.
Goodbye, my sweet little boy.
MA-MAAA
SOB!

We find The Shark's ass trying to hobble off down the alley way to safety. He's a big damn mess when we come up to him. His ankle was damn near broke in two. Still, he was well enough to say...

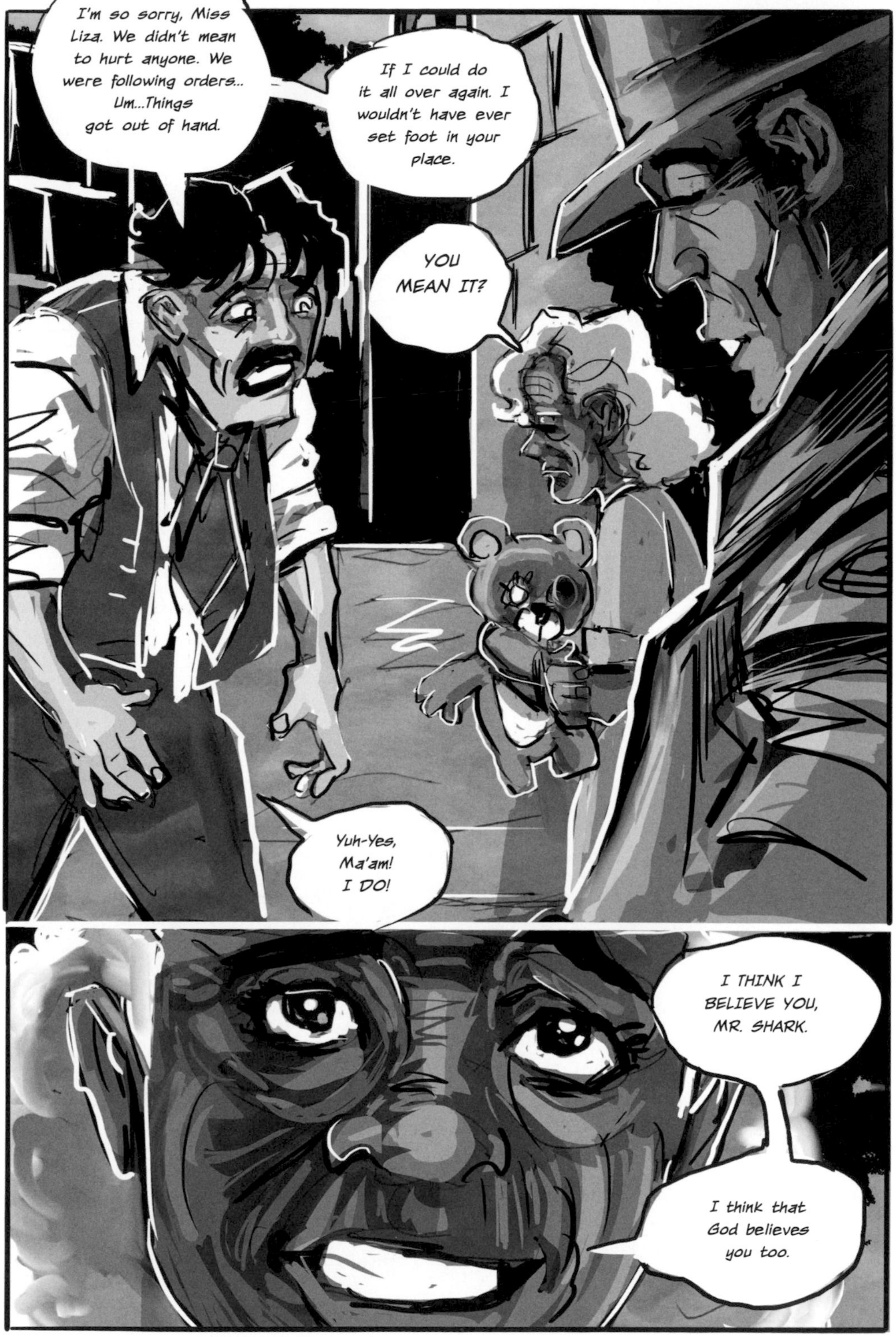

I'm so sorry, Miss Liza. We didn't mean to hurt anyone. We were following orders... Um...Things got out of hand.
If I could do it all over again. I wouldn't have ever set foot in your place.
YOU MEAN IT?
Yuh-Yes, Ma'am! I DO!
I THINK I BELIEVE YOU, MR. SHARK.
I think that God believes you too.

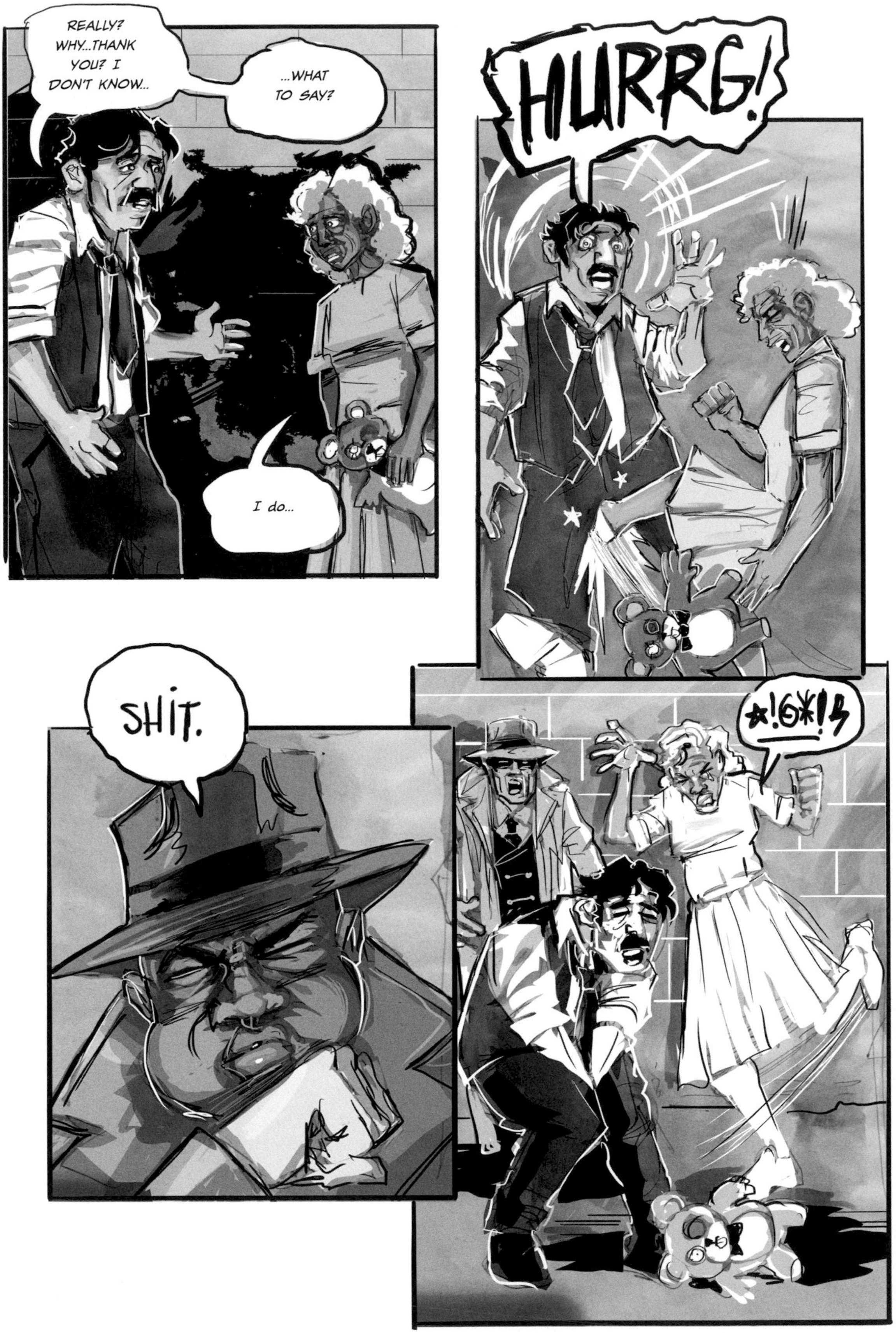
REALLY? WHY...THANK YOU? I DON'T KNOW...
...WHAT TO SAY?
I do...
HURRG!
SHIT.

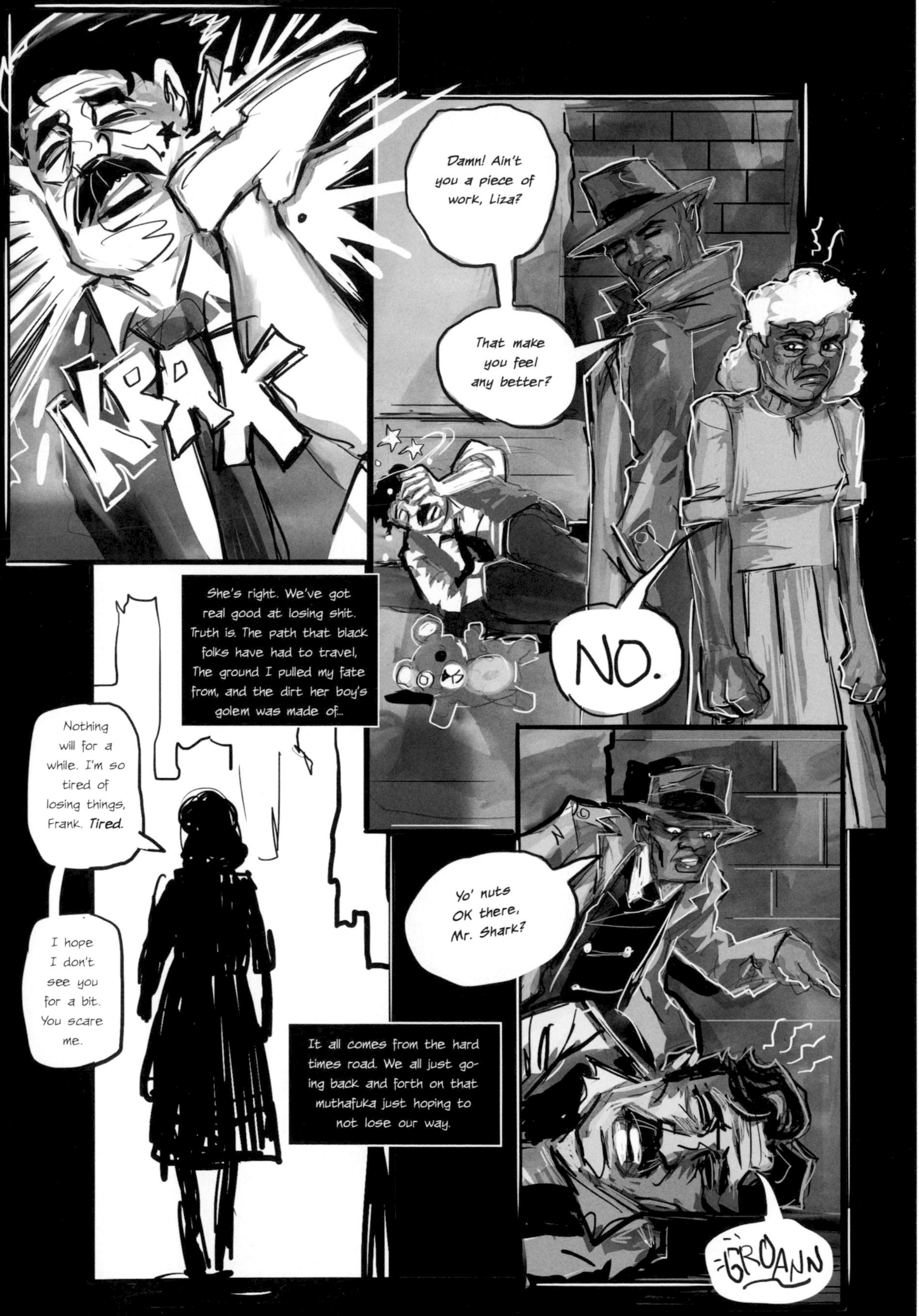

KRAK
Damn! Ain't you a piece of work, Liza?
That make you feel any better?
NO.
She's right. We've got real good at losing shit. Truth is. The path that black folks have had to travel, The ground I pulled my fate from, and the dirt her boy's golem was made of...
Nothing will for a while. I'm so tired of losing things, Frank. *Tired.*
I hope I don't see you for a bit. You scare me.
It all comes from the hard times road. We all just going back and forth on that muthafuka just hoping to not lose our way.
Yo' nuts OK there, Mr. Shark?
GROANN

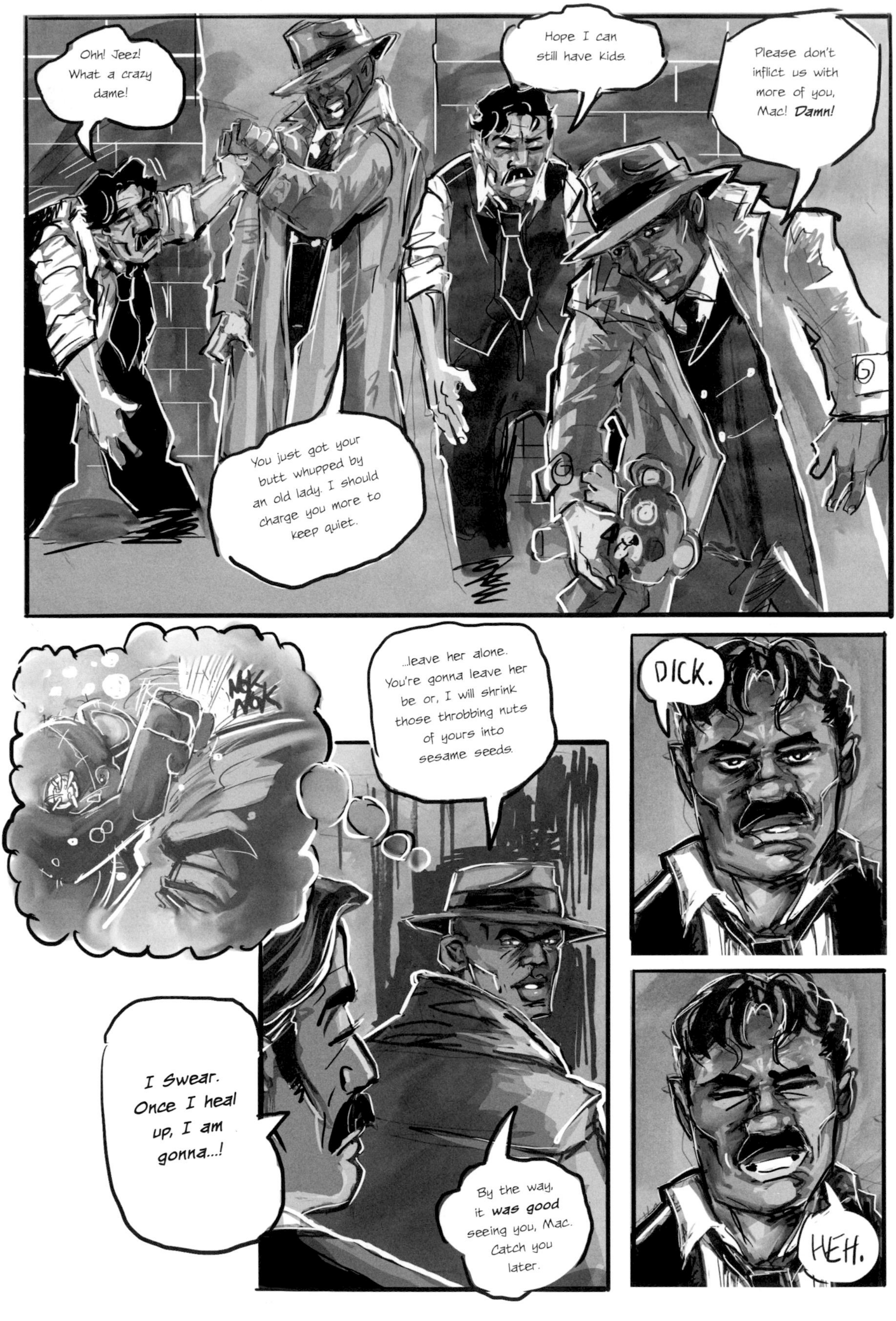
Ohh! Jeez! What a crazy dame!
You just got your butt whupped by an old lady. I should charge you more to keep quiet.
Hope I can still have kids.
Please don't inflict us with more of you, Mac! **Damn!**
...leave her alone. You're gonna leave her be or, I will shrink those throbbing nuts of yours into sesame seeds.
I Swear. Once I heal up, I am gonna...!
By the way, it **was good** seeing you, Mac. Catch you later.
DICK.
HEH.

CHAPTER 10

RED SAID...

So, three months pass, and things get back to their normal self. Papa John thought I'd forgotten about his ass. I decided to pay him a visit as a reminder...

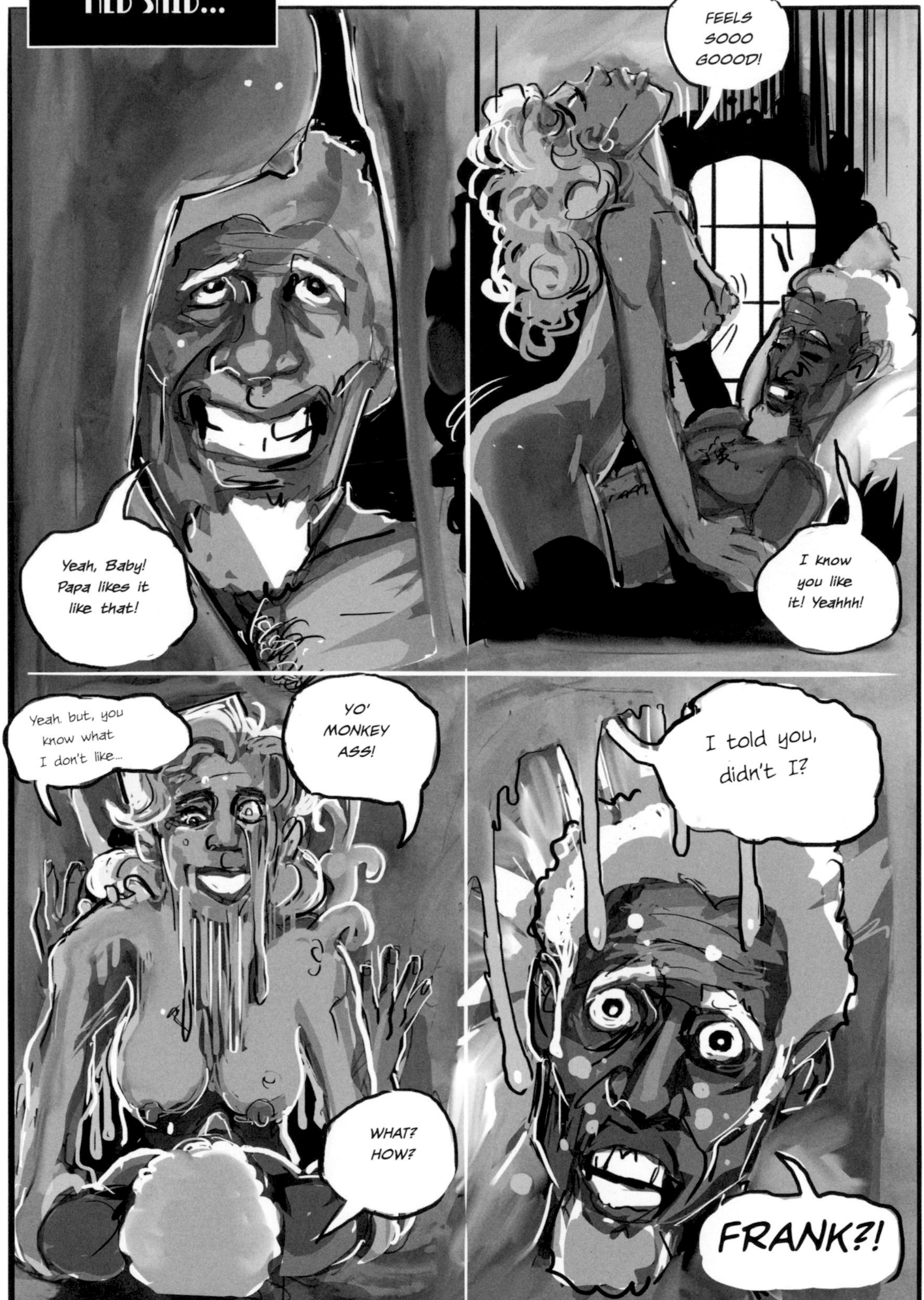

Yeah, Baby! Papa likes it like that!
FEELS SOOO GOOOD!
I know you like it! Yeahhh!
Yeah. but, you know what I don't like...
YO' MONKEY ASS!
WHAT? HOW?
I told you, didn't I?
FRANK?!

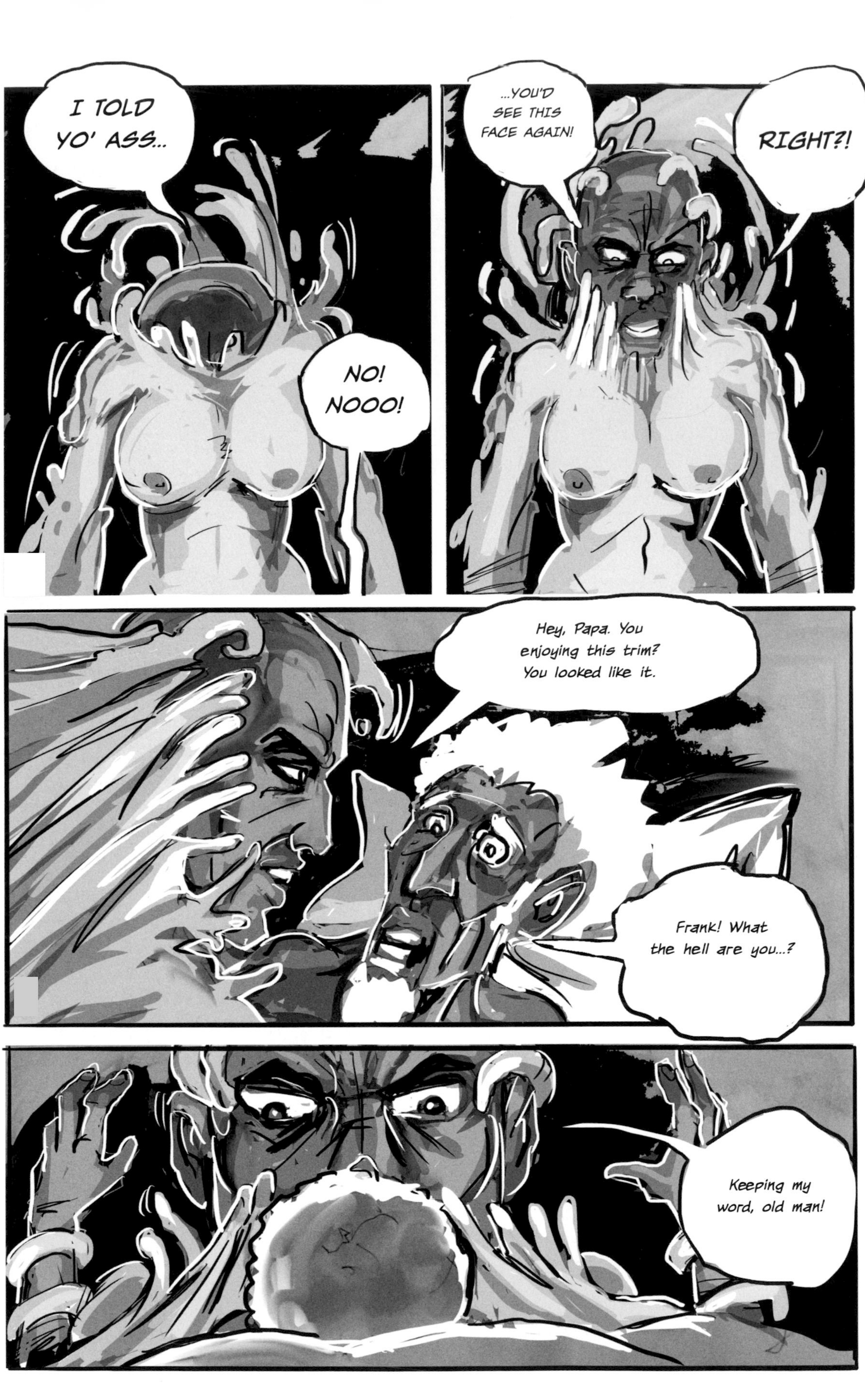
I TOLD YO' ASS...
NO! NOOO!
...YOU'D SEE THIS FACE AGAIN!
RIGHT?!
Hey, Papa. You enjoying this trim? You looked like it.
Frank! What the hell are you...?
Keeping my word, old man!

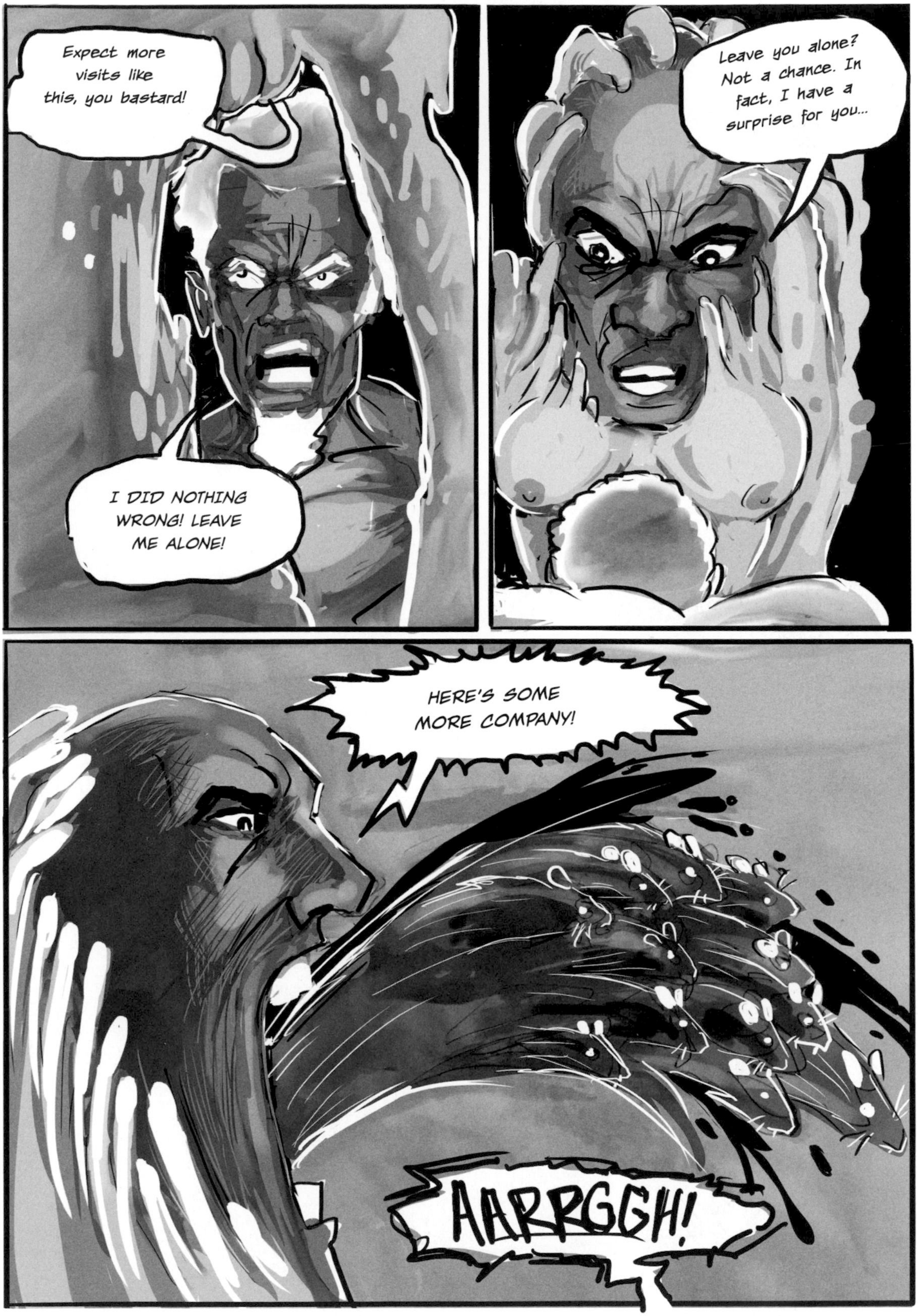
Expect more visits like this, you bastard!
I DID NOTHING WRONG! LEAVE ME ALONE!
Leave you alone? Not a chance. In fact, I have a surprise for you...
HERE'S SOME MORE COMPANY!
AARRGGH!

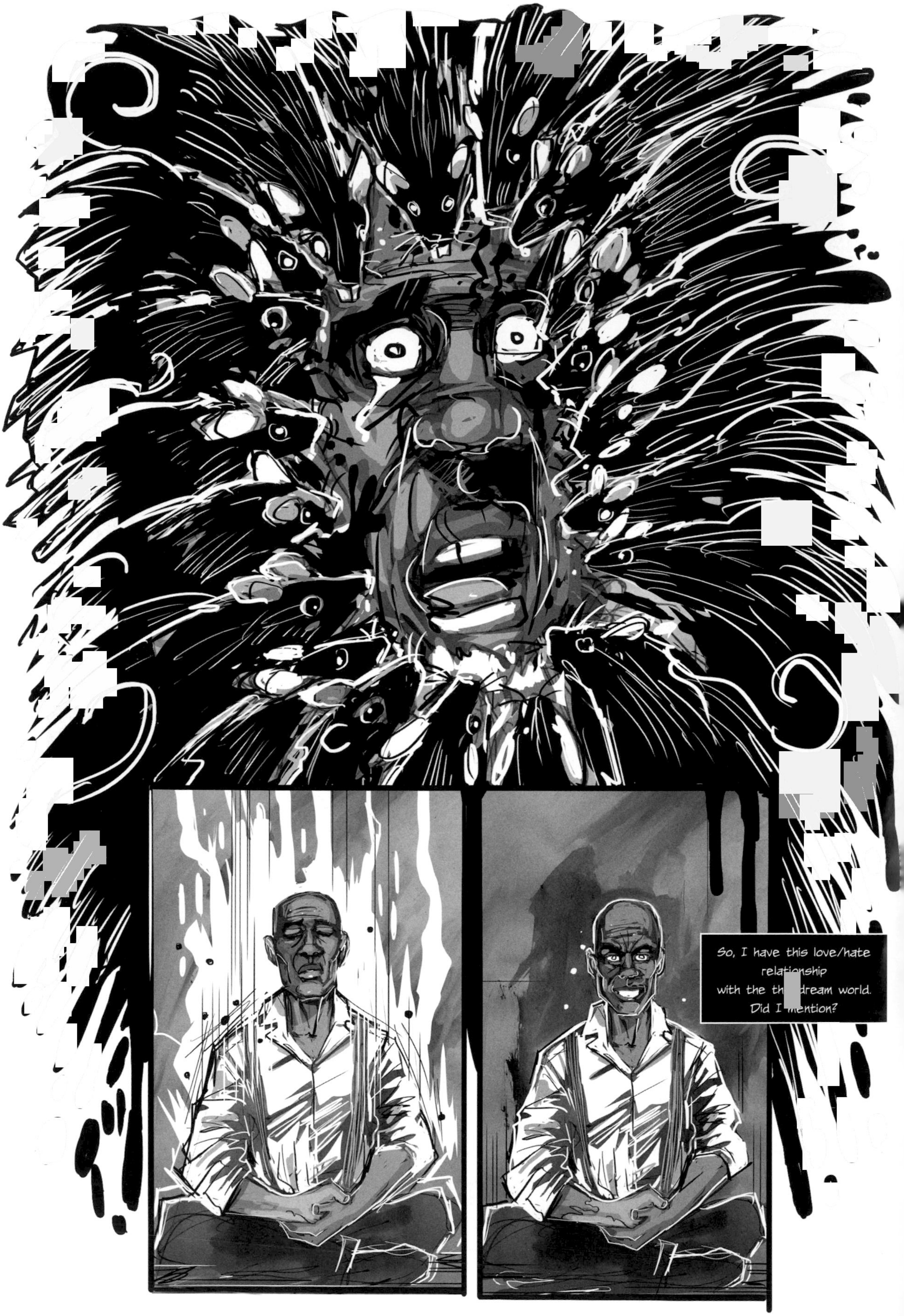
So, I have this love/hate relationship
with the th dream world.
Did I mention?

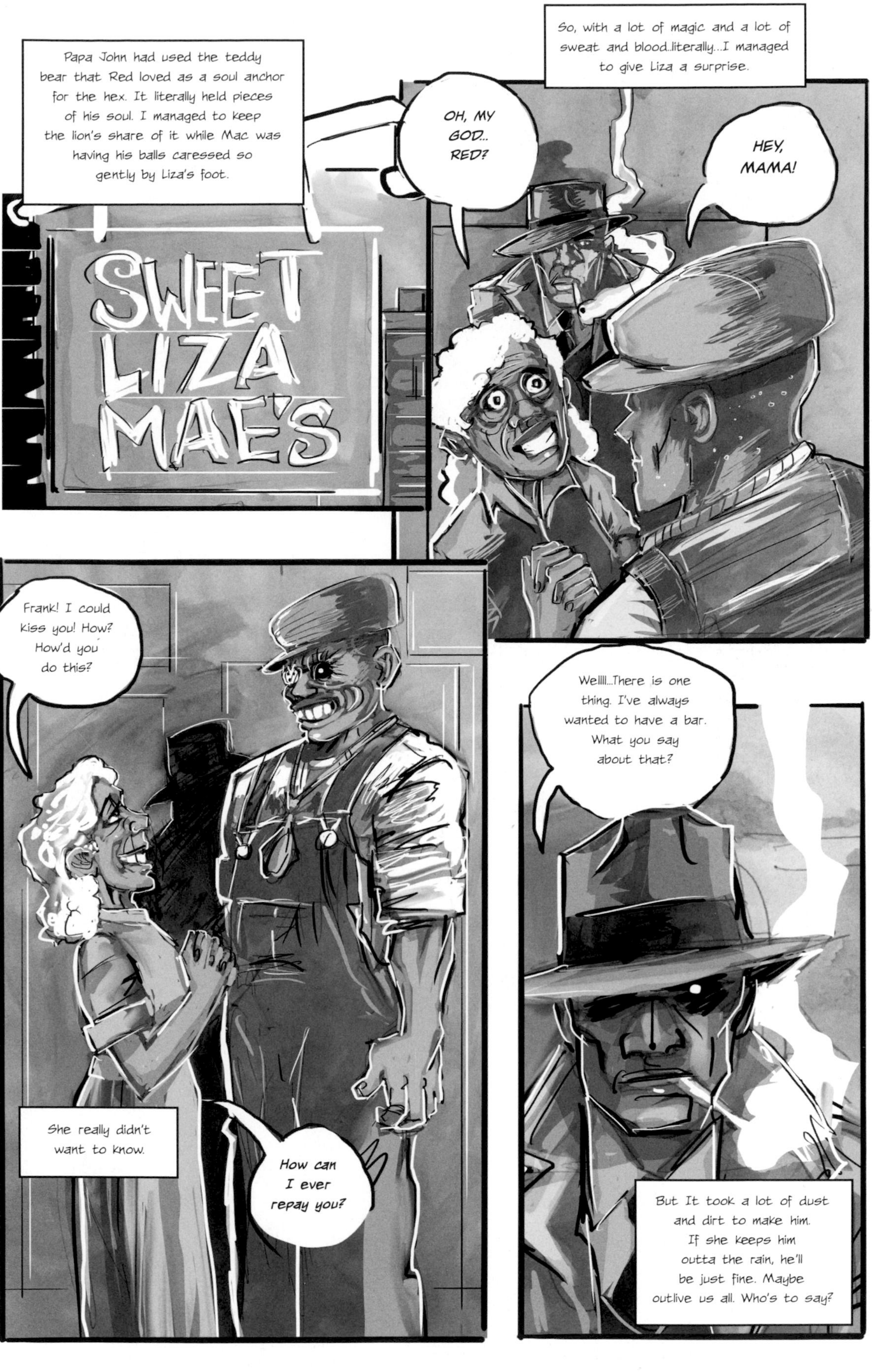
Papa John had used the teddy bear that Red loved as a soul anchor for the hex. It literally held pieces of his soul. I managed to keep the lion's share of it while Mac was having his balls caressed so gently by Liza's foot.
SWEET LIZA MAE'S
So, with a lot of magic and a lot of sweat and blood..literally...I managed to give Liza a surprise.
OH, MY GOD... RED?
HEY, MAMA!
Frank! I could kiss you! How? How'd you do this?
She really didn't want to know.
How can I ever repay you?
Wellll...There is one thing. I've always wanted to have a bar. What you say about that?
But It took a lot of dust and dirt to make him. If she keeps him outta the rain, he'll be just fine. Maybe outlive us all. Who's to say?

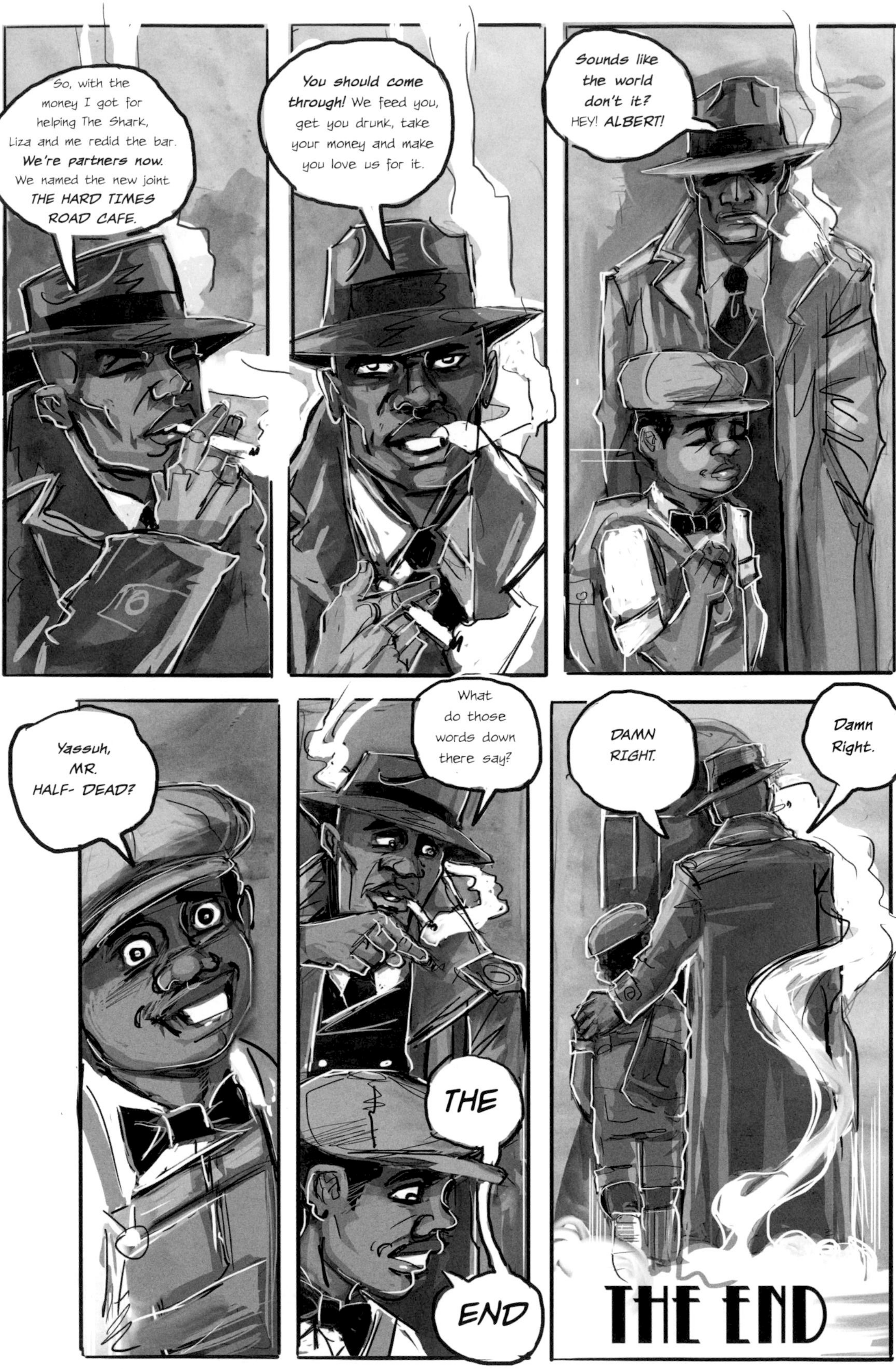
So, with the money I got for helping The Shark, Liza and me redid the bar. We're partners now. We named the new joint THE HARD TIMES ROAD CAFE.
You should come through! We feed you, get you drunk, take your money and make you love us for it.
Sounds like the world don't it? HEY! ALBERT!
Yassuh, MR. HALF- DEAD?
What do those words down there say?
THE
END
DAMN RIGHT.
Damn Right.
THE END

BLUE HAND MOJO

pin-ups by **John Jennings**

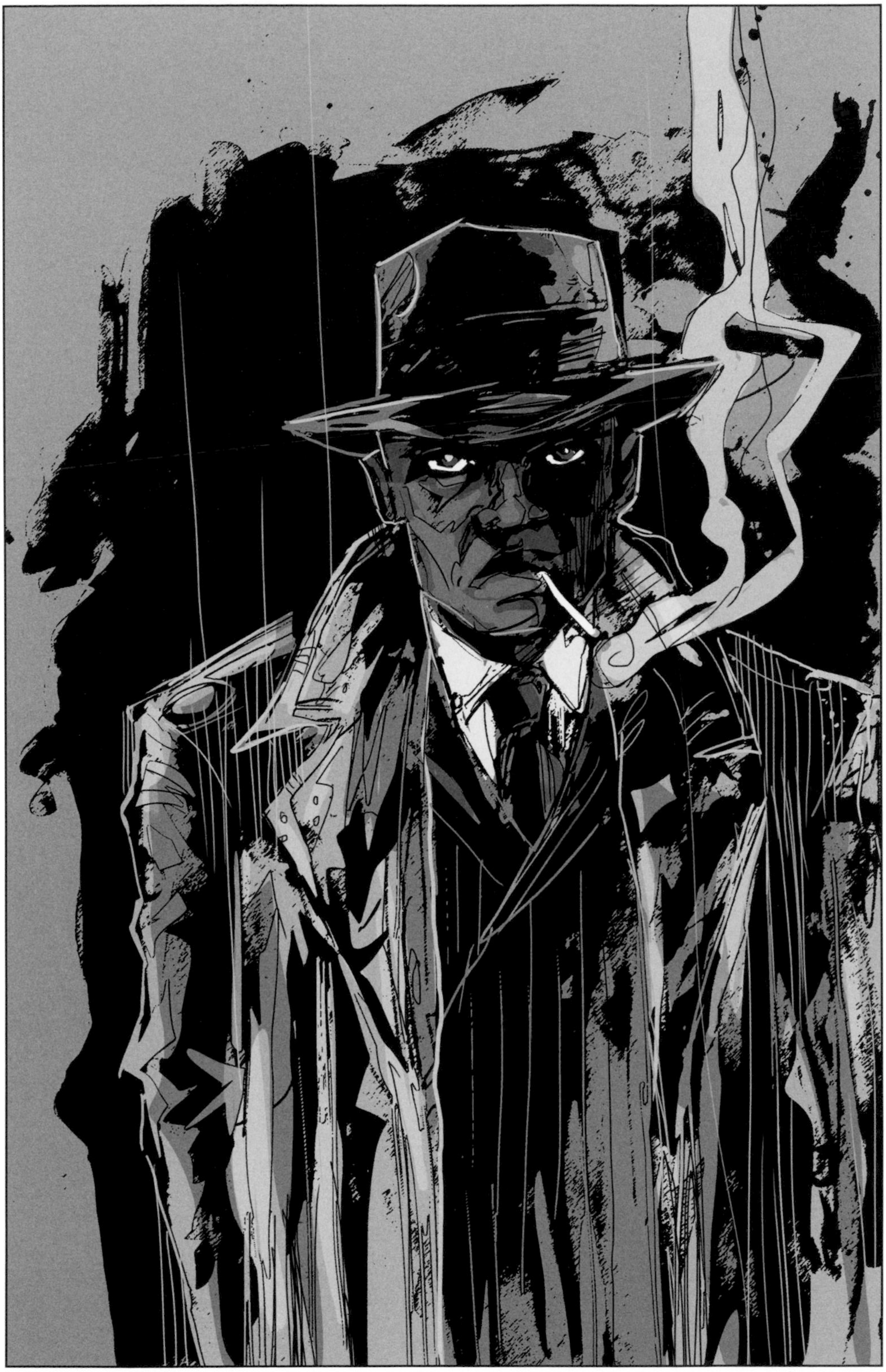

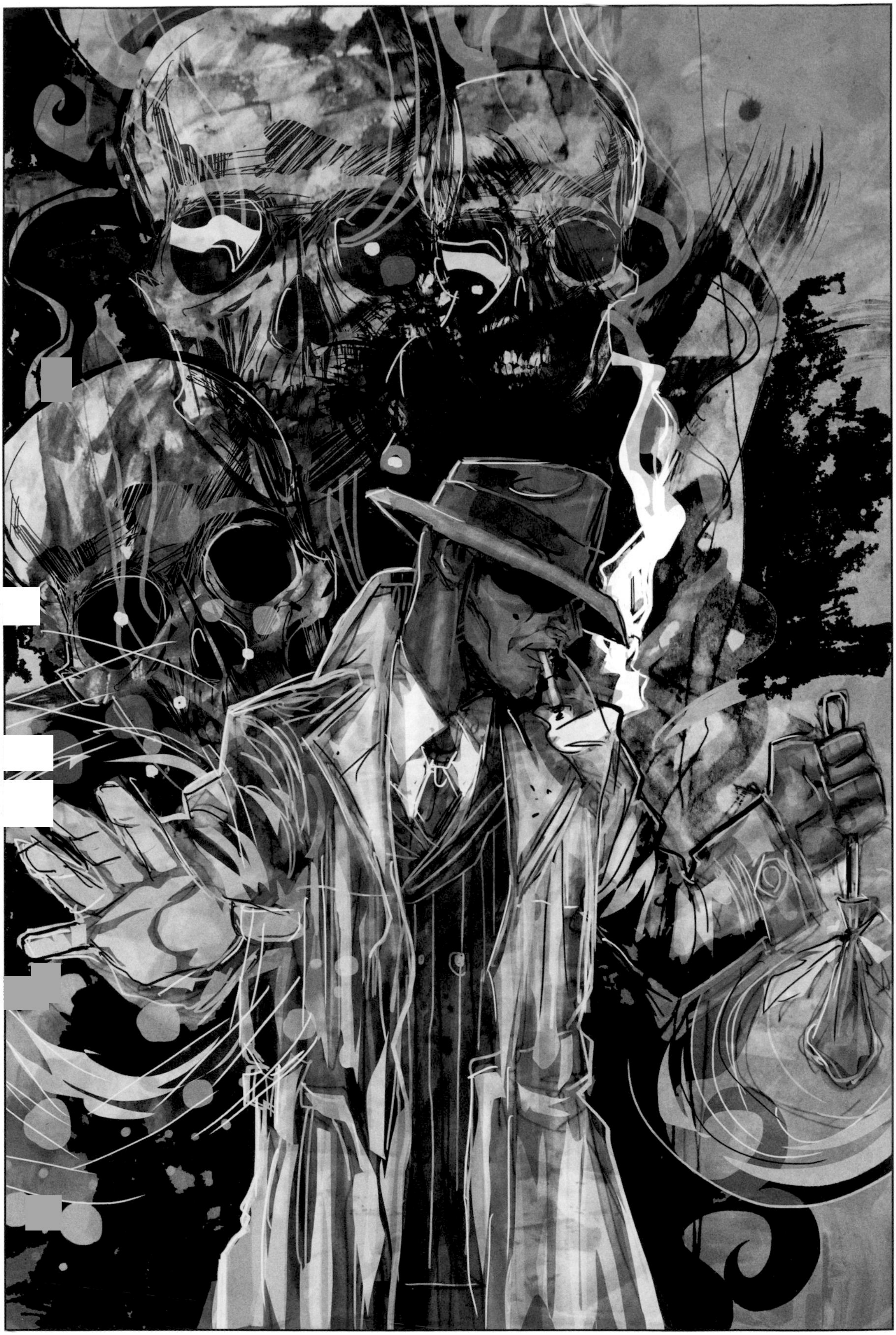

2015 GLYPH AWARD WINNER

BEST WRITER

DayBlack
MYA
CROSS

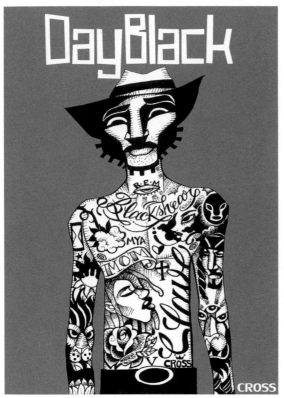

VOLUME ONE

"DayBlack is a remarkable visual accomplishment … It's like you're watching a series of stunning paintings."

–Comic Book Resources

COMING SUMMER 2017

DayBlack
CROSS

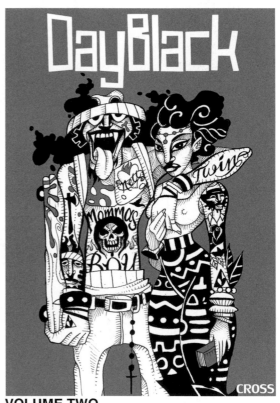

VOLUME TWO

"The story has a vibrant pop, portraying the characters and action with immense originality."

–Publishers Weekly

COMING SUMMER 2017

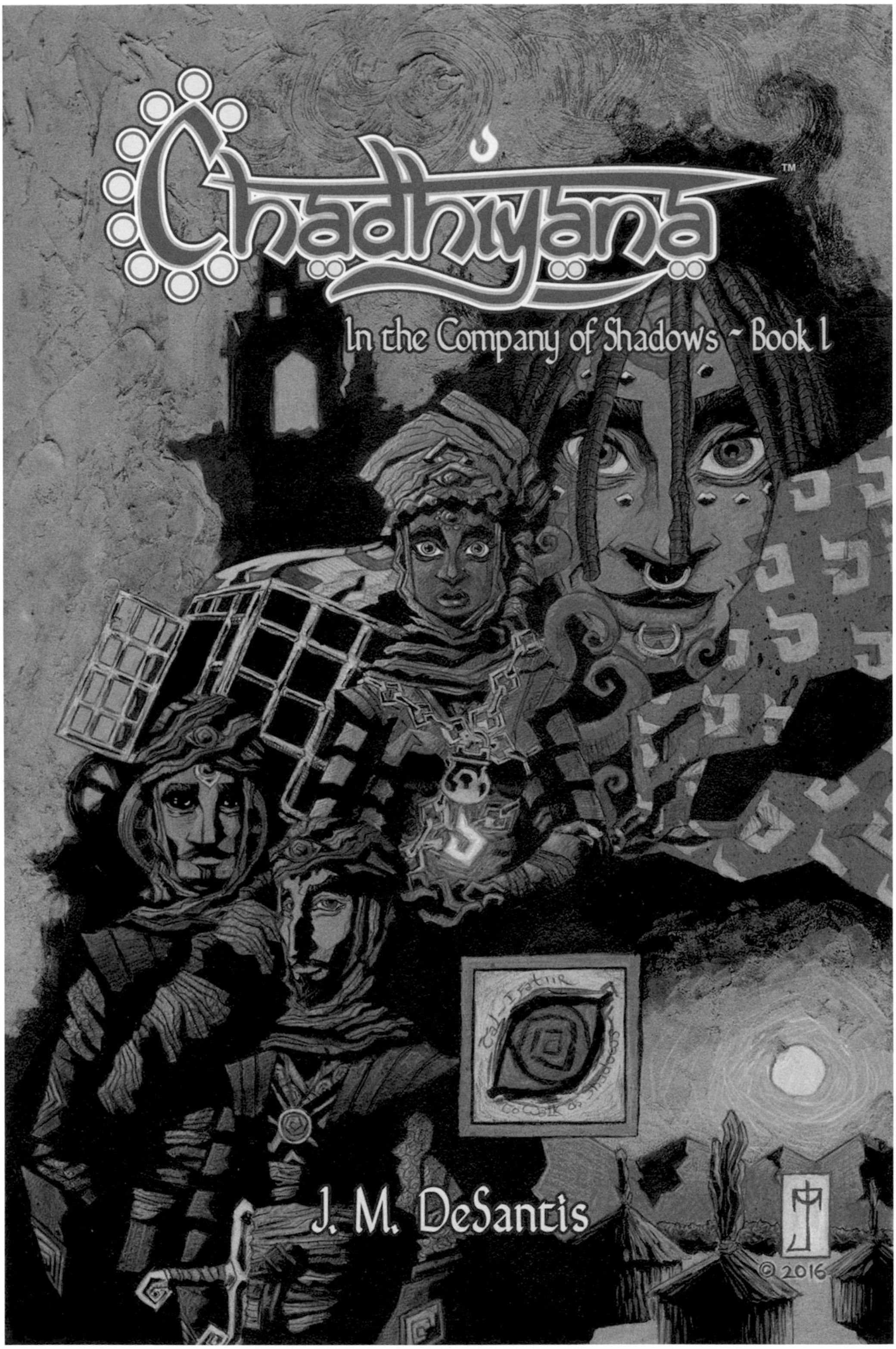

Chadhiyana™
In the Company of Shadows ~ Book 1
J. M. DeSantis
© 2016

"This comic is wonderfully different [from] than anything I've picked up before—from the art and coloring, to the story itself."

–Sequential Tart

"Manticore has so much to offer its readers and the creative team behind it of Keith Miller and Ian Gabriel, go really well together."

–Graphic Policy

OTHER COMICS FROM ROSARIUM

Bread & Butter #1
Liz Mayorga
ROSARIUM

Tallerman
Sammey
C21ST GODS
ROSARIUM

WARP
ZONE

THE LITTLE BLACK FISH

THE ADVENTURES OF
WALLY FRESH

TACO EL GATO
ROSARIUM
CANDY B.

Echo Gear
Vincent Sammy
ROSARIUM

vol. #1
in
OVENLAND
Story and Art by
Micheline Hess

The Little Red Fish

KID CODE
ROSARIUM PUBLISHING
PRESENTS
KID CODE
CHANNEL ZERØ
1
JUL
FIRST SENSES SHATTERING ISSUE!
IT'S TIME FOR SOME ACTION!

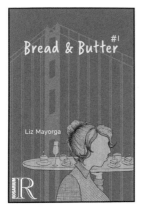

Found on Amazon, ComiXology, and Peep Game Comix!